The Best

Professional Write and File

RELATED TITLES

The Best Book of WordPerfect® 5.1
Vincent Alfieri,
Revised by Ralph Blodgett

The Best Book of: WordStar® (Features Release 5.0)
Vincent Alfieri

The Best Book of Microsoft® Word 5
Kate Miller Barnes

The First Book of WordPerfect® 5.1
Kate Barnes

The Best Book of: dBASE IV™
Joseph-David Carrabis

The First Book of Microsoft® Word 5
Brent D. Heslop and David Angell

The First Book of Paradox® 3
Jonathan Kamin

The First Book of PC Tools® Deluxe
Gordon McComb

The First Book of Quicken
Gordon McComb

The Best Book of DESQ®View
Jack Nimersheim
(forthcoming)

Understanding MS-DOS, Second Edition
Kate O'Day, John Angermeyer,
Revised by Harry Henderson

The Best Book of: DOS
Alan Simpson

The Best Book of: Lotus® 1-2-3®, Third Edition, Release 2.2
Alan Simpson

The First Book of Lotus® 1-2-3® Release 2.2
Alan Simpson and Paul Lichtman

The First Book of The Norton Utilities
Joseph Wikert
(forthcoming)

The Best Book of Microsoft® Works 2.0 for the PC, Second Edition
Ruth K. Witkin
(forthcoming)

For the retailer nearest you, or to order directly from the publisher, call 800-257-5755. International orders telephone 609-461-6500.

The Best Book of Professional Write and File

Douglas J. Wolf and Joe Kraynak

*To the College of St. Thomas in
St. Paul, Minnesota, for its dedicated effort
to promoting higher education*

© 1990 by Douglas J. Wolf

FIRST EDITION
FIRST PRINTING—1990

All rights reserved. No part of this book shall be reproduced, stored in a retrieval system, or transmitted by any means, electronic, mechanical, photocopying, recording, or otherwise, without written permission from the publisher. No patent liability is assumed with respect to the use of the information contained herein. While every precaution has been taken in the preparation of this book, the publisher and author assume no responsibility for errors or omissions. Neither is any liability assumed for damages resulting from the use of the information contained herein.

International Standard Book Number: 0-672-22726-6
Library of Congress Catalog Card Number: 89-64236

Acquisitions Editor: *Richard K. Swadley*
Development Editor: *Marie Butler-Knight*
Production Coordinator: *Becky Imel*
Cover Design: *DGS&D Advertising, Inc.*
Cover Photography: *Cassell Productions, Inc.*
Compositor: *Cromer Graphics*
Production: *Sally Copenhaver, Tami Hughes, William Hurley, Jodi Jensen, Dave Kline, Lori A. Lyons, Jennifer Matthews, Dennis Sheehan, Mary Beth Wakefield*
Indexer: *Joelynn Gifford*

Printed in the United States of America

Overview

1 Getting Started, 1
2 Formatting Your Document, 27
3 Using Block Commands, 51
4 Working with Files, 71
5 Using the Professional Write Dictionary and Thesaurus, 99
6 The Drawing and Calculating Functions, 117
7 Using the Write Fonts, 133
8 Previewing a Document, 143
9 Printing with Professional Write, 165
10 The Address Book and Form Letters, 175
11 Macros, 197
12 Creating a Professional File Database Form, 205
13 Working with Records, 231
14 Using Data Tables, 253
15 Using Macros in Data Entry, 263
16 Printing Records and Reports, 271
Appendix: Installing Professional Write and Professional File, 293

Contents

1 Getting Started — 1

Starting Professional Write on a Hard Disk System — 2
Starting Professional Write on a Floppy Disk System — 3
Computer Menus — 3
The Write Screen — 3
The Keyboard — 6
    The Function Keys — 6
    Special Keys — 9
Entering Text — 11
    Wordwrapping — 12
    Moving the Cursor — 12
    Moving to a Different Page — 13
    Insert versus Overstrike Mode — 14
    Deleting Characters — 14
    Deleting a Word or Line — 15
    Double-Spacing the Text — 18
    Inserting Hard Spaces — 19
    Formatting Characters — 19
    Using the List and Outline Format — 20
Saving a Document — 22
    Saving to a Floppy Disk — 22
    Saving to a Hard Disk — 23
    Special Features for Saving Files — 24
Printing the Document — 25
Summary — 26

2 Formatting Your Document 27

- Getting a Saved Document File 27
    - Getting a File from a Floppy Disk 28
    - Getting a File from a Hard Disk 28
- Setting Left and Right Margins 29
- Resetting Margins 32
- Setting a Temporary Left Margin 33
- Inserting Page Breaks 34
- Setting Tab Stops 35
    - Setting Typewriter Tab Stops 36
    - Setting Decimal Tab Stops 37
- Centering Text 39
- Setting Top and Bottom Margins 42
- Setting the Page Size 43
- Making the New Settings Permanent 43
- Creating Headers and Footers 44
- Entering the Print Page Number Command 45
    - Formatting the Header or Footer 45
- Adding a Title Page 48
- Summary 48

3 Using Block Commands 51

- What Is a Block? 51
    - Working on a Block 52
    - Text Blocks and Rectangular Blocks 52
- Marking a Block of Text 52
- Text Block Operations 53
    - Understanding the Clipboard 55
- Taking Action on a Block 56
    - Moving a Block of Text 56
    - Copying a Block of Text 57
    - Changing the Typestyle of a Block 59
    - Changing the Character Fonts 61
    - Changing Block Margins 61
    - Changing Block Indentation 64

Changing Line Spacing	65
Printing a Block	65
Saving a Block	66
Working with Rectangular Blocks	67
Erasing a Rectangular Block	67
More Rectangular Block Operations	70
Summary	70

4 Working with Files — 71

Understanding the Files Directory	71
DOS and Professional Write	72
Files on a Hard Disk—The Directory System	72
Viewing the Files Directory	73
Viewing a Directory on a Hard Disk	73
Viewing a Directory on a Floppy Disk	74
Changing the Default Data Directory	76
Using the Files Directory	77
Getting the Most out of Filenames	78
Sorting the Directory	79
Searching for a File	82
Working with Individual Files	86
Creating a Subdirectory	86
Saving a Document	86
Saving a Document in Other Formats	87
Getting a File	89
Erasing the Working Copy	90
Deleting a Document File	92
Removing a Directory	93
Copying Documents	93
Copying Files from a Hard Disk to a Floppy	93
Copying Files to a Different Hard Disk Subdirectory	94
Combining Documents	95
Inserting a Document into the Working Copy	95
Inserting a Worksheet File	95
Summary	97

Contents

5 Using the Professional Write Dictionary and Thesaurus 99

    The Spell Checking Feature 99
        Using the Spell Checker 100
        The Personal Dictionary 107
        Using Multiple Personal Dictionaries 107
    Using The Professional Write Thesaurus 108
    The Find and Replace Feature 111
        Finding Text 111
        Find and Replace 113
        Using Wild Cards 114
        Finding and Erasing All Occurrences of a Word 115
        Counting Words 115
    Summary 116

6 The Drawing and Calculating Functions 117

    Drawing with Professional Write 117
        Creating a Drawing 118
        Editing the Drawing 122
    Calculating with Professional Write 125
        Performing a Calculation 125
        Using Parentheses 127
        Inserting Numbers into the Calculator 128
        Calculating Averages 130
        Rounding Off Your Results 131
    Summary 131

7 Using the Write Fonts 133

    What Are Fonts? 133
        Fixed-Pitch and Proportional Fonts 133
        Portrait and Landscape 134
    Consider the Source 134
        Setting Up Fonts 134
    Changing Fonts 138
        Changing to Fonts That Your Printer Supports 138
        Changing Fonts with a Block Command 139

Seeing Fonts on Screen	140
Preventing Problems with Fonts	141
Accommodating a Large Font	141
Adjusting Tables and Tab Settings	141
Accommodating Fonts in Graphics Elements	142
Summary	142

8 Previewing a Document — 143

Before You Begin	144
Hardware Requirements	144
Preview's Page Limitation	144
The Printer Setup	144
Getting Started	145
Starting the Preview	146
Using the Full-Page View	147
Moving the Word Cursor in Full-Page View	147
The Split Screen	148
Starting Preview at a Selected Page	149
Using the Preview Menus	149
F1-Help	150
F2-Options	150
F3-Fonts	153
F4-Return	155
The Close-Up View	155
Moving the Word Cursor in Close-Up View	157
Correcting Problems	158
Correcting Wordwrap Problems	158
Correcting Page Breaks	159
Correcting Unjustified or Uncentered Lines	160
Adjusting Tables, Lists, and Outlines	161
Using Font Format to Adjust for Different Fonts	161
Overlapping Lines	162
Summary	163

9 Printing with Professional Write — 165

- Setting Print Options — 165
  - Number of Copies — 166
  - Starting Page, Ending Page — 166
  - Pause Between Pages — 167
  - Printing an Envelope — 167
  - Data File to Merge — 168
  - Indent — 168
  - Print Style — 168
  - Print to — 169
  - Download Soft Fonts — 170
- Inserting Printer Control Codes — 170
- Joining Files — 171
- Inserting a Graph During Printing — 172
- Summary — 172

10 The Address Book and Form Letters — 175

- Creating the Address Book — 175
  - Creating an Address Book File — 176
  - Entering Records — 178
  - Adding Records — 179
- Finding a Record — 180
  - Flipping Pages — 180
  - Adding Search Criteria — 180
  - Using Wild Cards — 181
  - Adding Criteria to Narrow the Search — 181
- Copying an Address into a Letter — 182
  - Modifying the Address Copy Format — 183
- Updating Your Address Book — 184
  - Editing Records — 184
  - Deleting Records — 185
- Creating and Using Several Address Books — 186
- Form Letters — 186
  - Composing the Letter — 186
  - Merging Letter and Database — 187
- Using Data from Professional File or dBASE — 188

      Exporting Address Book Data to
          Professional File 192
    Printing Mailing Labels or Envelopes 194
    Summary 195

11 Macros 197

    Creating a Macro 197
        The File Print Macro 199
        The Pause Macro 201
    Starting Over 202
    Listing Macros 203
    Deleting a Macro 203
    Editing a Macro 203
    Summary 203

12 Creating a Professional File Database Form . . 205

    Understanding Databases 205
    Starting Professional File 206
    Designing a Form 206
    Creating the Form 207
        Entering Field Names 210
        Saving the Form 214
    Editing the Form 214
        The Edit Menu 215
        Adding a Field 216
        Moving a Field Name 217
        Deleting a Field Name 217
        Changing Field Names 217
        Reordering Records after Editing 217
        Field Attributes 218
        Adding Field Attributes to the Form 219
        Format Attributes 220
    Using Formulas 224
        Subtotal Formula 226
        Using a Conditional Formula 227
        A Final Formula 227

Using Field Validations 228
    Including Validation Messages 228
    Validation Comments 229
Summary 229

13 Working with Records 231

Getting the Form 231
Entering Information 233
    Erasing a Field 233
    Entering a Date 234
    Using Quick Entry to Enter Date and Time . . . 234
    Testing Formulas 235
    Using the Formula Entries to Play What-If 236
    Checking the Conditional Formula 237
    Adding Comments 238
Modifying the INVOICE Form 239
Creating More Records 240
    Quick Entry 241
    Referring to the Previous Record 242
Finding Records 244
    Browsing 245
    Using Search Criteria 245
Sorting Records 250
Editing a Record 250
Editing Several Records at Once 251
Deleting a Group of Records 252
Summary 252

14 Using Data Tables 253

When to Use a Table 253
Creating a Table 254
    Designing the Table 254
    Saving Your Design 256
Viewing Data in the Table 257
    Moving the Cursor in the Table 258
    Using the Table to Enter Data 259

Viewing the Table from Search/Update	260
Modifying Table Instructions	260
Printing a Table	261
Summary	261

15 Using Macros in Data Entry 263

Creating a Macro	263
The Get Database Macro	266
The Merge Write and File Macro	266
The Print Mailing Labels Macro	268
Summary	269

16 Printing Records and Reports 271

Printing Records	271
Printing a Record as a Form	272
Printing Mailing Labels	274
Printing the Current Record	277
Printing Messages	278
Printing Reports	281
Printing a List	282
Creating Crosstab Reports	287
Modifying Column Headings	290
Summary	290

Appendix: Installing Professional Write and Professional File 293

Index 305

Introduction

Professional Write and Professional File were designed to help professionals do the work they most frequently encounter without knowing a lot about computers. From writing letters to developing proposals, from keeping track of clients' names and addresses to scheduling production deadlines, Professional Write and File are there to guide you with user-friendly menus and messages ... and shortcut keys that let you bypass the menus as you gain experience. If you're planning on using Professional Write by itself, you'll find it to be a fully featured word processing program that can handle the most demanding writing job. With Professional Write, you'll be able to develop simple business letters or complex proposals, adjusting and readjusting the format until it suits your taste, and even checking the spelling of a document before you print it out.

Similarly, Professional File has a power of its own, offering a flat file database that can hold thousands of names and addresses. In addition, File can keep track of hundreds of lists, part numbers, inventories, and invoices that would otherwise create an unmanageable heap of paper.

The combination of Write and File makes these two packages even more powerful. Together, they let you insert elements, even lists, from your database into your documents. Just compose a letter with Write and drop in an address from File—the letter is ready to print. With Professional Write's merge feature, the drudgery of mass mailings is no longer yours; just merge Write and File, and all you have to do is stuff the envelopes.

Before You Get Started

I'll try to keep it brief, but there are a few terms and concepts concerning computers that you should be familiar with before we get down to details. If you're an experienced user, skip ahead to the next section. If this is your first encounter with computers, the following information will give you some idea of where Professional Write and File fit into the big picture.

Your Computer, DOS, and Applications Programs

Your computer (the *hardware* of the system) is essentially useless without some instructions (*software*) that tell it what to do. First, the computer needs a program that monitors all the components of the system, keeping the keyboard, disk drives, screen, and other elements all in step. This go-between program is called the *Disk Operating System* (DOS, pronounced DAWSS). Without it, you can't run Professional Write and File.

Once DOS is loaded into your computer, the computer is able to understand and use *applications programs*, such as word processing, database, and spreadsheet programs. These applications programs get all the glory, performing the specific tasks that users require. Professional Write and Professional File are two such applications programs.

Documents and Files

With Professional Write and File, you create what are called *documents*, in this case, electronic documents. Each document is stored in a separate *file* on a disk, much the same way as paper documents are stored in a filing cabinet. To work on the document, you just tell Professional Write to get a particular document file (you'll learn how later). Professional Write retrieves the document and displays it on screen so you can work on it.

File Management

If you're storing your documents on floppy disks, there's not much file management to worry about. In general, you should keep related documents, say for a single project, on a separate disk devoted to that project, and keep all disks free of unnecessary files—files have a habit of multiplying on floppy disks. You also need to determine a system for naming your files that will keep all files for a single project organized.

If you're using a hard disk, file management is a little more complicated. You need to work with what are called *directories* and *subdirectories* that essentially break down your hard disk (a high-capacity storage unit) into smaller, easy-to-manage subunits. For example, to install Professional Write, you would create a directory (call it PRO) and store all the Professional Write program files in that directory. Whenever you wanted to use Professional Write, you would access that directory and start running the program. You could also create a separate directory called WDATA to store all the files you create using Professional Write.

You could then create several subdirectories under the WDATA directory (for example, MEMOS and LETTERS) to store the documents that you create using Professional Write. This breaks down an otherwise unmanageable list of files into smaller lists.

By creating directories and subdirectories, you form a structure that's similar to a family tree. An example of such a tree is shown in Figure 1.

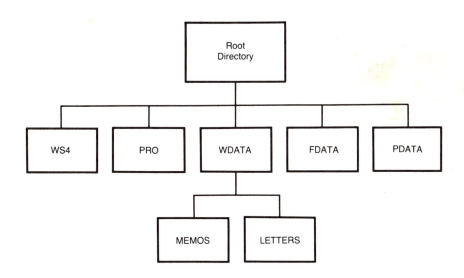

Figure 1 A hard disk directory system

How to Use This Book

This book is designed to teach you to use each program (Write or File) by itself. If you own both programs, this book will help you use them together to fully exploit their power.

The beginning chapters explain how to use Write and assume that this is your first attempt at word processing. These chapters focus on getting the programs up and running through simple exercises. After that, you'll explore the more powerful features. If you're a word processing intermediate, you can glance through the beginning exercises to familiarize yourself with Write's menus and keyboard conventions. Then, you can jump to the feature you want to learn in detail.

The later chapters explain how to use File both by itself and with Professional Write. These chapters include an introduction to the concept of creating a database and teach how to correctly structure the database in order to avoid problems. You will learn to use Write and File together to create form letters, reports, and any type of output that would require the merging of the two programs. Because the programs were designed to work together, joining files is simple, and you'll be producing customized letters in no time.

Conventions

The following conventions explain how the author presented various types of information in the book.

Instructions: Most tasks in this book are broken down into numbered lists that present step-by-step instructions. If there's more than one way to perform a step, the options are handled in a bulleted list under the step.

Two-Key Keystrokes: Certain keys are used in combination with other keys to give a command. These two-key keystrokes are joined with a hyphen—for example, Ctrl-F1. To use the keystroke, hold down the first key and press the second key.

Options: Professional Write and File are menu-driven programs; each menu contains a list of numbered options. The options in this book are presented in a computer-like font—for example, option `1. Create/Edit`. To choose an option, either type the number or use the arrow keys to highlight the option and press Enter.

Icons: Small graphic images, called *icons*, appear next to certain blocks of text. These icons flag the text, alerting you that special information is coming up.

| SC | This icon marks a shortcut key—a two-key keystroke that lets you eliminate time-consuming steps. |

| CAU | The caution icon warns you ... proceed carefully. |

| NOTE | This icon tells you to keep some important information in mind. |

| TIP | The tip icon marks a suggestion for using a feature. |

Using this Book

Don't just read the book—use it. Sit down in front of your computer with Professional Write and File and work through the examples. Don't be afraid to make mistakes at first. If you get tired of reading, feel free to play around with your documents and files; you might lose some text here or there (or gain some), but the practical experience you'll gain is a lot more valuable than the few lines of examples you might lose.

Acknowledgments

The Professional Write and Professional File development teams at Software Publishing Corporation deserve most of the credit for making this book possible. They developed word processing and database programs that anticipate the requirements of any job and simplify even the most complex task. Before encountering Professional Write, I used macros cautiously, if I used them at all, and creating a boilerplate was more trouble than it was worth. But the Professional Write and File menu-driven programs make these tasks easy and understandable.

I would also like to thank William "Groundstrokes" Gladstone, President of Waterside Productions, and Carol Underwood for helping launch this book. Without them, the book would still be an idea.

Thanks also to Richard Swadley of Howard W. Sams & Company, who gave timely advice and support in the initial stages to keep the book moving.

Finally, I'd like to thank Marie Butler-Knight for patiently guiding the development of the book throughout the project. Her editorial expertise and questioning eye helped clarify the instructions, and her knowledge of bookmaking ensured that all elements of the book came together at the end.

Trademark Acknowledgments

All terms mentioned in this book that are known to be trademarks or service marks are listed below. In addition, terms suspected of being trademarks or service marks have been appropriately capitalized. Howard W. Sams & Company cannot attest to the accuracy of this information. Use of a term in this book should not be regarded as affecting the validity of any trademark of service mark.

brother is a registered trademark of Brother Corporation, Ltd.
dBASE is a registered trademark of Ashton-Tate.
Hercules is a trademark of Hercules Computer Technology.
Hewlett-Packard and LaserJet are registered trademarks of Hewlett-Packard Corporation.
Lotus and 1-2-3 are trademarks of Lotus Development Corporation.
Macintosh is a registered trademark of Apple Computer, Inc.
Microsoft Word is a trademark of Microsoft Corporation
MS-DOS is a trademark of Microsoft Corporation.
Professional is a registered trademark of Software Publishing Corporation.
WordStar is a registered trademark of MicroPro International Corporation.

O N E

Getting Started

In the early 1950s, when computer technology was invented, word processing was one of the least anticipated uses of computers. In fact, one respected government study predicted that the entire world would need, at the very most, 50 computers! Since then, word processors have become as common as typewriters, and we look back wondering how people ever wrote "back then."

What's made the word processor such a useful tool is that it creates an electronic sheet of paper that is wider, longer, and easier to manipulate than any physical piece of paper. This electronic sheet scrolls from top to bottom, feeding you more "paper" as you type and allowing you to scroll up or down to look at your text.

Once you're finished typing, you can store your creation in a *file* on a magnetic disk just as you might save a piece of music on a cassette tape. To retrieve a stored file, simply tell the computer to play back that portion of the disk, and presto! the document appears, awaiting your command. We'll see just how to do this later.

You can edit your document on screen before printing it out on paper.

Because your document is stored magnetically and you edit it electronically, making changes is simple. Adding, deleting, or moving text is nothing more than an electronic process of cut-and-paste. For instance, if you write a concluding paragraph and then decide that it would make an excellent introduction, just lift the paragraph from the end and move it to the beginning.

Chapter 1

Starting Professional Write on a Hard Disk System

> If you have not already installed Professional Write, go to the Appendix and follow the installation instructions.

To run Professional Write, you first need to make the drive that holds the Professional Write program files active. If the program files are in drive C and `C:>` is displayed on screen, you're ready to begin. If the program files were in drive D, however, you would need to type `d:` and press Enter. DOS would activate drive D and display `D:>`.

Once you're in the correct drive, you're ready to start Professional Write. First, you must tell DOS the name of the directory that contains the program files. To do this, type `cd\pro`, telling DOS, "Change Directory to PRO." DOS responds as before with the prompt `C:\PRO>`, indicating that the PRO subdirectory is active. You can now run the files in that directory. Type `pw` to launch Professional Write. Your screen should resemble Figure 1-1.

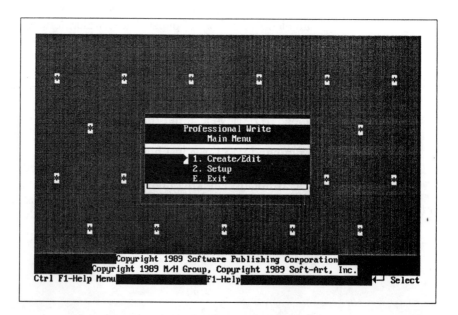

Figure 1-1 The opening Professional Write screen

Starting Professional Write on a Floppy Disk System

> If you haven't made a backup copy of the Professional Write program files, follow the instructions in the Appendix for making backups.

Make certain a DOS disk is in drive A and the drive door is closed. Turn on your computer. The disk drive will read the DOS disk and load the operating system. DOS may ask you to enter today's date and the current time. After you type in this information, DOS will display the prompt A:>, indicating that drive A is currently active.

When A:> appears on the screen, remove the DOS disk and replace it with your backup copy of the Professional Write startup disk. Type pw and press Enter. Professional Write will ask you to insert the program disk in drive A. Take out the startup disk, and insert your backup copy of the program disk in Drive A. Press Enter. After a moment, the screen should resemble Figure 1-1.

Your computer may need information from both the startup and program disks to run a command, such as Help. In these cases, Professional Write will prompt you to swap disks. To avoid swapping disks so often, put your startup disk back in drive B.

Once you're up and running, Professional Write offers you three choices for what to do next. This set of choices is the first you will see of what are called *menus*.

Computer Menus

The menus will lead you through your tasks.

To make it easy for you to access the available options, software programs provide lists (menus) of the options; these menus include a brief description of each option.

For example, the opening menu shown in Figure 1-1 lists three options:

1. Create\Edit
2. Setup
E. Exit

To activate one of the options listed, you can move the highlight (using the Up and Down Arrow keys) to the option you want, and then press the

Enter key. You can also select the option by typing the number or letter that corresponds to the option. For example, you could type **1** to select the Create/Edit option.

At the bottom of the screen are three more options:

```
Ctrl F1-Help Menu
F1-Help
          Select
```

The first option indicates that by pressing Ctrl-F1 (that is, by holding down the Ctrl key while pressing the F1 key), you open a Help menu that further explains your choices. Pressing the F1 key alone brings up a message screen that tells you how to start and lists some suggestions. The bent arrow to the left of Select represents the Enter key; pressing Enter selects the highlighted option in the menu.

Type **1** now to open the Write word processing screen, as shown in Figure 1-2.

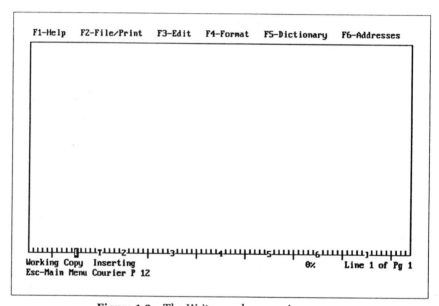

Figure 1-2   The Write word processing screen

The Write Screen

Let's take a moment to get acquainted with the features on this screen. If it seems overwhelming, remember your first driving lesson. At first,

Function keys provide access to even more options.

everything seemed to be happening at once, but after some time, the flow of events became second nature. The same is true with Write. Once you get past the beginning, the rest will come naturally.

Across the very top of the screen is a list of keys and a title for each, beginning with F1-Help and ending with F6-Addresses. These are the function keys and their associated capabilities. By pressing any of the function keys, you pull down a menu, which overlays the Write screen. These menus let you access even more options.

The next line down is part of a border that surrounds the workspace. At the bottom border are the markings for the left and right margins, the tab stops, and the character by character increment markings. The bottom of the border is called the *ruler line* because it indicates where the tab stops and margins are set. In the upper left of the workspace is the *cursor*. This blinking light lets you know where the next character you type will appear. When you type a character, it is inserted exactly where the cursor is located. The cursor then moves to the next position to the right, awaiting the next character.

Type in the Insert mode at first, so you won't delete important information.

At the very bottom of the screen is the *status line*. The first entry on the left is Working Copy followed by the word Inserting. Working Copy appears when you're creating a new document; it indicates that your new document doesn't have a name. Inserting indicates that when you type, you insert characters into the document rather than write over what's already there. The difference between the use of Insert and Overwrite is covered a bit later.

Across the screen to the right is an indicator that shows the percent of *RAM* (random access memory) being used by your document. When you begin a new document, the indicator displays 0%, as it does in Figure 1-2. As your document becomes longer, the number increases, indicating that you're using increasing amounts of computer memory. When the indicator approaches 100%, you need to split your document into two pieces, in order to continue working. Later, when you print the document, you can join the pieces to recreate the single document.

The next message in the status line shows the *location of the cursor* relative to the document. Even though the cursor is several lines down from the top of the document border, the status line indicates Line 1 of page 1. The reason for this seeming discrepancy is that Write is assuming a top margin of six lines for the document. Hence, Write is telling you that the cursor is located on the first line after the top margin. In addition, the indicator lets you know what page you're working on.

Last, in the bottom left corner of the screen is Esc-Main Menu. Pressing the Esc (Escape) key at this point takes you from the word processing workspace to the Main menu shown in Figure 1-1. To see the effect of pressing Esc, do so now.

Write protects you from yourself.

Even if you had entered a line of text, Write would let you escape to the Main menu. However, if you then tried to select option E (Exit), Write would not let you exit. Why? Because when you open a document and type in any text, Write assumes you want to save the document before you exit. Exiting without saving the document causes it to be lost permanently; that could be a real disaster! Of course, if you saved the document to a disk previously, you'd still have the old version.

Okay, now that you have been in the workspace and back out to the Main menu, reopen the workspace by choosing option 1. Create/Edit.

The Keyboard

Although your computer keyboard contains the usual typewriter keys, it has several keys not found on a normal typewriter keyboard. One important key that is different is the Enter key. The Enter key is used to signify that you want to end a line of text or activate a menu choice, as you did when selecting the beginning option from the Main menu.

The Function Keys

Across the top or to the left side of the main typewriter keys are the function keys, which let you access menus in Write. The keys are numbered 1 to 10 or 12, but for the time being we will focus only on the first six.

F1-Help

The F1 function key lets you access a context-sensitive help screen. Context sensitive just means that Professional Write "knows" what you're working on and displays a Help screen that specifically addresses the task you're trying to perform.

To see one of these Help screens, press the F1 key. Since you're in the Create/Edit mode, Professional Write assumes you need help moving the cursor, and it presents the Cursor Movement Keys screen shown in Figure 1-3.

This particular Help screen contains the directions for moving the cursor in the document. At the bottom of the Help screen are instructions for controlling the screen:

- To close the screen, press Esc.
- To see more of the screen, press the Down Arrow or PgDn key.

Getting Started

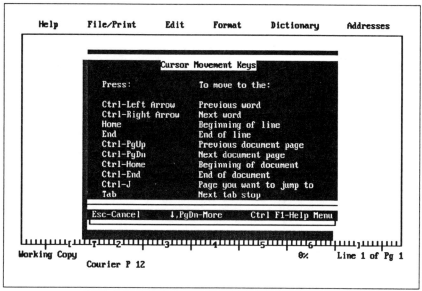

Figure 1-3 The Cursor Movement Keys screen

- To get help concerning some other task, press Ctrl-F1 (that is, hold down the Ctrl key and press the F1 key). This displays the Help menu that lists a variety of tasks you may need help with. Just highlight the task you need help with and press Enter.

The Help screens can be accessed at any point in the creation of a document, to assist you as you learn to use Write. For now, close the pulldown menu by pressing Esc.

F2-File/Print

Press the F2 key to see the File/Print menu, shown in Figure 1-4. As you can see, this menu lets you perform various operations, such as saving and getting a file. This is the same menu you'll access when you're ready to print your document.

This time, instead of pressing the Esc key to close the menu, let's try using the Right Arrow key to close the F2 menu and open the F3 menu. The Right Arrow key may be the same as the 6 key on the numeric keyboard. If it is, make sure the light on the Num Lock key is off, meaning the key is not activated. (If the Num Lock key is activated, pressing the Right Arrow key will select option 6. If the present menu has fewer than 6 options, pressing the Right Arrow key will do nothing.) Now, press the Right Arrow key, closing the File/Print menu and opening the Edit menu. (The Left Arrow key works in a similar way, closing the present menu and opening the previous one.)

Chapter 1

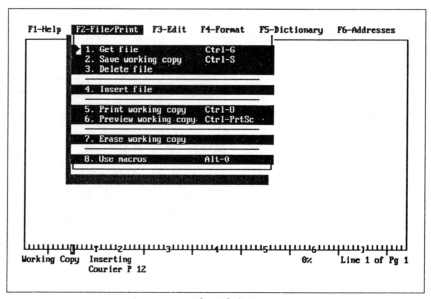

Figure 1-4 The File/Print menu

F3-Edit

The menu you'll use most frequently when creating and perfecting your document is the Edit menu. This menu lets you boldface or underline words and phrases, cut and paste blocks of text, and search for individual words. Professional Write will even replace each instance of a word with whatever word you choose.

F4-Format

Press the Right Arrow key again to open the Format menu. This menu lets you set all the attributes that determine how the document will appear when you print it. Write offers common default settings for margins and tab stops, but makes it easy to change these settings for your convenience.

F5-Dictionary

Use Write's dictionary to find the less-obvious typos.

Write is equipped with a 77,000 word dictionary. When you're finished typing your document, before printing it, you can tell the Dictionary to check your spelling, stop on suspect words, and ask for your input. Write will suggest a correct spelling, too. But be careful; if you typed in when you meant to type on don't expect the Dictionary to catch the mistake—in *is* spelled correctly.

F6-Addresses

In addition to all these useful word processing features, Write includes an Address Book. This lets you insert the names and addresses of the people you write to most frequently into any document you wish to send.

Special Keys

Figure 1-5 shows the IBM 101-key keyboard. The keys that differ from those on a normal typewriter keyboard are labeled.

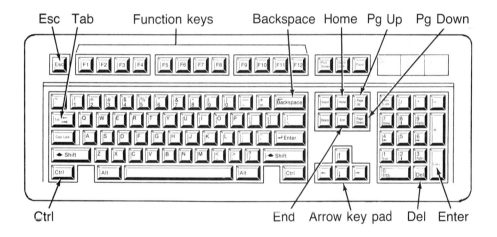

Figure 1-5 A schematic of a keyboard: arrows indicate which keys are different

Esc (Escape)

This key is used to *go back* from the present screen to the previous screen. When you're typing a document in the workspace, this key takes you to the Main menu. Esc is also used to abort an action. For example, if you start to print a document and then decide to use the spell checker first, pressing Esc will stop the print sequence.

Ctrl (Control)

Ctrl helps you get the most out of your keystroke.

The Control key (Ctrl) is used in conjunction with other keys. Think of it as being similar to the Shift key, which activates capital letters. For example, pressing only the F1 key displays a Help screen, but holding down the Ctrl key while pressing the F1 key (Ctrl-F1) opens the Help menu.

Backspace

The Backspace key moves the cursor back one space to the left and erases the character at that position. Avoid the temptation to use the Backspace key the same way you'd use an arrow key; this key eats letters!

Arrow Keys

Arrow keys move the cursor within a document (without affecting the text), and move the highlight from option to option within a menu. The Left and Right Arrow keys move the cursor one character at a time in a single line of text, while the Up and Down Arrow keys move the cursor up or down one line at a time. You can hold any of the arrow keys down to move the cursor in a machine-gun fashion. Or, better yet, make use of the Ctrl key; press Ctrl-Left Arrow or Ctrl-Right Arrow to move the cursor word by word.

The arrow keys are located either on a separate pad or in the numeric keypad area. Before using those keys, make sure the Num Lock key is not activated (the light should be off). It acts like a toggle switch, so pressing the key turns it on until you press it again.

Del (Delete)

The Del key erases the character that the cursor is on. Holding down Del erases characters continuously. Professional Write also lets you delete a single word or line or an entire block of text, but we'll look at those features later.

Home

When typing a line of text, you may want to move the cursor quickly back to the beginning of a line. To do this, simply press the Home key. Want to go all the way back to the beginning of the document? Press Ctrl-Home, and you're there.

End

The End key moves the cursor to the end of the line you're working on. To jump to the very end of the document—you guessed it, press Ctrl-End.

Enter

Professional Write automatically wraps words from line to line, so don't press Enter at the end of a line.

Letter keys aside, the most frequently used key is the Enter key. Similar to a carriage return on a typewriter, the Enter key inserts a hard return in the text. Because Professional Write moves the cursor automatically to the next line as you type, you don't have to press Enter at the end of each line. But when you want a distinct space between lines, such as in a paragraph break, you need to use the Enter key.

Enter is also used to confirm an action; it gives you that one last chance to change your mind. For example, if you choose to print your document, Write waits for you to confirm the command, by pressing Enter, before it starts printing.

PgUp (Page Up), PgDn (Page Down)

If you're used to working with paper, the word "Page" here may be a little misleading; you might expect these keys to move the cursor one printed page—about 55 lines of text plus the top and bottom margins. But the page we're referring to here is the page displayed on screen—about 24 lines of text. Use the PgDn key to move to the next screenful of text; use the PgUp key to move to the previous screen.

If you want to move the cursor one bona fide page (55 lines plus margins), just press Ctrl-PgUp or Ctrl-PgDn.

Tab

The Tab key works the same way on a computer as it does on a typewriter; that is, it moves the cursor a specified number of spaces across the line. You can set the tab stops wherever you like and use as many as you need. Pressing Shift-Tab moves the cursor back to the previous Tab stop.

Entering Text

Type characters just as you would on a typewriter.

Now let's enter some text, so we can try these keys out on some real stuff. Suppose you're the boss and you want to send a brief memo to all the people in your department about your upcoming trip to Africa. To enter the text shown in Figure 1-6, perform the following steps:

1. Type `To: Members of the Staff`.
2. Press Enter, moving the cursor to the next line.
3. Continue typing until you type `Boss`.

4. Press Enter twice: once to move the cursor to the next line, and once to insert a blank line.

5. Continue typing the rest of the memo as shown in Figure 1-6.

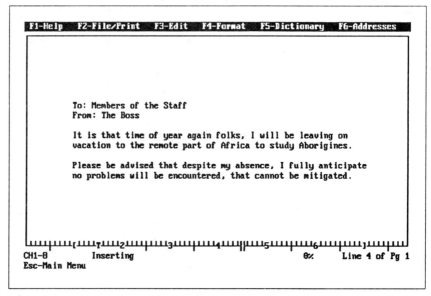

Figure 1-6   The MEMO document

Wordwrapping

Professional Write adjusts and readjusts text to fit the margins.

Whenever you reach the end of a line, Write automatically *wraps* the words around to the next line. Write does this by counting the number of characters you type and calculating the space remaining on the line. That calculation tells Write if there's enough room for a certain number of words. If you run out of room, Write automatically wraps the word or words to the next line down. This feature makes it easy to type away without worrying about pressing Enter.

Moving the Cursor

As you typed the example above, the cursor moved ahead of the characters, one at a time. One character at a time is fine for typing, but when you decide to edit, that gets to be mighty slow. So now that we have some text to play with, let's move the cursor around to get a feel for the different ways we can move it.

Note the present position of the cursor in the memo you just created. Now, press the Home key; the cursor jumps to the beginning of the line. Press Ctrl-PgUp, moving the cursor to the first character in the memo, in this case the letter T in To.

Press the Tab key once, and the cursor moves to the letter e in Members. Look at the line at the bottom of the screen. The cursor is mimicked in the Ruler line, moving as you type. Because you just pressed the Tab key, the cursor is over the T in the ruler line. If you were to press Tab again, the cursor wouldn't move because no other tab stops have been set.

Now, press Ctrl-Right Arrow, moving the cursor to the next word. Press Ctrl-Left Arrow, and the cursor jumps back to the previous word.

To move the cursor to the beginning of the next line, press Ctrl-Enter.

Moving to a Different Page

Make the cursor jump to a specific page.

If your document contains a number of pages, you can move the cursor from page to page. But first, you have to access the Jump to Page screen shown in Figure 1-7. Pressing Ctrl-J accesses the screen.

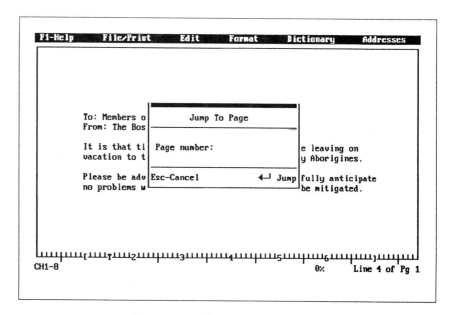

Figure 1-7 The Jump to Page screen

The only problem here is that you have to know what page you want to jump to. Because formatting changes the way a page prints, page 7 on screen may differ from page 7 on paper, but it'll be close.

Insert versus Overstrike Mode

Professional Write lets you type characters in either of two modes: Insert or Overstrike. Insert is the default setting. (Default just means that unless you specify otherwise, the computer will choose for you. Usually, the default is the safest option.) As you type or press the spacebar in the Insert mode, the characters to the right of the cursor are pushed ahead, making room for the characters you type. To let you know that you are in the Insert mode, the program displays the cursor as a tall bar and displays Inserting in the status line.

If you wish to type over the characters you've already entered, you can use the Overstrike mode. To change to Overstrike, just press the Ins key once. Inserting disappears from the status line, and the cursor shrinks to a small line below the characters.

Use the shortcut keys Ctrl-Y to switch from Insert to Overstrike and back. Or, simply press Ins.

Typing in the Overstrike Mode

With the memo still on screen, move the cursor to the B in Boss. Now, press the Ins key changing to the Overstrike mode. Inserting disappears from the status line. Type Chief. As you can see, Boss is gone, and Chief is in its place.

Be careful in the Overstrike mode. Until you return to the Insert mode, the cursor will continue to gobble up letters. To return to the Insert mode, press the Ins key.

Typing in the Insert Mode

Professional Write automatically readjusts your text to accommodate a change.

Let's say that you want to further enhance the name by changing The Chief to The Big Chief. To insert the word Big, move the cursor to the space between The and Chief. Make sure Inserting is displayed on the status line. If it's not, press the Ins key once.

Next, press the spacebar once, and type Big. The screen should look like Figure 1-8.

Deleting Characters

Suppose you want to delete the word folks from the memo. Move the cursor to the space to the left of folks, and press the Del key until all of

Getting Started

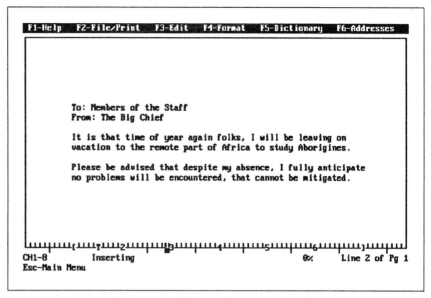

Figure 1-8 The word Big is inserted

the letters in folks are erased. Notice that as the word is erased, the words following are pulled in to fill the gap, vacation jumps up one line, and the rest of the characters shift as needed (see Figure 1-9). Professional Write automatically adjusts the text around insertions and deletions to maintain the integrity of the document. You no longer have to worry about spacing and formatting when you're absorbed in the compexities of editing.

Deleting a Word or Line

You can delete an entire word or line with the use of a menu option. Let's eliminate the word Big in the From: line:

1. Move the cursor to any character in Big.
2. Press F3, opening the Edit menu as shown in Figure 1-10.
3. The second option on this menu is Delete word. You can activate that option in either of two ways:
   - Use the arrow keys to move the highlight to the option, and press Enter.
   - Type 2.

   In either case, the word disappears immediately.

15

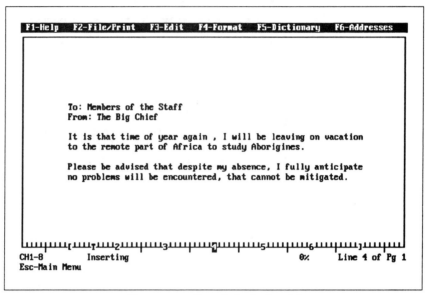

Figure 1-9 Text shifted after deletion

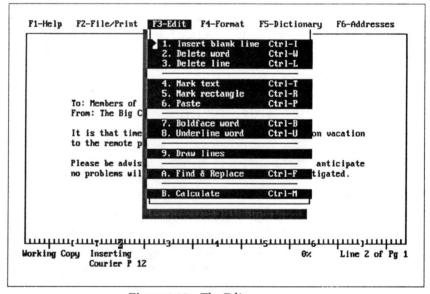

Figure 1-10 The Edit menu

Finally, let's remove the entire From: line, using the same menu:

1. Press F3, opening the Edit menu.
2. Select option 3. Delete line. The entire line is deleted, as shown in Figure 1-11.

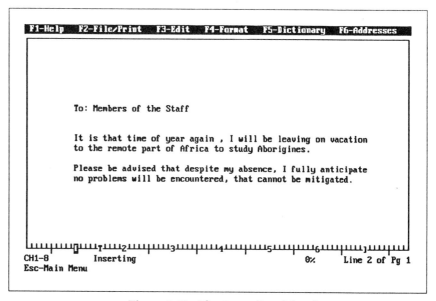

Figure 1-11 The From: line deleted

Do not use the Edit menu's delete options to delete several words or lines; a safer way is to use the block commands described in Chapter 4.

On the Edit menu, to the right of the Delete word and Delete line options are the notations Ctrl-W and Ctrl-L, respectively. What this means is that instead of pressing F3 to open the Edit menu and then selecting option 2 or option 3, you can simply move the cursor to the word or line you want to delete and press Ctrl-W (to delete a word) or Ctrl-L (to delete a line). Once you get used to these key combinations, they save loads of time.

The Edit menu offers shortcut keys for almost every option. This is true of the other menus as well. To make these combinations easier to remember, most of them are abbreviations for the option's name: Ctrl-B for **B**oldface, Ctrl-U for **U**nderline, and Ctrl-M for calculate (**M**ath). You may have to stop and think at first, but these shortcuts soon become as natural as pressing a Shift key to capitalize.

Double-Spacing the Text

The default setting for line spacing is single space. To change to double space, perform the following steps:

1. Press F4, opening the Format menu shown in Figure 1-12.
2. Choose option 7. Turn double spacing on/off. Double appears after Inserting in the status line. Text typed from this point on will be double-spaced.

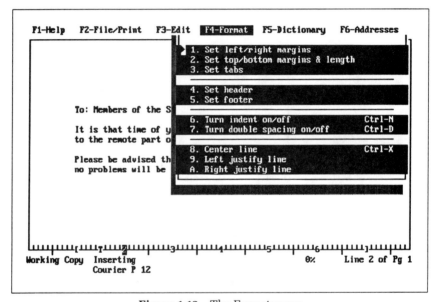

Figure 1-12 The Format menu

Option 7 is a toggle command that turns double spacing on or off. Selecting this option makes the document double spaced from that point forward but does not affect previously entered text. To change previously entered text, make sure the cursor is in the first line of the paragraph you want to change, then choose option 7. This changes the spacing in that paragraph only; you must repeat the process to change the spacing of other paragraphs. You can also change line spacing by using a block command, but we'll deal with that later in Chapter 3.

Use the shortcut keys to change the line spacing without opening the Format menu. Whenever you want to change the spacing, press Ctrl-D.

Inserting Hard Spaces

Use hard spaces to override the Wordwrap feature.

Professional Write automatically wraps words from one line to the next, whether you want it to or not. Occasionally, you may want a name or title in a document to remain together on one line. Unless you tell it otherwise, Wordwrap may split it.

To override the Wordwrap feature, you can insert hard spaces between the words in the name. Professional Write treats the hard spaces as characters and won't split what it considers to be a single long word.

To type a hard space, press Ctrl-spacebar. Professional Write displays a dot where the space would normally appear, as shown in Figure 1-13.

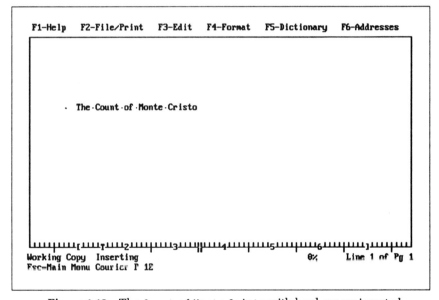

Figure 1-13 The Count of Monte Cristo with hard spaces inserted

Formatting Characters

Format characters for emphasis.

With Professional Write, you can add two enhancements to the characters you type: Boldface or Underline. The same steps are used to add either enhancement to your characters:

1. Move the cursor to the word you wish to boldface or underline.
2. Press F3, opening the Edit menu shown in Figure 1-14.
3. Choose option 7. Boldface word or option 8. Underline word.

Chapter 1

Figure 1-14 The Edit menu

The word you enhanced is displayed with the enhancement. (On a color monitor, the boldfaced word is a different color; on a monochrome monitor, the word is brighter than the others.) To verify the type of format a word has, move the cursor to the word in question. The status line indicates the format used.

If you try to use character enhancement on a single word in a title consisting of several words with hard spaces, Professional Write will treat the entire title as a single word, enhancing all the characters in every word. Figure 1-15 shows The Count of Monte Cristo underlined. Under appears in the Status line, indicating the word is underlined.

If you decide later that you really don't like the enhancement, you can remove it by simply deleting the enhanced word and retyping it or by using the block commands explained in Chapter 3.

A quicker method for boldfacing or underlining characters is to use the shortcut keys. Move the cursor to the word you want to enhance and press Ctrl-B (to boldface) or Ctrl-U (to underline).

Using the List and Outline Format

Let Professional Write add structure to your lists and outlines.

Professional Write gives you the power to type lists and outlines in an indented format. The indenting is done automatically, so you can concentrate on the content while Write does the formatting.

Getting Started

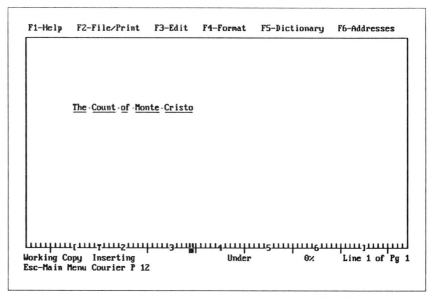

Figure 1-15 The Count of Monte Cristo underlined

To indicate that you want to indent, type a leading bullet character, in the case of a list, or a number or letter, in the case of an outline. A bullet can include any of the following characters: − * + . Figure 1-16 shows a list with a variety of leading characters.

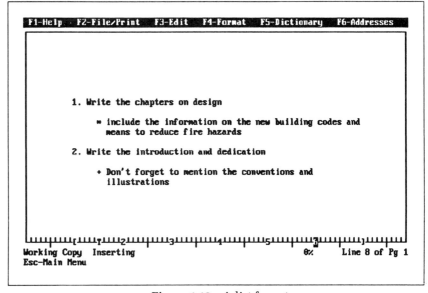

Figure 1-16 A list format

The outline format includes further indentations for subcategories of topics. Figure 1-17 presents an example of the outline format. As you can see, typing a letter, number, or Roman numeral followed by a period, right parenthesis, greater than sign, frontslash, backslash, dash, or colon tells Professional Write to create an outline format.

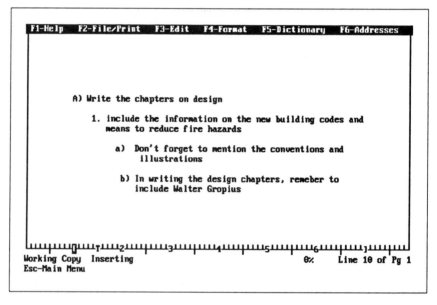

Figure 1-17 An outline format

Saving a Document

Save your work every fifteen minutes or so, to prevent losing important information.

As you typed the memo shown in Figure 1-11, it was saved in RAM (random access memory); the status line shows how much RAM you've used. If you turn off the computer without saving the document to a disk, you will lose the document forever. To prevent this loss, you need to save the document. The process of saving files depends on the type of disk you're using.

Saving to a Floppy Disk

To save the memo to a floppy disk, perform the following steps:

1. Press F2, opening the File/Print menu shown in Figure 1-18.

2. Choose option 2. Save working copy to see the Filename screen shown in Figure 1-19. This screen displays the disk drive where Professional Write will try to save the file.
3. Remove the disk from drive B, and replace it with a blank formatted disk.
4. Press Ctrl-E to erase the disk drive displayed on screen, then type b:memo and press Enter. This tells Professional Write, "Save document to drive B and call the file MEMO."

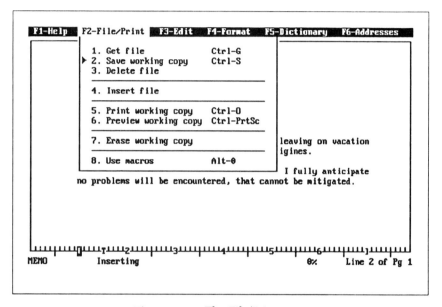

Figure 1-18 The File/Print menu

The shortcut keys offer a quicker way to save files. When you decide to save your file, just press Ctrl-S to access the Filename screen.

Saving to a Hard Disk

To save the memo to a hard disk, perform the following steps:

1. Press F2, opening the File/Print menu shown in Figure 1-18.
2. Choose option 2. Save working copy, opening the Filename screen shown in Figure 1-19. This screen displays a path to the subdirectory where Professional Write will try to save the file.

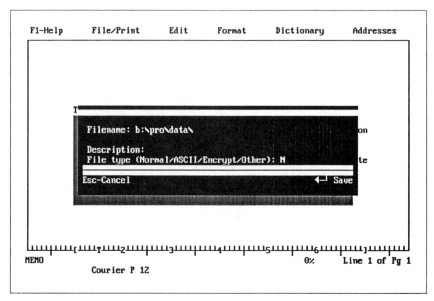

Figure 1-19 The Filename screen

3. If the path is correct, type the name of the document, for exampl memo, and press Enter. If not, press Ctrl-E to erase the path, type the path of the subdirectory where you want to save the document, and type the name of the document. For example, type c:\wdata\examples\memo. This gives Professional Write directions to the subdirectory and a name for the file.

The shortcut keys offer a quicker way to save files. When you decide to save your file, just press Ctrl-S to access the Filename screen.

Special Features for Saving Files

Professional Write's built-in conversion program lets you share files with others and use files that were not created with Professional Write.

Professional Write offers two important features that you should be aware of when saving files. First, in order to make it easier to remember what you have written in a particular document, Professional Write offers a Description option that lets you add a brief description of your document file. This is a terrific feature because the operating system, DOS, does not allow for long filenames, and the short names give you little clue as to what's in the file. Although the description does not appear in the list of document files, you can get to it quickly by opening the PFS.DIR file. This file displays your description of the document next to the DOS filename.

Second, Professional Write lets you save the document in a special kind of file other than a normal Professional Write file. This allows you to share files with others by saving the file in a generic format, called ASCII (pronounced ASKee), which can be read by virtually all word processing programs. You can also save the file as an Encrypted file to prevent other Professional Write users from seeing the contents of your file without a password. But don't forget your password!

To use the two other options, don't press Enter after typing the filename. Instead, press the Tab key moving the cursor to the description area and type your description. Then press Tab again, moving to the File Type entry area, and type the first letter of the file type you want. Finally, press Enter to save the document file.

Printing the Document

Now that the memo is stored in a safe place, let's print out a real-live version of it. To print the document, Professional Write sends it to the printer. If you haven't selected a printer, go to the Appendix and read the section on setting up a printer. The setup consists of telling Professional Write which printer you're using, so Write can talk to the printer in a language that the printer understands. With the printer set up, perform the following steps:

1. Press F2, opening the File/Print menu.
2. Choose option 5. Print Working Copy, opening the Print Options screen in Figure 1-20. The options are discussed in detail in Chapter 9, but we'll get the printer up and running for now.
3. Press the Tab key to move the highlight to any option you want to change, then type in the desired change. For example, if you want the printer to pause between pages so you can check how the format looks on a page, press the Tab key three times to move the cursor to the right of Pause between pages (Y/N), and type Y. Once you're sure the Print Options are set as you wish, press Enter.

If everything is set up correctly, the printer should start. Wait until the printing stops before typing anything.

To print the working copy using the shortcut keys, press Ctrl-O, opening the Print Options screen, then continue from there.

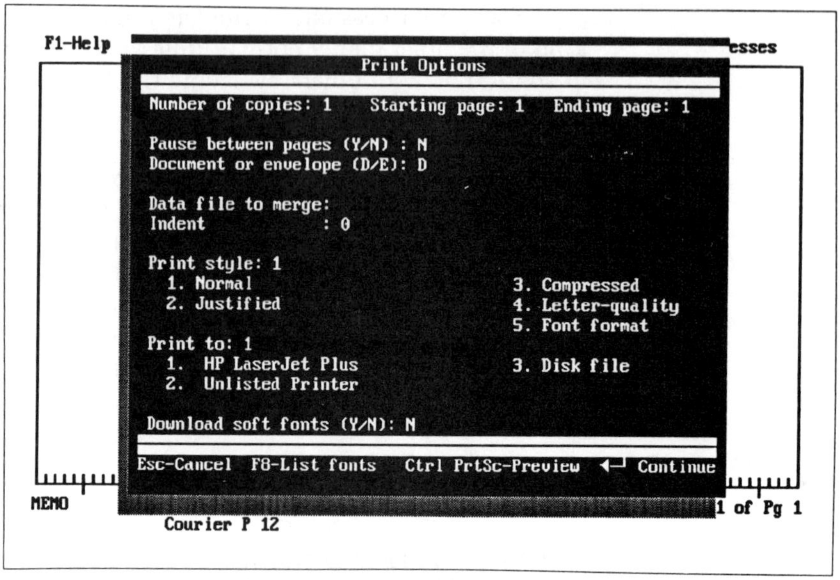

Figure 1-20 The Print Options screen

Summary

In this chapter you learned to use the function keys and other special keys to enter and edit text, and to add enhancements such as underline and boldface. You also learned how to save a document to a disk so you can retrieve it later for editing or printing. And you learned to print a hard copy of your document. Not bad for a chapter's worth of work!

In the next chapter, we'll do a little fine-tuning. You'll learn to retrieve the saved MEMO document, add text to it, and then use more extensive formatting options to spruce it up.

T W O

Formatting Your Document

In the previous chapter, you began to see the results of different formatting techniques on entered text. In this chapter, you'll acquire new skills to give you even more power over your document.

But first, you have to retrieve your document from disk, so you'll have something to work with.

Getting a Saved Document File

Professional Write "gets" your file for you.

Professional Write uses the term "Get" for retrieving a file from disk and putting it into RAM. To get your file, you first need to access the file directory where the file is located. To do that, start Professional Write on your computer and perform the following steps:

1. Choose option 1. Create/Edit from the Main menu. A blank work screen opens.
2. Press F2, opening the File/Print menu as shown in Figure 2-1.
3. If you're using a floppy disk, make sure the disk with the file you want is in drive B. Since we'll be working with the MEMO document, make sure the disk with that file is in the drive.
4. Choose option 1. Get file.

Chapter 2

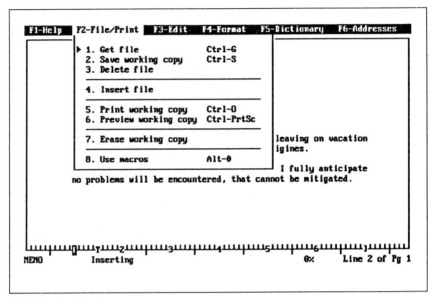

Figure 2-1 The File/Print menu

The shortcut keys provide quick access to the file directory. After choosing the Create/Edit option, just press Ctrl-G.

Depending on the type of disk you're using, you see either of two displays. If you have a floppy disk, the directory is displayed, and all you need to do is select the file you want. If you're using a hard disk, however, you need to know the name of the subdirectory where you stored the file.

Getting a File from a Floppy Disk

Since the directory is already on screen, simply press the Down Arrow key until the highlight is over MEMO and press Enter to open the file.

Getting a File from a Hard Disk

If you customized Professional Write as suggested in the Appendix, you created a directory called WDATA with a subdirectory called EXAMPLES to hold the files created with this book. You may also have changed the default directory so Professional Write would access the EXAMPLES subdirectory whenever you wanted a file. If you performed this setup, Professional Write now displays:

Formatting Your Document

```
Filename: C:\WDATA\EXAMPLES
```

We'll explore subdirectories more deeply in Chapter 4, but for now let's get your file. In Chapter 1, we saved the MEMO document in the EXAMPLES subdirectory. If that directory is displayed on the Filename screen, just type the name of the file you want—for example, memo—and press Enter. If a different drive, directory, and subdirectory are displayed, perform the following steps:

1. Press Ctrl-E, erasing the subdirectory path presented by Professional Write.

2. Type c:\wdata\examples and press Enter. The directory of files, including MEMO is displayed on screen. Figure 2-2 shows a sample File directory.

3. Move the highlight to MEMO and press Enter, loading the document into RAM. Your memo will soon appear on screen.

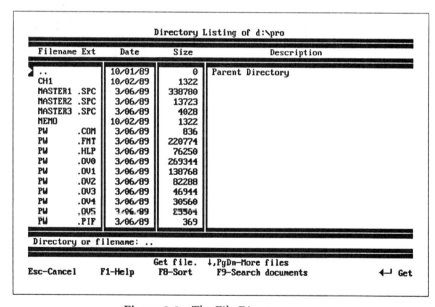

Figure 2-2 The File Directory screen

Setting Left and Right Margins

With the MEMO document on screen, let's change the left margin. First, you must move the cursor to a line in the workspace that contains no text. Press the Down Arrow key until the cursor is in the line below the last line of text. If you left the cursor in a line of text, Professional Write would tell you via a message screen that you can't change the margins until you move the cursor. With the cursor on a blank line, perform the following steps:

1. Press F4, opening the Format menu shown in Figure 2-3.
2. Choose option 1. Set left/right margins and press Enter. The Set Left and Right Margin submenu appears as shown in Figure 2-4, presenting you with two options.

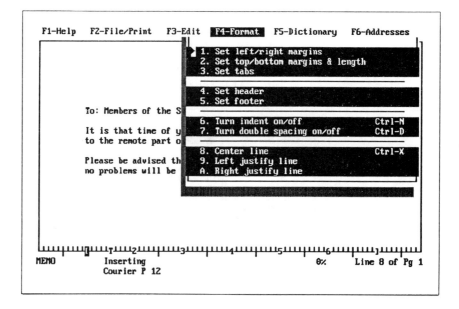

Figure 2-3   The Format menu

For quick access to the Set Left and Right Margins submenu, position the cursor on a blank line, and press Ctrl-[.

Professional Write gives you a choice of setting new margins for the rest of the document or for only a portion of the text. In either case, the margins will affect only the text entered after you changed the margin; text entered earlier remains unchanged. This means that even if you left the cursor at the top line of the MEMO document and made a change, the previously entered text would not be altered.

You can set the margin in either of two ways. One way is to simply move the brackets on the ruler line. Let's change the left margin using this method:

Formatting Your Document

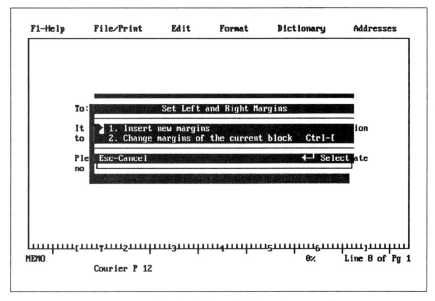

Figure 2-4 The Set Left and Right Margins submenu

1. Press the Right Arrow key, moving the cursor to the right until it is on the 2 in the ruler line.
2. Type [and press Enter. You've just succeeded in setting a new left margin.

The second method is to type the exact values for the margins. We'll use this method to set the right margin:

1. Press F4, reopening the Format menu.
2. Choose option 1. Set left/right margins. This opens the Set Left and Right Margins submenu.
3. Choose option 1. Insert new margins.
4. Press F8, accessing the Margin Settings screen as shown in Figure 2-5.

    The default margins in Professional Write are 10 and 70; that is, 10 spaces are reserved on the left, and characters can be typed up to the 70th space to the right. However, we moved the left margin, so the screen displays the new left margin setting of 20.
5. Press the Tab key once, moving the cursor to Right margin:.
6. Type 50, and press Enter.

Margin settings are displayed in the ruler line.

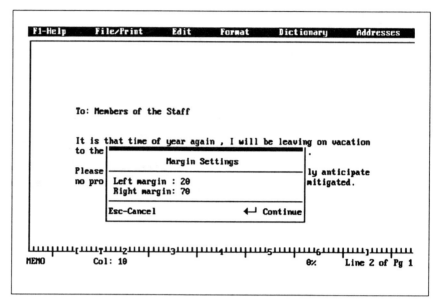

Figure 2-5 The Margin Settings screen

Look at the ruler line, and you'll see the new margin settings. These new margins are in effect for the text that you enter from this point on. Move the cursor up several lines into the body of the text; the ruler line indicates the old margin settings—those used for the previous text.

Now, let's see the effects of the new margins. Leave the cursor where it is, then type the following:

```
If anyone has a serious problem that absolutely
requires my attention, call my home number and leave a
message on my answering machine. I will check daily
for messages.
```

Your screen should match the one in Figure 2-6. The margins remain at the new settings until you change them.

Resetting Margins

Now, let's reset the margins to the default settings of 10 and 70. Just perform the following steps:

Formatting Your Document

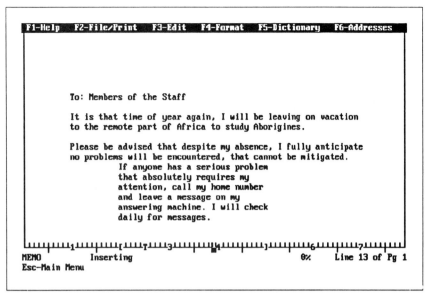

Figure 2-6 The effects of the new margin settings

1. With the cursor in the line below the last line of text, press F4, opening the Format menu.
2. Select option **1. Set Left/Right margins**.
3. Choose option **1. Insert New Margins**.
4. The default margins are 10 and 70, so move the cursor on the ruler line to 1 and type [. Move the cursor to 7 and type].

Of course, you could follow the other procedure by opening the Format menu, pressing F8, then typing 10 and 70.

In either case, the margins return to the default settings. By letting you change the margins so quickly, Professional Write makes it easy to set off lines of text for special emphasis throughout the document.

Setting a Temporary Left Margin

Use a temporary left margin for bulleted or numbered lists.

An even easier way of setting off text is to use a temporary left margin, which is indented from the normal left margin. It's a lot like a tab stop except in this case you don't have to press Tab to indent each successive line.

Like the margin settings, the temporary left margin affects only the portion of the document that you type after creating the margin. To make a temporary left margin, perform the following steps:

1. Move the cursor to the place where you want the indented text to begin.
2. Press F4, opening the Format menu.
3. Select option 6. Turn indent on/off.

Professional Write displays where the temporary left margin is located. Any text you type will be wrapped around to that margin. The temporary left margin is a toggle switch, so follow the same steps above to turn it off; that is, open the Format menu and select Turn indent on/off.

Inserting Page Breaks

You can override Professional Write's page breaks.

Like most word processing programs, Professional Write calculates the length of a document and then divides the lines of text to print neatly on individual pages.

As you enter longer documents, however, you may create tables or set off chunks of text, such as long quotes, that should be printed on a single page. Because Professional Write automatically divides text, your text or tables may get split by one of Write's automatic page breaks.

To override this page break, you must manually insert a page break command at the beginning of the table or text you want kept together. This requires the use of what's called an *embedded* command. (Embedded just means that the command is actually somewhere within the text.) In this case, you need to type the embedded command

NEW PAGE

at the point where you want to insert a page break.

For example, the text in Figure 2-7 has a small table that should remain as a single unit. At the top of the table is the *NEW PAGE* command.

The *NEW PAGE* command is entered at the beginning of the table at the left margin, to make sure Professional Write reads the command before it starts printing the table. When Professional Write reaches the *NEW PAGE* command, Write recognizes the asterisks and reads NEW PAGE as a command instead of as text.

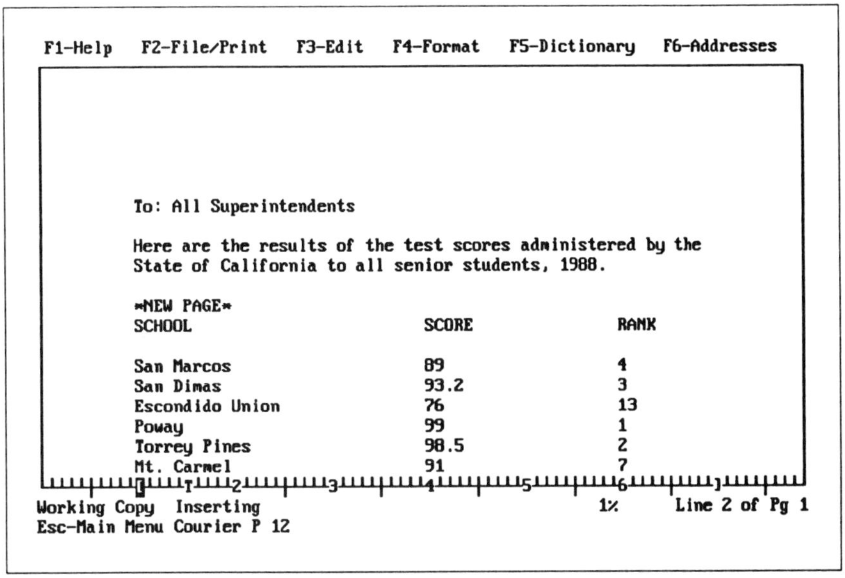

```
    F1-Help    F2-File/Print   F3-Edit   F4-Format   F5-Dictionary   F6-Addresses




    To: All Superintendents

    Here are the results of the test scores administered by the
    State of California to all senior students, 1988.

    *NEW PAGE*
    SCHOOL                          SCORE                    RANK

    San Marcos                      89                       4
    San Dimas                       93.2                     3
    Escondido Union                 76                       13
    Poway                           99                       1
    Torrey Pines                    98.5                     2
    Mt. Carmel                      91                       7
|....|....T....|....2....|....3....|....4....|....5....|....6....|....7....|....
Working Copy   Inserting                              1%       Line 2 of Pg 1
Esc-Main Menu  Courier P 12
```

Figure 2-7 The *NEW PAGE* command embedded in the text

As soon as Professional Write reads the *NEW PAGE* command, it feeds paper through the printer until reaching the beginning of the next page. Write then begins printing the table at the top of the new page.

Setting Tab Stops

The default tab stop in a new Professional Write document is 15 characters from the left margin. That's 5 characters in from the left default margin. (Remember, a space is considered a character.) This default setting is convenient for indenting paragraphs, but if you're interested in doing more with tabs, read on.

Professional Write offers two kinds of tab stops: the traditional typewriter tab stop and a decimal tab stop for aligning numbers. The typewriter tab stop, displayed on the ruler line as T, lines up text in columns, tables, and in other similar constructions.

The decimal tab stop, D on the ruler line, lines up the decimal points in columns of numbers. When you use the decimal tab stop, numbers to the left of the decimal point are inserted to the *left* of the tab stop, the decimal point lands on top of the tab stop, and the numbers after the decimal point are inserted to the *right* of the tab stop.

Setting Typewriter Tab Stops

As was true with changing margins, the cursor must be in a line that contains no text; otherwise, Professional Write will not accept the change. Move the cursor to the bottom of the MEMO document. Then,

1. Press F4, opening the Format menu.
2. Choose option 3. Set tabs, opening the Set Tabs submenu as shown in Figure 2-8.
3. Select option 1. Insert new tabs. Professional Write responds with a message at the very bottom of the screen:

   Type T or D at each Tab location

4. Move the cursor to the tab stop desired and type T. T appears in the ruler line, indicating the position of the new tab stop.

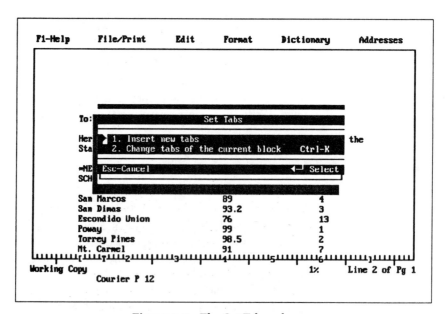

Figure 2-8 The Set Tabs submenu

To make sure the tab stop is where you want it, check the Col (Column) number in the status line. Computer screens are deceptive; a character at the top of the screen may appear to be in a different position from a character at the bottom, even though they're at the same tab stop.

After inserting the new tab stops, press Enter to go back to the workspace. Now that the tab stops are set, you can use the Tab key just like the Tab key on the typewriter, except that now you can move the cursor backward. To move the cursor forward to a Tab stop, just press the Tab key. To move back to a previous tab stop, press Shift-Tab.

Setting Decimal Tab Stops

If you've been typing the previous examples, the MEMO document is probably displayed on screen. Let's save the revised document and clear the screen, so you can try out the decimal tab stops. To save the document, perform the following steps:

Professional Write remembers the location of the file on disk.

1. Press F2, opening the File/Print menu.
2. Choose option `2. Save Working Copy`. Professional Write responds with the Filename screen. Notice the difference from the first time you saved the MEMO document. This time, Professional Write remembers the location of the file and assumes you want to replace the old version of the MEMO document with the new, edited version.
3. Press Enter, saving the document to disk.

Now that you've saved the file in a safe place, Professional Write will let you clear it from the screen:

1. Press F2, opening the File/Print menu.
2. Choose option `7. Erase working copy`. This clears the screen, so you can start with a fresh workspace.

The Warning screen protects your work.

Had you tried to clear the screen before saving the revised MEMO, Professional Write would have presented a Warning screen as shown in Figure 2-9 to make you reconsider.

Now that you have a clear workspace, try out the decimal tabs. In this example, you will enter a couple of numbers in a short letter and line up the numbers with the decimal tab.

1. Type `Dear Dave:` and press Enter twice.
2. Press the F4 key to open the Format menu.
3. Choose option `3. Set Tabs`.
4. Choose `Insert new tabs`.

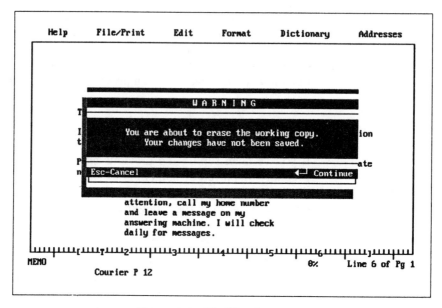

Figure 2-9 The Warning screen

5. Move the cursor to 2 in the ruler line and type D.
6. Move the cursor to 4 type D.
7. Press Enter to return to the workspace.
8. Type:

   ```
   The new cost and sales prices for the fall promotion
   are as follows:
   ```

9. Press Enter twice to move the cursor to line 6.
10. Press the Tab key twice to move the cursor to the location of the first D tab.
11. Type 456. Notice that the numbers are inserted to the left of the cursor. This works in both Insert and Overstrike mode, as long as you use the Tab key to move to the decimal tab.
12. Type . (period) to indicate the decimal point, and type 12. These numbers are inserted to the right of the decimal tab stop, which is in the same place as the decimal point.
13. Press the Tab key again and type 547.34. The screen should resemble Figure 2-10.

Formatting Your Document

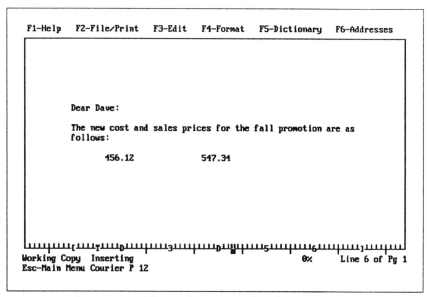

Figure 2-10 The numbers inserted at decimal tab stops

Professional Write lines up the decimal points effortlessly. If you've used other word processing programs that don't offer this feature, you'll really appreciate it now.

Save your new document as COST by using the F2 File/Print menu. We will return to the document later to use Professional Write's calculation function.

Centering Text

The task of centering text can intimidate even the most highly-skilled typist. If you've ever tried it on an ordinary typewriter, you know the script: count the characters, divide by 2, and then backspace from the center of the page. But with Professional Write, centering is a snap.

Let's say you're Dave at Dave's Appliance Service and you want to design your own company letterhead. Begin with a clear screen. If the COST document is on screen, press F2 to access the File/Print menu, and choose option 7. Erase working copy. Then, type the following:

```
Dave's Appliance Service
1450 Midway
San Diego, CA 92313
```

The cursor is now in the line with the city, state and zip code. To center that line, perform the following steps:

1. Press F4, opening the Format menu.
2. Choose option **8. Center line** and press Enter.

Bingo! The line is centered. Look at Figure 2-11 to see the results of all your hard work.

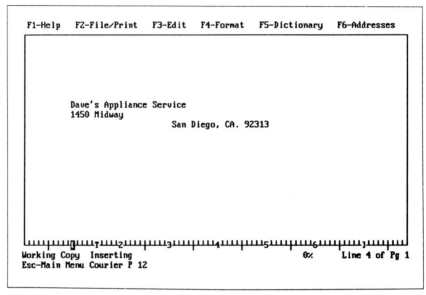

Figure 2-11 The last line of the address centered

You must recenter a line after editing it.

To center the street address, move the cursor to that line of text. Instead of using the Format menu, press Ctrl-X, and the line is centered. Repeat the procedure with the top line of the address, so your screen resembles the one in Figure 2-12.

If you edit a single line in the address, Professional Write does not automatically recenter the line. For example, type **Drive** after **1450 Midway**. Notice that the line is heavy to the right. To fix this, press Ctrl-X recentering the line. Your address should now look like the one in Figure 2-13. Press Ctrl-S, and save the document as LHEAD.

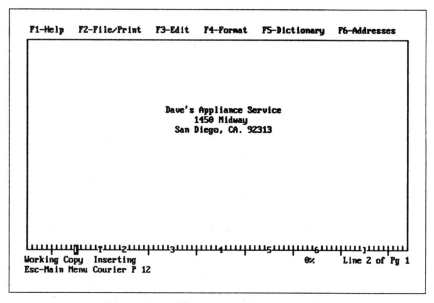

Figure 2-12 The entire address centered

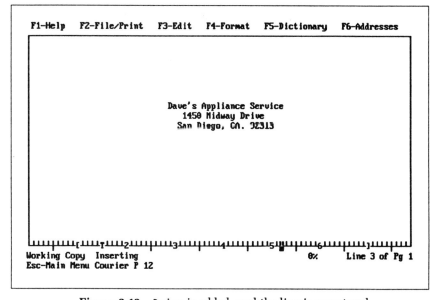

Figure 2-13 Drive is added, and the line is recentered

Chapter 2

Setting Top and Bottom Margins

Earlier in this chapter, you modified the left and right margins and created a temporary left margin. Now you'll modify other attributes of the page, such as top and bottom margins, to prepare the document for printing.

First, we need to access the screen that will let us change the settings. Press the F4 key and choose option 2. Set top/bottom margins & length to display the screen shown in Figure 2-14.

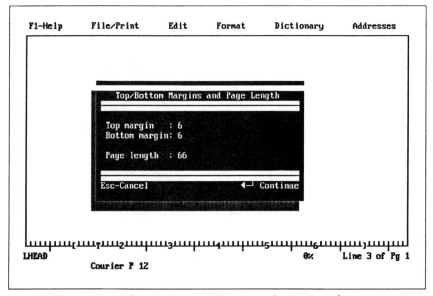

Figure 2-14   The Top/Bottom Margins and Page Length screen

The default settings for the top and bottom margins are 6 lines. Press the Tab key to move to the setting you want to change, then type the new setting. For example, press the Tab key to move the cursor to the top margin setting, then type 10. Don't press Enter yet; we'll use the same screen to set the page size.

> Choose your top and bottom margin settings carefully. Later, we'll add headers or footers that require 2 lines each. If you plan on using a header, leave at least 4 lines at the top of the page; for a footer, leave 4 lines at the bottom.

Setting the Page Size

Tell Professional Write the size of the paper you plan to print on, so the page on screen will correspond to the physical page.

The page length capability lets you change the page breaks within your document to correspond with the length of paper you're using. For example, if you're printing the document on legal paper (8½ by 14 inches), you can change the default setting of 66 lines to 84 lines. (The setting for ledger paper, 11 by 17 inches, is 102 lines.)

To change the present setting, just press the Tab key to move the cursor to the page length setting, then type the new setting. When you're finished changing the margin and page settings, and you're sure you want to keep them, press Enter. If you've decided not to change the default settings after all, press Esc.

Making the New Settings Permanent

You can change the default settings to the settings you use more often.

The modifications you just made are permanent for the particular document you're working on but not for every document you create. That's fine if you're using Professional Write's default settings for most of your documents. However, if you use other settings more often, you probably want to change the default settings.

Replacing the default settings with the settings of your choice requires the same basic procedure as the one used to save changes to an existing file. You just create and save an empty file that contains the format settings you use most often.

If you're using a floppy disk, make sure your backup copy of the Professional Write Program Disk is in the drive (if you're using a hard disk, Professional Write is in a directory on the disk). Make sure the screen is clear, then:

1. Press F4, opening the Format menu.
2. Select the element you want to change, and change it as described above.
3. Save the change by pressing Enter.
4. Repeat the process until you've changed every element on the Format menu that you wanted to change.
5. Save the file as PW.DEF, by using the F2 key or Ctrl-S.

Now, every time you use Professional Write, the settings of your choice will be in force. To return to Professional Write's default settings, simply delete the PW.DEF file and restart Professional Write.

Chapter 2

Creating Headers and Footers

You can opt to use a number as your sole entry in the header or footer.

Some documents may call for a *header* or *footer*; that is, a title, comment, or reference that is set off from the rest of the page. For example, you may want to use a header on the first page of a document to set off the title. You might also want to use a *running header* (one that appears at the top of every page) to include the document's name, the date it was created, and the name of the author. Or, more simply, you might use a number as the sole entry in a header or footer.

Creating a header or footer requires the same steps. Press the F4 key and select the option you desire from the Format menu. If you choose Set header, you open the Header screen shown in Figure 2-15.

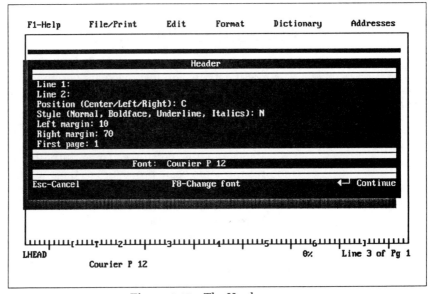

Figure 2-15   The Header screen

Type your text (up to 64 characters) in the space behind the title, then press Tab to move the cursor to line 2. Type your text (again 64 characters or less).

> Headers and footers are printed in the top and bottom margins. If you plan on using a header or footer, make sure you provide enough room in the margins.

Entering the Print Page Number Command

Enter the print page number command to have Professional Write number your pages.

Professional Write will not print page numbers automatically. To print page numbers, you must type a print page number command in the Header or Footer screen. The print page number command can come at the end of the header or footer, or it can be the sole entry.

The print page number command consists of a number bracketed by asterisks; for example, *2* tells Professional Write to begin printing the page numbers starting with the number 2. All of the numbering schemes shown in Table 2-1 are acceptable to Professional Write.

Table 2-1 Numbering Schemes

Header/Footer Entry	What Prints on Each Page
1	1,2,3,4,...
Page *1*	Page 1, Page 2, Page 3, ...
-*100*-	-100-, -101-, -102-, -103- ...
5.*1*	5.1, 5.2, 5.3 ...

Usually, you'll match the print page number command with the first page entry so the header and page numbers will begin printing on the same page. For example, Figure 2-16 shows the print page command and first page entry both as 1; the header will begin printing on page 1, and the number 1 will be on the first page of the document.

However, you may have a title page that is not considered a page of the document. In that case, you would want the header and page numbering to start on the second page of the document. Since the header will start on the second page, your first page entry will be 2. Since the title page is not numbered, the second page will be page 1, so the print page command will be *1*. As shown in Figure 2-17, the heading will start printing on the second page with the number 1.

Formatting the Header or Footer

Change the appearance of your header or footer to give each page a look of grandeur!

Now that your header or footer is typed in, you can play with it a little to alter its appearance on the page. The first choice Professional Write offers you is Position (Center/Left/Right):C. This choice represents the overall positioning of the header or footer. Center is self-explanatory. Left and Right stand for left justify and right justify; if you

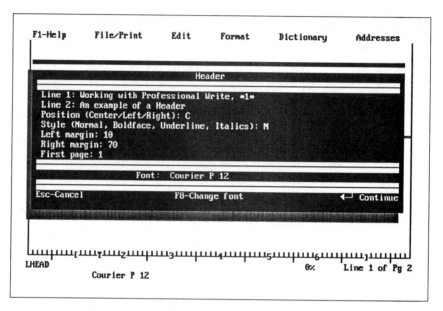

Figure 2-16 The print page number command matched to the first page entry

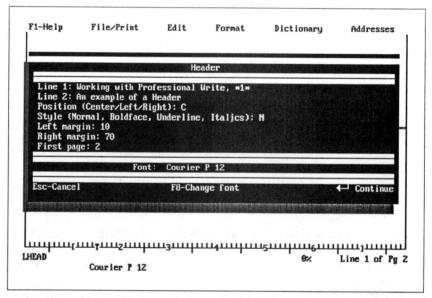

Figure 2-17 The first page entry and print page number command differ

choose left justify, for example, the header will be printed flush with the left margin. The C after the colon is the default setting—Center. If that's what you want, press Tab to move to the next choice; otherwise, type the first letter of the position you desire, then press Tab.

You can choose more than one typestyle to combine styles.

Your second choice concerns the typestyle you want for the characters in your header. Professional Write offers four choices: Normal, Boldface, Underline, and Italics. The default setting is N, Normal; if that's the setting you want, press Tab to go to the next choice. If not, type the first letter of the typestyle you want, then press Tab.

The default margin settings shown on the screen match the default settings that Professional Write uses for documents. If you changed those settings, you'll want to change these settings to match the new ones. You can also play with the margin settings here to alter the overall position of the header or footer. For example, say the margin settings for your document are 10 and 70. You can right-justify the header and set the right margin to 75 instead of 70, so the header will extend 5 spaces over the text.

Next, you can choose the page on which you want the header to begin printing. You may not always want the header to start on the first page; for example, you may have a special title page that sets off the title, the author's name, and the date. To change the default setting of 1, press the Tab key to move to this setting, then type the number of the page on which you want the header to start.

The final choice Professional Write offers you is Font. A *font* is simply a set of characters that have a uniform design and size. For example, 12-point Helvetica is a font. *Helvetica* is the design; 12-point is the size (height). (For reference, 72 points are in an inch.) Don't confuse type style, set earlier, with font; you can have a font, 12-point Helvetica, enhanced with a type style, bold. We'll look at type styles in more depth in Chapter 7, but for now take another look at the screen.

Look at the entry to the right of Font. If the entry is Normal font, Professional Write has determined that your printer can handle only one font. In that case, you don't have much choice.

If, on the other hand, the entry is a font name, you have the option of using a variety of fonts for your header or footer. To see the choices, press the F8 key, displaying a submenu with a list of fonts, orientations, pitches, and styles. Use the Up or Down Arrow key to highlight your choice, then press Enter. Your choice is displayed next to Font.

When you're satisfied with all your selections, press Enter. Professional Write returns to the Write screen and displays your newly created header or footer on screen.

Now is a good time to double-check the position of your header or footer. To see both the header and footer at the same time, as shown in Figure 2-18, just scroll down to a page break. Professional Write indicates the page break with two solid lines; the footer for the previous page is on top of the break, and the header for the next page is below the break.

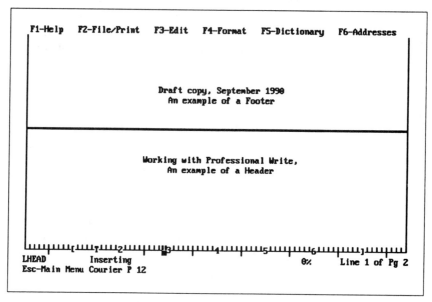

Figure 2-18 Header and footer displayed together at a page break

Adding a Title Page

A title page or cover page will enhance any document you create. With the myriad of fonts and typestyles available, and with the drawing functions we'll explore in Chapter 6, you'll be able to add a classy cover to any document as a finishing touch.

But let's hold off on that until you learn more about Write's capabilities. For now, just remember that when you do create a title page, you'll need to consider the first page entry and the print page number command to prevent problems with page numbering.

Summary

You've learned a lot in this chapter. You can get your saved document whenever you want to work on it, change a variety of settings to format the text, enhance characters for emphasis, create headers and footers, number the pages, and more! You've succeeded in learning the basics. Right now, you could create a professional-looking document that would impress even the most highly skilled typist.

If you thought the skills you learned in this chapter made typing easier, you'll appreciate the next chapter even more. We'll explore the use of block commands that let you copy, move, delete, or change entire blocks of text at one time.

T H R E E

Using Block Commands

In Chapter 2 you learned to change format settings to affect the lines of text typed after the format change. That's fine if you know exactly how you want the document to look, you don't make mistakes, and you never change your mind. If you're like the rest of us, though, you'll need to go back to the text and mold that basic stuff before it's the perfect sculpture you envisioned.

We did a little of this molding in the previous chapters, but those modifications focused either on lines of text or on the page as a whole. In this chapter, we'll be working with chunks of text called *blocks*.

What Is a Block?

A block is simply any word or group of words or phrases that you choose to consider a block. A word, a sentence, a paragraph, a page—any of these is a candidate for blockhood.

Manipulating blocks is no more than an electronic version of the old *cut-and-paste* method of editing. Picture yourself with a pair of scissors and a roll of tape, cutting out blocks of text and either pitching them in the garbage or pasting them in where they're more applicable. But with the electronic version, cutting and pasting is done by pressing buttons, and when you're done, you're done—no more retyping what you can't even read.

Working on a Block

Just mark the text and tell Professional Write what to do with it.

Working on a block of text is similar regardless of the action you intend to take. From deleting to copying, from inserting to moving, working with a block involves the same two basic steps:

- Identify and mark the text.
- Use a menu option or shortcut keys to take action on the text.

The first step is fairly straightforward; you're simply telling the computer which block of text you want to change. The second step introduces a little variation; once your text is marked, you can perform any of several operations.

Text Blocks and Rectangular Blocks

Professional Write makes a very helpful distinction between two types of blocks: text blocks and rectangular blocks. Text blocks are any blocks that Professional Write needs to rewrap after you move the block to a different location in the document. Say you move three sentences from one paragraph to the middle of another. If you mark the sentences as a text block, Professional Write automatically readjusts the paragraph to accommodate the additional lines.

The rectangular block feature lets you edit columns without reformatting surrounding text.

Sometimes, though, you may not want the text you edit to be rewrapped; for example, when you're editing a column of text. To preserve the original structure of the column, you'd need to mark the column as a rectangular block.

Marking a Block of Text

We'll use the MEMO document to practice manipulating blocks of text. Before we start, get the MEMO document you created earlier; it's shown in Figure 3-1. (If you need to refresh your memory on how to get a document, refer to the beginning of Chapter 2.)

The first step is to mark the text. We'll mark the two lines, 8 and 9, that precede the indented paragraph:

1. Move the cursor to the line of text that begins **Please be advised**. Make sure the cursor is on the first character you want to include in the block.

Using Block Commands

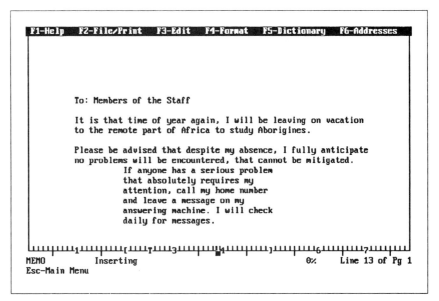

Figure 3-1 The MEMO document

2. Press F3, opening the Edit menu.
3. Choose option `4. Mark text`. The menu closes and the workspace reappears, as shown in Figure 3-2. `Marking text` is displayed in the status line. At the bottom of the screen is the message

   `Move the cursor to the end of the block and then press F10.`

4. Press the Down Arrow key once. All of line 8 is highlighted plus the first character in line 9.
5. To finish marking line 9, press the Right Arrow key, until the highlight is stretched over all of the text and the period at the end of the sentence. The result should appear as shown in Figure 3-3.

A quicker way to mark text is to bypass the Edit menu by pressing Ctrl-T. After moving the cursor to the first character you want to include in the block, press Ctrl-T, and you're ready to start highlighting.

Text Block Operations

Now that the lines are marked, press the F10 key opening the Text Block Operations menu shown in Figure 3-4. This menu lists all of the avail-

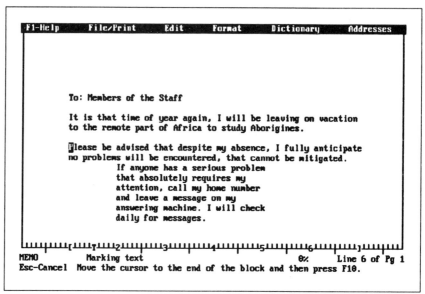

Figure 3-2 The Mark Text screen

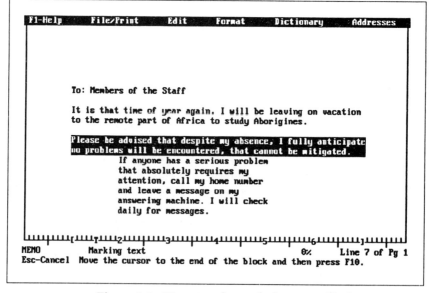

Figure 3-3 Lines 8 and 9 marked as a text block

able options. All you need to do is choose the option; Professional Write carries out the command. Note that the more common options have corresponding shortcut keys that allow you to bypass this screen as you gain more experience.

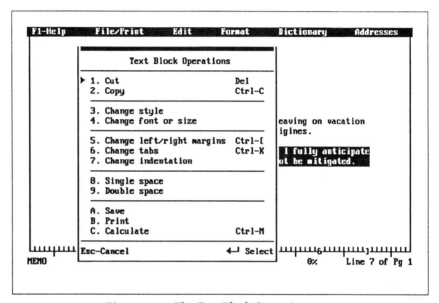

Figure 3-4   The Text Block Operations menu

Understanding the Clipboard

The Clipboard protects the block temporarily, just in case.

The options listed on the Text Block Operations menu can be divided into two categories: options that use the Clipboard and options that don't. If you choose an option such as changing the line spacing or typestyle of a block, you won't use the Clipboard. However, if you choose to cut, copy, move, or erase a block of text, that block retires to the Clipboard, a temporary holding cell for the text. This lets you move the block to a different location in the document or get the block back if you change your mind after erasing it.

Because the clipboard stores the block electronically in RAM, the Clipboard functions as an electronic purgatory. The block will remain on the Clipboard only up to the time that you perform one of the following steps:

- Move another block of text to the Clipboard.
- Exit from Professional Write.
- Turn off the computer.

You may need to work on one section of a block at a time.

The amount of text you can move to the Clipboard depends on the RAM of your computer. The more RAM available, the larger the Clipboard. If you need to move a large block to the Clipboard, you may need to break the block into two or more sections and work with one section at a time.

If you're trying to delete a large block of text that you're absolutely sure you don't need, and Professional Write alerts you that the Clipboard is full, press Enter. Professional Write will delete the block without saving it to the Clipboard.

If you mark a large area of text, you can check the boundaries of the block using two shortcut keys. Press Ctrl-Q to jump the cursor to the beginning of the block. Press Ctrl-Z to jump to the end. Ctrl-Q removes the highlighting, so be sure to replace the highlighting by pressing Ctrl-Z.

Taking Action on a Block

The cut text can be pasted back into the document.

Now that you understand how the Clipboard functions, let's cut the text you just marked. Type 1, cutting the highlighted text. The text disappears from the workspace, and Professional Write reformats the remaining text, moving and readjusting the margins to accommodate the change. Don't worry, the cut text isn't gone forever; it's safe and sound in the Clipboard. With the press of a key, it can be "pasted" back into the document.

The cursor should be on the first letter of the indented paragraph. Let's paste the cut text back into the same place from which we cut it. Press F3, opening the Edit menu, and choose option **6. Paste**.

Almost instantly, the lines of text relegated to the Clipboard reappear in the memo. Since you didn't do anything between steps to remove the text from the clipboard, you were able to restore the cut text. Had you cut more text between steps, the old text would have been overwritten and would be lost permanently.

Moving a Block of Text

To move a block, just delete it from one location and restore it in another.

Now suppose you want to change the memo to make lines 8 and 9 the conclusion. We'll use the same steps followed earlier to mark the text:

1. Make sure the cursor is on the P or in the space before the P in Please be advised.

2. Press the shortcut keys Ctrl-T. This puts Professional Write in the Mark Text mode. This time, mark the text by pressing the End key and then the Down Arrow key once. Lines 8 and 9 are now highlighted.
3. Press the Del key to remove the lines of text from the document to the Clipboard.
4. Move the cursor down to the line below the indented paragraph.
5. Instead of using the Edit menu, press Ctrl-P to paste the text from the Clipboard into the place where the cursor is located. The memo now looks like the one in Figure 3-5.

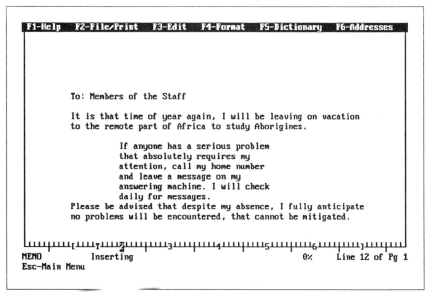

Figure 3-5 The memo with moved text

That cut block of text is still in the Clipboard. If you want to repeat it anywhere else, just move the cursor to the place where you want to repeat it and press Ctrl-P.

Copying a Block of Text

Copying a block of text is similar to cutting or moving the block. The only difference is that when you copy a block, you're not removing it from its original location. Instead, you're storing a duplicate of the marked text in the Clipboard. Once it's there, you can paste it into any location in the document.

To copy a block, perform the following steps:

1. Move the cursor to the beginning of the text you want to copy.
2. Press Ctrl-T, activating the Mark Text mode.
3. Use the arrow keys to stretch the highlight over the text you want to copy.
4. Press F10 to open the Text Block Operations menu.
5. Choose option 2. Copy.
6. Move the cursor to the place in the document where you want to insert the copy, and press Ctrl-P. The marked text remains in its original location and is pasted into the new location.

Bypass the Edit menu. After you mark the text, just press Ctrl-C, and your marked text is copied to the clipboard.

Cutting and Pasting between Files

Professional Write lets you cut and paste from one document to another.

Say you need to type a letter and you want to include a couple of passages from something you wrote a few days ago. If you had to do it on a typewriter, you'd have to retype the passages in the new letter. Besides all the added work, you'd be taking the risk of introducing new errors into the passages you spent so much time perfecting. In such a situation, the beauty of the Clipboard really reveals itself:

1. Save the document you're currently working on.
2. Get the document that contains the passages you want to copy. (If the file is on a different disk or in a different directory, you'll have to change the disk or directory.)
3. Press Ctrl-T and use the arrow keys to mark the text you want to copy.
4. Press F10 to display the Text Block Operations menu, and choose option 2. Copy Text (or press Ctrl-C) to copy the marked text to the Clipboard.
5. Clear the screen by pressing F2 and choosing option 7. Erase working copy.
6. Get the document you saved in step 1.
7. Move the cursor to the place where you want to insert the copy, and press Ctrl-P. Presto! The passage appears.

Get a little practice under your belt, and you'll be transferring text from document to document with no trouble at all. You'll find that it's a real time saver.

Changing the Type Style of a Block

Change the type style of an entire block without retyping it.

While you're reading through your document, you might decide that a particular word or passage needs a special enhancement to set it off or add emphasis. Without the block commands, you'd have to delete the passage, turn on the enhancement, and retype the entire passage. The block commands do away with all this work by adding the enhancement to what's already typed.

We'll use the MEMO document again to see how this feature works. You've decided you'd like to emphasize the middle paragraph. Here's what you need to do:

1. Move the cursor to the beginning of the indented paragraph that begins If anyone.

2. Press Ctrl-T.

3. Press the Down Arrow key to start highlighting the paragraph and finish with the End key. The paragraph is highlighted as shown in Figure 3-6.

4. Press F10, opening the Text Block Operations menu.

5. Choose option 3. Change style. This opens the Style submenu as shown in Figure 3-7.

6. Choose whatever enhancement you'd like to add to the marked text. For example, if you choose Underline, the marked text will be underlined as shown in Figure 3-8.

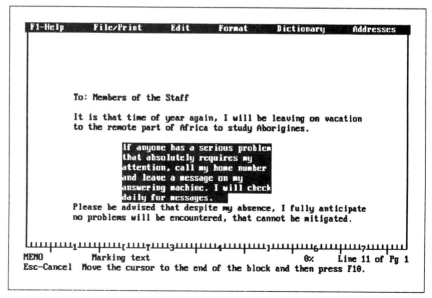

Figure 3-6 The indented paragraph highlighted

Chapter 3

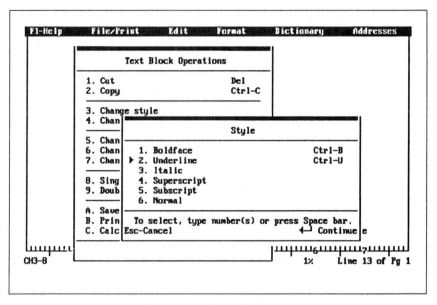

Figure 3-7 The Style submenu

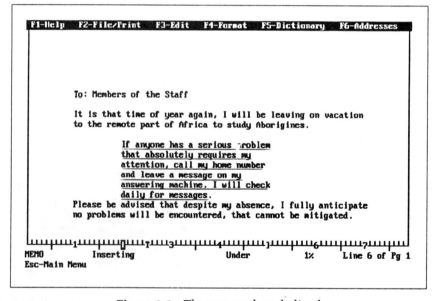

Figure 3-8 The paragraph underlined

How this enhancement will print is limited by your printer. That is, your printer may not be capable of printing italics, or it may not allow you to use a combination of styles, such as boldfaced italics. In such a case, the printer will default to the boldface enhancement.

How the enhanced text is displayed on your screen also depends on your hardware. On a monochrome (black and white) monitor, only underlining and boldface are shown. All other styles are displayed as boldface. On a color monitor, the text may appear as a unique color to indicate the specific enhancement.

Check the status line to determine the typestyle.

But no matter what the screen displays, the status line at the bottom of the screen always reveals the enhancement. Simply position the cursor on the text in question and look at the status line.

You can use shortcut keys for the two most common enhancements: boldface and underline. After marking the text, just press Ctrl-B to boldface it or Ctrl-U to underline.

Changing the Character Fonts

Check your Printer Manual to determine the fonts and point sizes your printer supports.

Professional Write includes a booklet that describes the capabilities of various printers. Professional Write lets you select from a variety of fonts, but you must make sure your printer has the capability to handle these variations. Chapter 7 handles fonts in greater depth, but let's look at how the block commands come into play here.

The procedure is pretty straightforward. After you mark the text, choose option 4. Change font or size from the Text Block Operations menu. If your printer supports different fonts and sizes, a submenu will reveal your choices. Choose the font and size, and Professional Write does the rest.

Changing Block Margins

You've added some enhancement to that middle paragraph, but it's still getting lost in the memo. So you decide to move the margins in a little more to set the passage off from the rest of the text. With the block commands, it's a snap:

1. Move the cursor to the beginning of the paragraph.
2. Press Ctrl-T.
3. Press the Down Arrow key to begin highlighting. Press the End key to finish highlighting.
4. Press F10, opening the Text Block Operations menu.

5. Choose option **5. Change left/right margins**. Professional Write responds with the Change Margins screen shown in Figure 3-9.

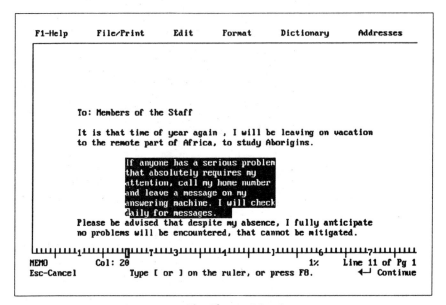

Figure 3-9 The Change Margins screen

At the bottom of the screen are instructions for changing the margins. You can change the margins in either of two ways. One way is to simply move the brackets on the ruler line. The other way consists of bypassing this screen by pressing F8 and then typing the numerical values of the new margins.

To set the margins with brackets, perform the following steps:

1. Use the Left and Right Arrow keys to move the cursor to the place where you want the left margin.

2. Look at the Col number in the status line to make sure the margin is where you want it. (This number gives a more accurate indication of the cursor's location.)

3. Once you're sure the margin is where you want it, type [, setting the left margin.

4. Move the cursor to the place where you want the right margin, and type].

5. Press Enter to lock in the margins you just set.

To type in the exact values of the margin settings, follow this procedure:

1. Press F8, opening the Margin Settings screen. In Figure 3-10 the current settings are 20 for the left margin and 50 for the right.
2. Type 5 for the left margin and 45 for the right.
3. Press Enter. The text is reformatted and appears as shown in Figure 3-11.

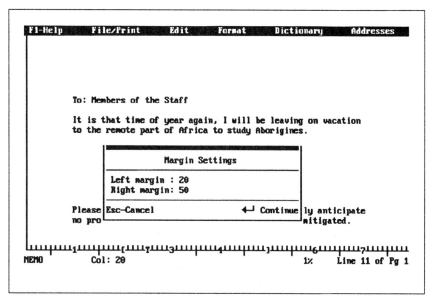

Figure 3-10   The Margin Settings screen

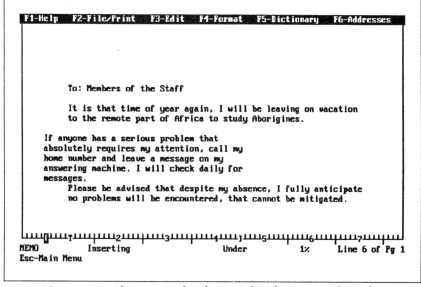

Figure 3-11   The paragraph reformatted with margins of 5 and 45

Although these new settings aren't very practical, they do illustrate Professional Write's flexibility in dealing with blocks of text. Even though the *document's* left margin setting is ten, we were able to set the *block's* left margin outside that constraint.

By the way, any tabs that were set within the margins are reset automatically relative to the new margins.

Changing Block Indentation

In Chapter 2, we looked at the temporary left margin. This margin is used when you want to indent a section of the text without changing the left margin setting.

With the block commands, you can use this temporary left margin for text that has already been typed. Professional Write will automatically rewrap and reformat the block to accommodate the indentation.

To indent a block of text, first mark the block. Then choose option **7. Change indentation** from the Text Block Operations menu. Professional Write tells you to move the cursor to the new indentation setting and press Enter. Use the Left and Right Arrow keys to move the cursor to the desired setting, then press Enter.

Professional Write fits the text to the new indentation and right margin. Figure 3-12 shows a block of text that has been squeezed by a left margin of 20 and a right margin of 45. As you can see, the text has been reformatted and rewrapped.

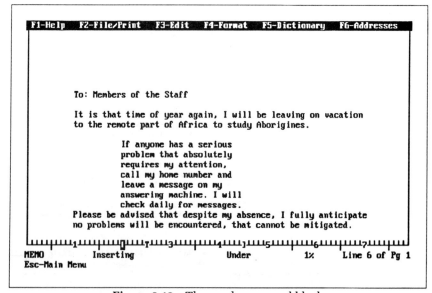

Figure 3-12 The newly squeezed block

Changing Line Spacing

Single-space extracted text to set it off.

One of the more frequently used block operations consists of changing line spacing. This is especially useful in setting off long quotations or extracts. For example, you may be typing a report that requires a reference to one or two paragraphs from a book. You might decide to double-space the entire report to make it more readable. But if you double-space the paragraphs you're lifting from the book, they'll get lost in your text, even if you do use quotes. The solution? Single-space the extracted paragraphs to set them off.

You might also decide to change line spacing to save your eyes. If you decide to create a single-spaced document, for example, that doesn't mean that you have to work with a single-spaced document on screen. If you've ever tried it, you know what I mean.

To prevent this unnecessary torture, double-space the document when you're typing and editing it. When you're done perfecting your masterpiece, single-space it.

To change the line spacing on an entire document, perform the following steps:

1. Press Ctrl-Home to move the cursor to the beginning of the document.
2. Press Ctrl-T, putting Professional Write in the Mark Text mode.
3. Press Ctrl-End, highlighting the entire document.
4. Press F10, opening the Text Block Operations menu.
5. Choose option **8. Single space** or option **9. Double space**. The entire text is reformatted.

Printing a Block

You can lift a table or list from your document and print it on a single page.

Suppose you've created a 40-page document and one of the pages has a list of addresses that you want to copy and send to your colleague in New Hampshire. You could print the entire page that the list is on, as you'll see in Chapter 9, but then you would end up with other text on the page that might distract from the list. With the block commands, however, you can print out only the portion of text you want.

First, mark the text you want to print. Then, press the F10 key opening the Text Block Operations menu. At the bottom of this menu are three choices: **A**, **B**, and **C**. Choose option **B**. Professional Write opens the Block Print Options screen, which is an abbreviated version of the normal Print Options screen. See Figure 3-13.

Chapter 3

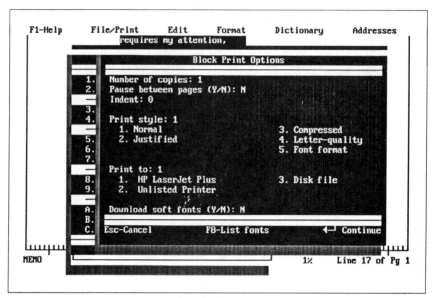

Figure 3-13 The Block Print Options screen

If you want to print a single copy, and do not want a special print format, press Enter to start the printer.

Saving a Block

Of course, you might foresee a need to use that same list of addresses in future documents. By saving the list in a special file, you can access it later and use the cut and paste function to insert an address wherever needed. To save a block to a special file, just perform the following steps:

1. Mark the text you want to save.
2. Press the F10 key, opening the Text Block Operations menu.
3. Select option A. Save.
4. Professional Write opens the Save File submenu.
5. If you're saving the block to the disk in the default drive, type a name for the block file and press Enter.

   If you're saving the block to a disk other than the default, press Ctrl-E to erase the default path. Type the correct path and a name for the block file (for example, d:\wdata\examples\block), and press Enter twice.

Working with Rectangular Blocks

Delete a portion of text without affecting the surrounding text.

Users of DOS-based computers have long been jealous of Apple and Macintosh users, who are able to cut out a portion of text without affecting surrounding text. Now, you can put your envy to rest. With Professional Write, you can erase a table or any rectangular block in a document without having to worry that the rest of the document will be reformatted incorrectly.

But that's not all. The rectangular block feature also lets you perform calculations on numbers in the block. We'll study this in more detail in Chapter 6. For now, let's see how the block feature works on columns.

Erasing a Rectangular Block

There's not much difference between marking ordinary text and marking a rectangle. You can mark the rectangle in either of two ways. The first way is to open the Edit menu and choose option 5. Mark Rectangle, then use the Arrow keys to mark the text. The other way is to press Ctrl-R and then mark the text. In essence, you're performing the same steps as you performed with text blocks but in a different mode.

Figure 3-14 illustrates an inventory memo consisting of a rectangular block of numbers within ordinary text. You don't want to send this memo to your boss with that clutter of meaningless numbers. So why not erase the quantities column? That way you can leave the cost of the items, and the memo won't look so bad.

Move the cursor to the Q in Quantities. Press Ctrl-R, putting the cursor in the Mark Rectangle mode. The status line declares Marking rectangle. Move the cursor to the right with the Right Arrow key and then use the Down Arrow key to move the highlight over the entire column of numbers, as shown in Figure 3-15.

Press F10, opening the Rectangular Block Operations menu, shown in Figure 3-16. Be careful; don't assume that since you're planning on deleting the column you want the Cut option. The Cut option here works a lot like the same option in the Mark Text mode; it reformats the text surrounding the deleted column. You might want to consider using another option on the menu, Erase, which eliminates the selected rectangle without affecting surrounding text.

In this example, choose option 3. Erase. After you erase the text, the document appears as shown in Figure 3-17.

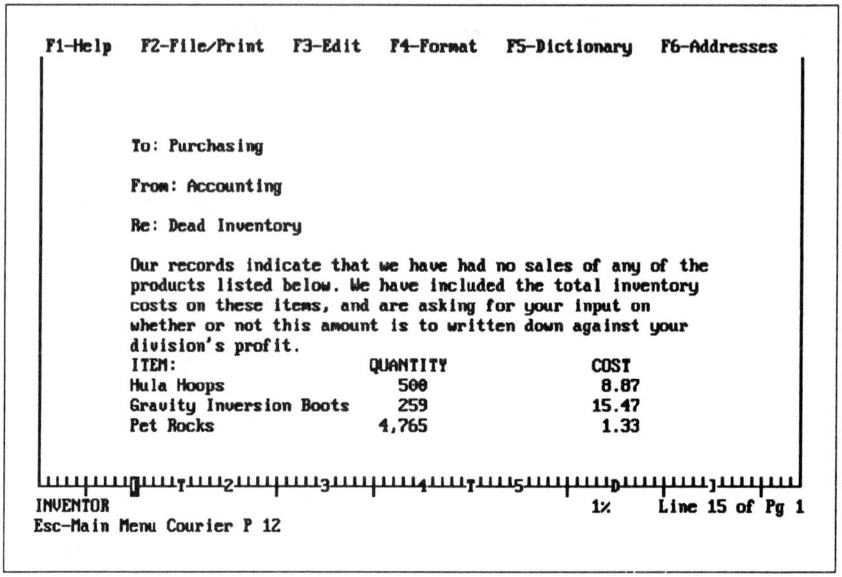

Figure 3-14 The inventory memo

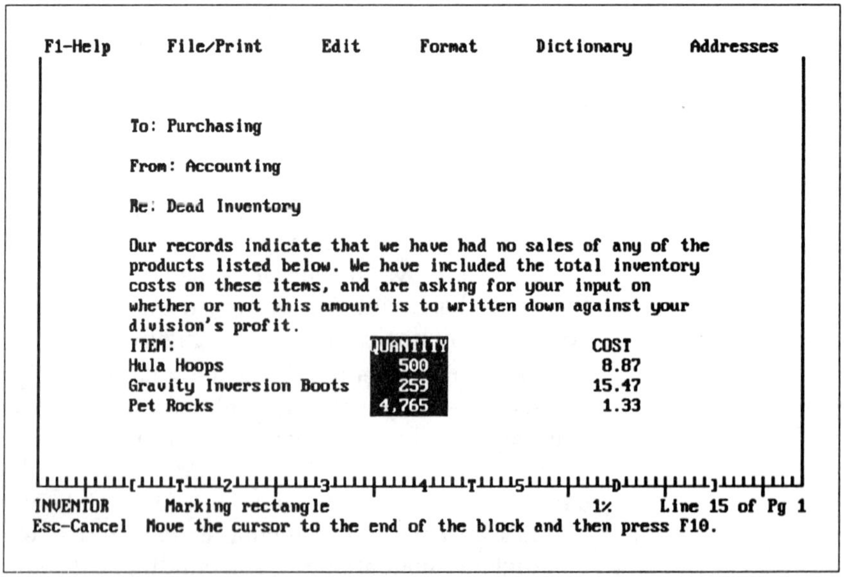

Figure 3-15 The QUANTITY column highlighted

Using Block Commands

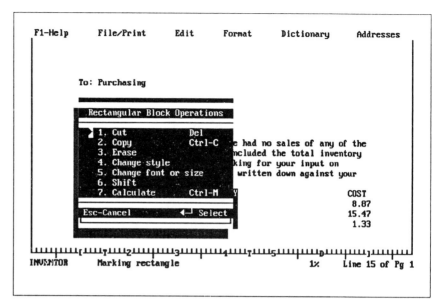

Figure 3-16 The Rectangular Block Operations menu

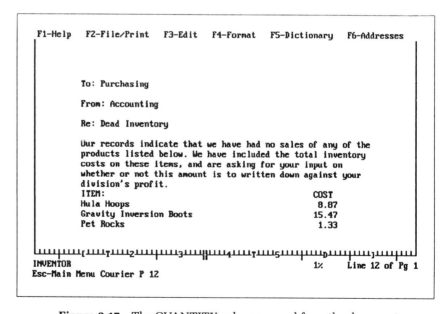

Figure 3-17 The QUANTITY column erased from the document

If you erased the wrong column, don't worry; the Clipboard is there to save you. Just move the cursor to the place where you want to restore the text and press Ctrl-P.

More Rectangular Block Operations

The Rectangular Block Operations menu shown in Figure 3-16 lists several other available options, most of which are similar to the options on the Text Block Operations menu. The following descriptions explain just what these other options offer.

Copy: As with copying lines of text, this option lets you keep the marked block in its original location and copy the block to other locations.

Change Style: With this option, you can add boldface, underlining, italics, subscripts, or superscripts to the marked rectangular blocks.

Change Font or Size: Depending on the capabilities of your printer, this option allows for rectangular blocks to be printed with the font you designate.

With `Shift`, you can adjust the position of an entire rectangular block.

Shift: This is another capability that DOS users covet from their Macintosh compatriots. After highlighting a rectangular block, you can use the arrow keys to adjust the position of the block. This option is good for small adjustments, but you won't be able to move the block over and between existing text as you could with the cursor. For these large adjustments, you still need to cut and paste.

Calculate: This option lets you perform mathematical operations on a column of numbers. Examples are covered in detail in Chapter 6.

Summary

In this chapter, you discovered the power of using the block as an editing tool. You moved, reformatted, enhanced, and deleted large areas of text easily and confidently, knowing that your block was stored safely in the Clipboard. You were also introduced to the rectangular block capability, which lets your DOS-based computer make Macintosh-like screen moves.
 In the next chapter, you'll look at some file management techniques that will help you organize all the files you'll be creating.

F O U R

Working with Files

Because of the way the disk operating system (DOS) is designed, you may find that "housekeeping" operations are the most difficult tasks associated with word processing. Moving, copying, deleting, and re-organizing files can be intimidating at first and bothersome later, especially if you're using a hard disk.

Fortunately, the designers of Professional Write recognized the need for a simplified filing system and included a file management module (the files directory) as part of the program. This simplified system not only helps you keep your house in order but also offers features that let you combine files and use files that were not created with Professional Write.

If you typed the sample documents that were described in the previous chapters and practiced saving and getting those files, you've probably encountered Professional Write's directory system already. In this chapter, we'll explore the files directory in depth to help you understand and use the system.

Understanding the Files Directory

A files directory is simply a list of files that makes the files more accessible to you. If you're familiar at all with DOS, you know that DOS offers a directory of its own. By typing dir at the DOS prompt, you can view a listing of the currently active directory or of the disk in the currently active drive. But you'll notice that a long list of files scrolls by too fast to read, and you can't move back up to see filenames that are off

The files directory helps you access your files.

the screen. Another drawback with the DOS directory is that when you want to open a file, you have to retype the filename *without typos* before DOS can open it.

What makes Professional Write's files directory so much more useful is that it lets you view the directory by scrolling through the list, lets you choose a file from the directory without retyping the filename, and helps you reorganize the files in a given directory. It even lets you add a brief description of the file to jog your memory. In short, Professional Write's directory is more user-friendly.

That's not to say that Professional Write's filing system is an entirely independent creation. Actually, it couldn't work without DOS.

DOS and Professional Write

DOS (the disk operating system) is a go-between program. It's purpose is to work with the disk drives, the monitor, and the applications program, such as Professional Write, to keep everything in step. Without DOS, you wouldn't be able to run Professional Write or any other applications program.

In the same manner, Professional Write doesn't bring its own file management system with it. Instead, Professional Write uses the same file management structure as DOS but gives it a friendlier face, making it easier to use.

Files on a Hard Disk—The Directory System

Because a hard disk system allows you to store hundreds of files, the only feasible way to keep track of all the files is to use what are called *subdirectories*. Assuming Professional Write's program files are installed on your hard disk, you're already making use of a subdirectory called PRO. If this subdirectory were not created, all of Professional Write's program files would be listed with whatever other files are on the disk you're using, making one very long list.

The directory system forms a sort of family tree. The main directory (the grandparents) consists of a list of directories (parents) that can be accessed. For example, your main directory may list PRO, WDATA, and FDATA, corresponding to applications programs and groups of data files you may have on your hard disk. Each of these directories may be divided into subdirectories. For example, you may have created a subdirectory called EXAMPLES under the WDATA directory. By doing so, you would keep the example files separate from other files in the

WDATA directory. You could create several other subdirectories under WDATA to keep all your various projects in their own directories. Your directory tree might look like the one in Figure 4-1.

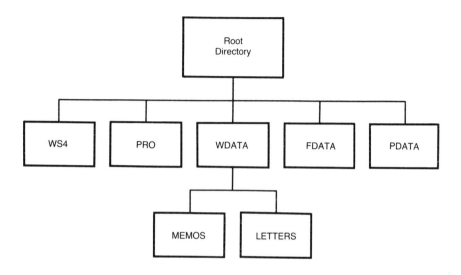

Figure 4-1 An example of a directory tree

We will work with the directory tree later in this chapter when we look at file management techniques. But since you will spend most of your time working with the files directory, let's look at that first.

Viewing the Files Directory

Before we can perform any tasks with the files directory, we need to open it so we can view its contents. The process you need to follow depends on whether you're using a hard disk or a floppy disk system.

Viewing a Directory on a Hard Disk

Since our PRO directory is chock full of files, let's take a look at its files directory. To view a directory, perform the following steps:

1. Choose option `1. Create/Edit` from the Main menu.
2. Press F2, opening the File/Print menu shown in Figure 4-2.

Chapter 4

3. Choose option 1. Get file. This opens the Filename screen, shown in Figure 4-3, that lets you type in the path of the directory you want to view. In Figure 4-3, the default path C:\PRO is displayed.

4. If the default path is correct, just press Enter. If not, press Ctrl-E to erase the default path, then type the correct path and press Enter.

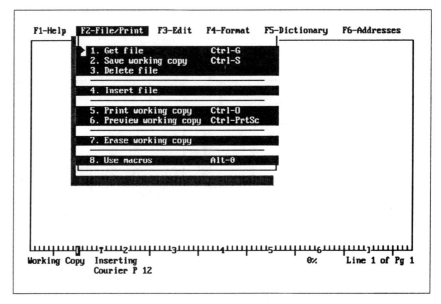

Figure 4-2 The File/Print menu

The files directory for C:\PRO is displayed on screen as shown in Figure 4-4.

Viewing a Directory on a Floppy Disk

To view a directory on a floppy disk, you just tell Professional Write which disk you want the files directory for; Professional Write does the rest. Here's the step-by-step process:

1. Load the floppy disk into drive B.
2. Press F2, opening the File/Print menu.
3. Choose option 1. Get file. This opens the Filename screen that lets you type the drive you want to access.

Working with Files

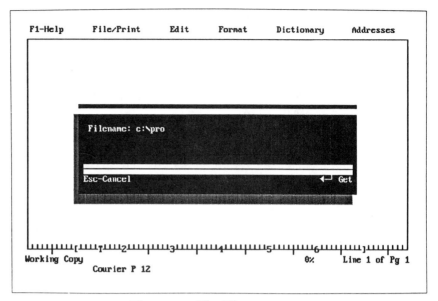

Figure 4-3 The Filename screen

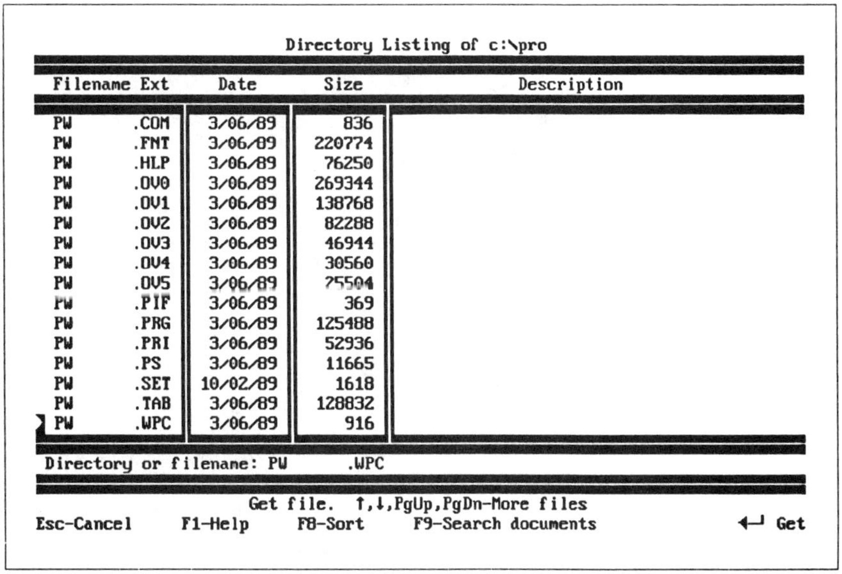

Figure 4-4 The files directory for C:\PRO

4. If **B:** is already displayed on the Filename screen, just press Enter to view the files directory of the disk in drive B. If something else is displayed, press Ctrl-E to delete it, then type **b:** and press Enter.

Chapter 4

Changing the Default Data Directory

Professional Write lets you change the default directory to the directory you most commonly use.

Up till now, you've had to press Ctrl-E and type a new path on the Filename screen every time you wanted to get a file. You'll be happy to hear that this bothersome step can be avoided. Professional Write lets you change the default directory to the one you intend to use most often. Here's how:

1. Start up Professional Write.
2. Choose option `2. Setup` from the Main menu. This opens a Setup submenu as shown in Figure 4-5.
3. Choose option `4. Change data directory`, opening the Current Data Directory screen as shown in Figure 4-6. Notice that the cursor is under the first letter of the current directory's name, and that the cursor is a blinking line below the letter; this means that the cursor is in the Overstrike mode.
4. Type the path of the subdirectory that you want to make the default directory. For example, type `c:\wdata\examples`.
5. Press Enter.

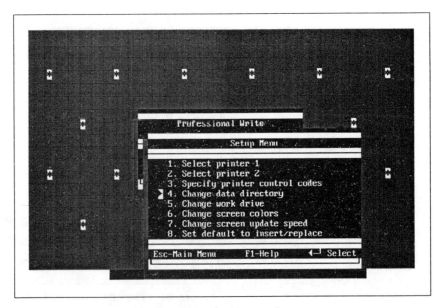

Figure 4-5 The Setup submenu

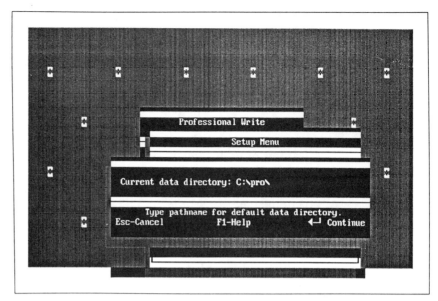

Figure 4-6 The Current Data Directory screen

Now, whenever you attempt to get, save, delete, or insert a file, Professional Write will assume that you want to access the EXAMPLES subdirectory. All you need to do is choose the action you want to perform from the File/Print menu, type the filename of the file you plan to act on, and press Enter.

Using the Files Directory

Now that you've encountered the directory, let's take a closer look at some of its features. At the very top of the screen is the Directory Listing of C:\PRO. The next line down contains the column headings. From left to right, the first entry is the Filename Ext that lists the files in this directory. Naming files is covered later in this chapter.

The next heading, Date, tells you the date the file was created. If your computer has an internal clock, Professional Write uses the date and time supplied by the clock. If not, Professional Write uses the date and time that you typed in when you started DOS.

The Size heading indicates the number of bytes in the file. A byte is a measure of how much memory it takes to store one character. A kilobyte is nearly 1000 bytes, actually 1024 bytes. This information is important when you try to copy a file to another disk. By comparing the size of the file and the remaining free memory on the disk you want to copy to, you can determine whether there's enough space before you attempt to copy the file.

You can use DOS to check the free memory of a disk. Exit Professional Write. At the DOS prompt, type the letter of the drive you want to access, and press Enter. Type `dir` and press Enter. At the end of the directory, DOS displays the free memory in bytes.

The Description column helps you remember what's in each file.

Next is the `Description` column. If you added a description to the document, it will be displayed here. This is one of the outstanding features of Professional Write. Once you've been away from a file for a couple of weeks, the filename you assigned may mean little or nothing to you. This added description gives a better indication of what exactly is in the file.

Beneath the list of files, is another line with the words `Directory or filename:` To the right of this entry is the name of the particular file currently highlighted. When you open the directory listing, the cursor highlights the first file in the list. Press the Down Arrow key to scroll through the list. As each file is highlighted, its name is displayed next to `Directory or filename:`.

The next line down indicates the action that you have undertaken. In this screen, the indicator reads `Get File` and follows with instructions as to how to access the other files.

At the very bottom of the screen is a list of keystrokes and what they do. Pressing Esc takes you back to the workspace without getting any file—just in case you change your mind. F1, as always, opens a help screen. The F8 and F9 keys offer the ability to Sort and Search the filenames; we'll look at these topics later in this chapter. The bent arrow next to `Get` represents the Enter key. Once the name of the file you want to get is highlighted, just press Enter to get the file.

Getting the Most out of Filenames

We've already named some files in order to save them, but we haven't yet looked at any system for naming files.

One of the more inscrutable aspects of DOS is the limitations you face when you try to name a file. In DOS, only eight characters or symbols may be used on the left side of a period, and only three characters on the right. Therefore a DOS filename looks like `AAAAAAAA.BBB` or `LETTERD1.LTR` or `SIX_THE.DOC`. Not very revealing, are they? Wait until you've been away from the document for six months.

Although the DOS filenames won't help you remember what's in a file, they do offer one especially useful feature—a filename extension, consisting of three letters to the right of the period. This extension can be used to classify documents of the same type. In the examples above, one of the documents has the extension .LTR. This could be used to classify all correspondence of a non-business nature, for example MOM.LTR and SISTER.LTR, from business correspondence like TERRY.BUS and KATE.BUS. The extensions also let you work with a group of files that share the same extension; for example, you can use a single command to copy all the files that have the same extension.

The problem is that when you write more than one letter to mom, you have to figure out how to distinguish between the letters. Now, the inventors of DOS would say that since all files are time-stamped, you can tell the letters apart by the date they were created. That's a good point, but it would still be helpful to have more detailed descriptions of the files.

With Professional Write, you get the best of both worlds. You can add extensions to the filenames to reap the benefits of extensions, and you can add detailed descriptions to the files to help you distinguish between files with similar names. We will look at how to do this later in the chapter.

Sorting the Directory

You can sort your directory by filename, date, size, or extension.

One of the features that sets Professional Write apart from other software programs is its ability to sort the files in a directory. You may have noticed already that Professional Write has sorted your files alphabetically in the EXAMPLES file. The program chooses this sorting arrangement by default. Filenames that start with numbers or symbols are listed first, then the remaining filenames are listed alphabetically.

Although you'll probably find the alphabetical sorting most useful, Professional Write offers three other sorting schemes. You can sort files by their extensions, by the dates when they were created, or by the size of the file.

To see the Sort Order screen, go back to the Main menu and perform the following steps:

1. Choose option `1. Create/Edit` from the Main menu.
2. Press F2, opening the File/Print menu.
3. Choose option `1. Get file`.
4. If the default drive or directory is correct, press Enter. If not, press Ctrl-E and type the drive or path of the directory you want to access. Professional Write displays the files directory. The directory may look like the one in Figure 4-7.
5. Press F8 to open the Sort Order screen as shown in Figure 4-8.

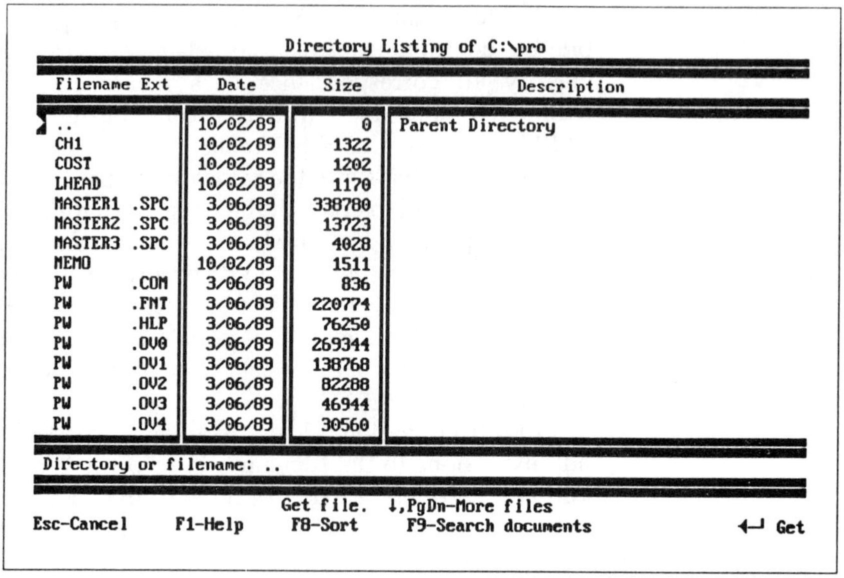

Chapter 4

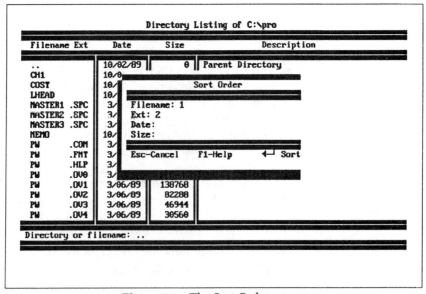

Figure 4-7 A files directory

Figure 4-8 The Sort Order screen

The 1 to the right of Filename indicates that the files are currently being sorted first by their filenames. The 2 to the right of Ext means the files are sorted next by their extensions. That is, if Professional Write discovers two files with the same name, it looks at the extensions to break the tie.

Sorting is always done alphabetically in ascending order: ABCD... 1234.... Professional Write doesn't let you change the sorting order; for example, you can't tell Professional Write to list the files in decending order (from Z to A).

Changing the Sorting Scheme

To change the attribute sort order, press the Tab key to move the cursor to the attribute that you want Professional Write to consider first when sorting the files, and type 1. For example, press Tab three times to move to the `Size:` field, and type 1. Notice that you have two 1's now. That won't do. Press Tab until the cursor is under the 1 next to `Filename:` and press the spacebar or Del, deleting that 1. If you wish, you can assign a number from 1 to 4 to all four fields, but make sure you don't use the same number twice. When you're done assigning numbers, press Enter. Your directory is now sorted according to the new scheme.

Figure 4-9 shows what the directory in Figure 4-8 would look like after being resorted according to size. As you can see, the files are listed from smallest to largest.

```
                  Directory Listing of C:\pro

   Filename Ext     Date        Size        Description

   ..              10/02/89         0    Parent Directory
   PW       .PIF    3/06/89       369
   PW       .COM    3/06/89       836
   PW       .WPC    3/06/89       916
   LHEAD           10/02/89      1170
   COST            10/02/89      1282
   CH1             10/02/89      1322
   MEMO            10/02/89      1511
   PW       .SET   10/02/89      1618
   SAMPLE   .LTR    3/06/89      2352
   MASTER3  .SPC    3/06/89      4028
   PW       .PS     3/06/89     11665
   MASTER2  .SPC    3/06/89     13723
   PW       .OV5    3/06/89     25504
   PW       .OV4    3/06/89     30560
   PW       .OV3    3/06/89     46944

   Directory or filename: ..

                          Get file.   ↓,PgDn-More files
   Esc-Cancel    F1-Help  F8-Sort     F9-Search documents        ↵ Get
```

Figure 4-9 The directory re-sorted

If you don't want your directory sorted, just delete all the numbers in the Sort Order screen. If you do this, Professional Write will display your directory more quickly because it doesn't have to sort it first.

Searching for a File

Professional Write will help you ferret out a specified word or phrase and tell you where to look.

As you've seen, adding a description to your file will help you remember the contents of your file in the future. But just imagine how much more helpful it would be to have a program that tracks down the file for you. Say you remember creating a memo with the word "Aborigines" in it, but for the life of you, you can't remember the name of the file you used the word in. Professional Write's Search feature can help.

Let's do it. First, display the EXAMPLES directory. Then:

1. Press F9, opening the Search Multiple Documents screen as shown in Figure 4-10.
2. Type `Aborigines`, and press Enter. The directory file shows only one file, MEMO, that contains the word "Aborigines."

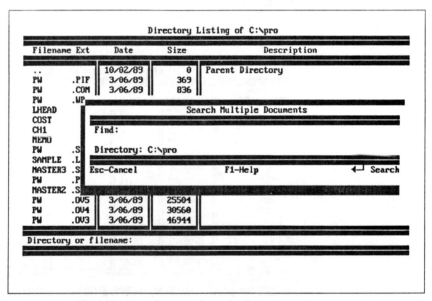

Figure 4-10 The Search Multiple Documents screen

You can also use this feature to find several files that use a word or phrase that's peculiar to the document. Let's suppose that as part of your work, you create several drafts of a contract before deciding on a final draft. You may want to save all the drafts, just in case you want to refer to those drafts in the future. (If you're like me, you'll type draft after draft never looking back, then decide later that you like the first draft better than all the others.)

With Professional Write's search feature, you could readily access all the drafts that share that particular word or phrase. For example, let's say that all the drafts contain the phrase "Arizona projects." Just open the Search Multiple Documents screen, and type `Arizona projects` next to `Find:`. Press Enter, and the directory will display all the files with that phrase.

Searching for Files outside the Present Directory

You can even look for a word in a different directory.

Professional Write does not limit you to searching for files in the current drive or directory. For example, if you were working in the WDATA directory in drive C, and the disk with your drafts was in drive A, you could open the Search Multiple Documents screen, press the Tab key to move the cursor to `Directory:`, type `a:`, and press Enter. Professional Write would begin searching the disk in drive A for all the files containing "Arizonal projects." See Figure 4-11. This is very useful if you want to insert a file from another directory into the file you're working on.

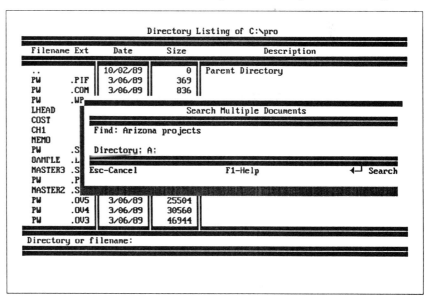

Figure 4-11 Write will search for "Arizona Projects" in Drive A

Searching for Files Using Wild Cards

The Search feature in itself is great, but if you're like the rest of us, you may forget exactly how a particular phrase was constructed, and since Professional Write is such a literal beast, it just won't help you out.

Use wild cards when you just can't remember.

Professional Write includes a feature that can help you with this problem. It lets you use *wild card* characters in place of the forgotten characters. These wildcard characters consist of two periods in place of the characters you can't recall. Say I used a word in the MEMO document that contains a word with the letter combination "gin" but I draw a blank trying to remember the rest of the word. I can type ..gin.. next to Find:, and Professional Write will find and display all the files that contain a word with the "gin" letter combination. When you open one of the files that's listed, Professional Write displays the text with the cursor on the first occurrence of the term you were looking for. Try it! You may never have to use your memory again.

Figure 4-12 shows another example of a wild card search. Here, the entry directs Professional Write to find any words that have the word "work" or the word "work" with any characters following. This includes words such as "working," "workout," and "workspace." Notice that each period does not represent a character; the two periods together represent any and all characters that may follow "work."

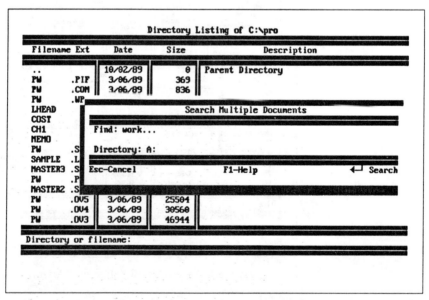

Figure 4-12 A wild card search entry

The wild card can also be used effectively for finding words when you're unsure of the spelling. If one of your business contacts was named Smyth and you forgot the spelling, you could use the wildcard Sm.th to find all the documents with Smyth and Smith. Of course you would still have to filter through the files for the ones you want.

Narrowing the Search

If you use a common word or letter combination in your search, you may end up with a long list of files that doesn't do you much good. To help you narrow your search, Professional Write lets you specify the group of documents you want to search. For example, you may know that the document you're looking for has the filename extension .LTR. In this case, you could tell Professional Write to search only the documents with the .LTR extension.

Figure 4-13 shows a wild card directory name used to narrow the scope of documents to search. In this example, Professional Write will search for the letter combination "work" in only those documents that have the .LTR extension.

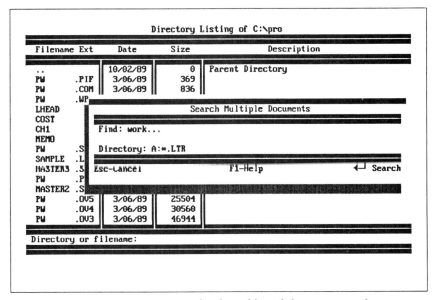

Figure 4-13 An example of a wild card directory search

Working with Individual Files

Up to this point, you have seen the big picture. You've seen Professional Write's files directory system and how it organizes your files. You've also seen the benefits of this system—how the system helps you access your files. Now you will look at some more specific tasks, those dealing with individual files.

Creating a Subdirectory

Create a subdirectory before beginning any project.

Before you begin working on a particular project that may eventually result in the creation of several files, you should create a subdirectory to hold those files. For example, if you're writing a book about keeping lizards as pets, it would be a good idea to create a special subdirectory (called LIZARDS) to hold all the chapter files.

Unfortunately, you have to go outside Professional Write to create a subdirectory; fortunately, creating a subdirectory is not very difficult. To go outside of Professional Write, save whatever you're working on, clear the screen, and choose option `E. Exit` from the Main menu. Now you're at the DOS prompt, and you can use the DOS Make Directory command to create a subdirectory.

Let's make a subdirectory called LIZARD under the WDATA directory:

1. First, make sure you're in the WDATA directory; that is, `D:\WDATA` should be displayed. If it's not displayed, type `cd\wdata`, telling DOS, "Change directory to WDATA." (You need to be in the WDATA directory so the LIZARD subdirectory will be within the WDATA directory.)
2. Type `md lizard` and press Enter. This tells DOS to make a subdirectory called LIZARD.
3. Press Enter.
4. To return to Professional Write, type `cd\pro` and press Enter. Then type `pw`.

The LIZARD subdirectory is now available whenever you decide to start writing your book.

Saving a Document

Protect your work by saving it to disk.

You may already have saved some of the example documents you created earlier. But if you need to refresh your memory, here's the step-by-step process:

1. Press F2 to display the File/Print menu.
2. Select option 2. Save working copy. This opens the Filename screen.
3. If the default drive or directory is correct, just type a name for the file. If not, press Ctrl-E, type the path of the directory or type the drive you want to save the file to, and type a name for the file.
4. Press the Tab key to move the cursor to the Description: field, and type in a brief description of what's in the document.
5. Press Enter to save the document.

You can bypass the File/Print menu by using the shortcut keys. When you're ready to save your document, press Ctrl-S, opening the Filename screen. If you're working on a document you had previously saved, just press Enter to resave the file with changes. If the document is brand new, you need to type the path, filename, and description as outlined above, and then press Enter.

Saving a Document in Other Formats

Professional Write offers a built-in conversion program.

Every word processing program performs its functions a little differently. If you open a document in one program that was created in another, you might see a bunch of characters that look very strange. In order to share documents or run documents in another program, it is often necessary to convert the document from one program to another. Some software companies offer special conversion programs exclusively for this purpose, but with Professional Write, the conversion program is built in.

Saving a Document in the ASCII Format

ASCII is a universal word processing format.

The most common format for sharing word processing files is called ASCII. If you plan on sending a file via modem, you'll probably use ASCII. This format uses very basic codes that are understood by several word processing programs. The only drawback is that the ASCII format deletes any fancy trimmings that you may have added to your text. That means your file will lose its underlining, boldface, headers and footers, and whatever else goes beyond the basic text. So be careful.

To prevent losing your special formatting elements for good, consider saving your file first as a Professional Write document, then resave the file in ASCII with the filename extension .ASC.

You can save a document as an ASCII file right from the Filename screen as shown in Figure 4-14.

Chapter 4

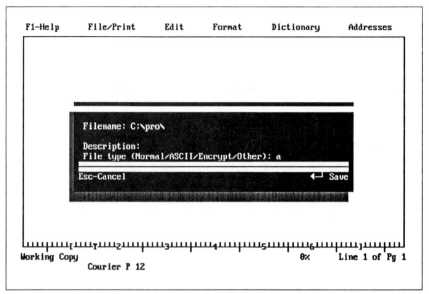

Figure 4-14 The Filename screen

After typing the path and filename, press the Tab key to move to the File type field. Type a to change the file type from Normal to ASCII. A warning screen appears, letting you know that most of the formatting you used in this document will be lost. If you're absolutely sure you want to do this, press Enter to continue the process.

If the document has already been saved in the Normal format, another warning screen will appear, alerting you that this document is about to be overwritten. If you want to save the original from destruction, press Esc. The warning screen will not appear if the document is being saved to a different subdirectory or disk or if it has a different filename.

Saving a Document in a Different Word Processing Format

Professional Write can convert your files to several other common word processing programs.

If you want to save a document so that it can be read by another word processing program, you need to know the name and version of the program that will be used. It's also important to know the filename format that the target program requires. Some word processors, such as Microsoft Word, demand that the filename have the extension .DOC. To save a file in another word processing format, perform the following steps:

1. Press F2, opening the File/Print menu.

2. Choose option 2. Save Working Copy.

3. Type the path, a filename, and a description if desired.
4. Press Tab, moving the cursor to the File type field, opening an information screen regarding filenames.
5. Press Enter, opening a submenu of the word processing programs as shown in Figure 4-15.
6. Choose the format you want, and Professional Write will save your file in that format.

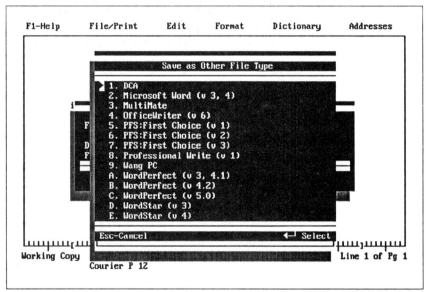

Figure 4-15 The Save as Other File Type submenu

It's a certain bet that some of your formatting will be lost or changed in the conversion process. Don't assume the conversion is 100% complete; compare the two versions to determine if anything is missing.

If the word processing program to which you're converting your file does not require a specific extension, consider using an extension, such as .WS for WordStar, to help you remember that the file is not in Professional Write format.

Getting a File

Professional Write uses the term "get" to retrieve a file that was previously saved to disk. To get a file, perform the following steps:

Chapter 4

1. Press F2, opening the File/Print menu.
2. Choose option 1. Get file, opening the Filename screen.
3. If you have a hard disk and the file you want is in the subdirectory that's displayed, press Enter, opening the directory listing.
   - If the document is in a different subdirectory, press Ctrl-E, and type the path leading to the subdirectory and the name of the subdirectory. Then press Enter, opening the directory listing.
   - If you're getting a file from a floppy disk, press Ctrl-E, then type the letter of the disk drive you want to access followed by a colon. Press Enter, opening the directory listing.
4. Use the Up and Down Arrow keys to highlight the document you wish to retrieve, then press Enter.

Getting a File Saved in a Different Format

Professional Write's conversion program lets you use files that were created using a different word processing program.

You've seen how to save a document in a different format in order to share it with others. Now, you'll look at how Professional Write can help you use files that you may receive in a different word processing format. Just tell Professional Write what format the document is in; when you get the document, Professional Write automatically converts it to the Professional Write format.

To convert a file, perform the following steps:

1. Press F2, opening the File/Print menu.
2. Choose option 1. Get file, opening the Filename screen.
3. Enter the name of the document, including the extension.
4. Press Enter. Professional Write attempts to retrieve the document. If Professional Write recognizes the format, it displays a working copy. If not, Professional Write displays the Get File format menu—a list of word processing formats—as shown in Figure 4-16.
5. Assuming you know the format of the document that you are trying to get, select the format and press Enter.

It's a fair bet that some aspects of formatting will be lost, but Professional Write reveals what it can't do by displaying a backslash (\ ) in place of the format element that's been left out.

Erasing the Working Copy

To clear the screen, erase the working copy.

When you're done editing your document and you've saved it to a disk, you'll need to clear the document from the screen so you can start

Working with Files

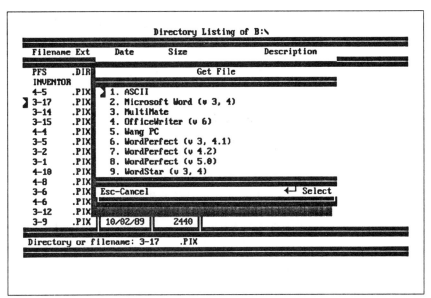

Figure 4-16 The Get File format menu

working on another project. Professional Write lets you clear the screen at any time with its Erase Working Copy option.

Because the working copy is stored only in random access memory until you save it to a disk, be careful about performing this step; you could lose an important document.

To erase a working copy, perform the following steps:

1. Press F2, opening the File/Print menu.
2. Choose option 7. Erase working copy.

If the document has not been saved since the last edit, Professional Write displays a warning that the text will be lost. If the text has been previously saved, the workspace is clear.

You can bypass these steps if you're absolutely sure you don't want to save what's on the screen. Begin performing whatever task you need to perform, such as getting a different file. If what's on the screen has been previously saved, Professional Write clears the screen and carries out your command. If the document on screen hasn't been saved, you'll be warned that if you proceed, you will lose what's on screen. If you're sure you don't need to save the document, press Enter, and Professional Write will carry out your command.

91

Chapter 4

Deleting a Document File

A working copy of a document is held only temporarily in random access memory. If you erase the working copy or turn off your computer, the working copy is gone. If you have saved the document to disk, however, the document still exists in a more stable location. You can retrieve the document at any time by choosing the Get file option.

Deleting a document from disk means that it is gone for good, so don't perform this step without reconsidering. You can bet that as soon as you get rid of a file, someone will rush into your office and ask you for it. As a precaution, before deleting any file (from a hard disk especially), copy the file to a floppy disk. This process is known as *archiving*. By archiving the files that you're *done* with, you free up valuable disk space without losing files you might need later. To delete a document, perform the following steps:

1. Press F2, opening the File/Print menu.
2. Choose option 3. Delete file.
3. If you have a hard disk and the file you want is in the subdirectory that's displayed, press Enter, opening the directory listing.
   - If the document is in a different subdirectory, press Ctrl-E, then type the path leading to the subdirectory and the name of the subdirectory. Press Enter, opening the directory listing.
   - If you're retrieving from a floppy disk, press Ctrl-E, then type the letter of the disk drive you want to access followed by a colon. Press Enter, opening the directory listing.
4. Highlight the file you wish to delete, and press Enter. Professional Write will give you one last warning before deleting the file. Press Enter to complete the deed.

As time passes, an often-used subdirectory may become crowded. Finding a specific file may get more and more difficult. The solution to this problem is to break the directory into two or more parts. You can reorganize your files in a three-step process:

- Create a new subdirectory.
- Copy files from the crowded subdirectory to the new one.
- Delete the copied files from the crowded subdirectory.

Removing a Directory

Once your directory is empty, you can remove it.

If you deleted all the files from a directory in order to "clean house," you may have noticed that the directory is still very much in existence. To remove this directory, you'll need to use the DOS Remove Directory command:

1. Make sure the directory is empty. DOS will not let you remove a directory that has files in it.
2. Exit Professional Write.
3. At the DOS prompt, type `rd` and the complete directory path to tell DOS to "remove directory." The directory is immediately eliminated. For example, to remove the LIZARD subdirectory, type

   ```
   rd
   d:\wdata\lizard
   ```

Copying Documents

Copying documents is as simple as getting the document and saving it somewhere else.

At times you may wish to save a document to a disk or a subdirectory other than the default. You may want to make a backup copy of a file just in case anything would happen to the original, or you may want to save a file to a separate floppy disk to share with a colleague. You may also find that a subdirectory is getting crowded and you need to move the file to a different directory. Professional Write's files directory system simplifies these tasks.

Copying Files from a Hard Disk to a Floppy

The process of copying a file from hard disk to floppy is fairly straightforward. All you do is get the file from the hard disk and save it to the floppy. Here's the step-by-step procedure:

1. Press F2, opening the File/Print menu.
2. Choose option `1. Get file`, opening the Filename screen.
3. If the default directory is correct, press Enter. If not, press Ctrl-E, type the subdirectory path, and press Enter. This opens the files directory.

4. Use the Up and Down Arrow keys to highlight the document you wish to retrieve, then press Enter.
5. Press the F2 key, reopening the File/Print menu.
6. Choose option 2. Save Working Copy.
7. Insert a floppy disk into the floppy disk drive.
8. Type the letter of the floppy disk drive followed by a colon. Press the spacebar, and type the name of the file you want to save. For example, type a: memo to save the MEMO document to a floppy disk in drive A.
9. Press Enter.

Copying Files to a Different Hard Disk Subdirectory

Copy files from a crowded directory to a less crowded one.

If you use a software product other than Professional Write as a desktop publishing system, you might want to create a document in Professional Write and then save it to the subdirectory that contains the desktop publishing program. Or you may just want to copy files from a crowded directory to a less crowded one. To copy to a different hard disk subdirectory, perform the following steps:

1. Press F2, opening the File/Print menu.
2. Choose option 1. Get file, opening the Filename screen.
3. If the default directory is correct, press Enter. If not, press Ctrl-E, type the subdirectory path, and press Enter. This opens the files directory.
4. Use the Up and Down Arrow keys to highlight the document you wish to retrieve, then press Enter.
5. Press the F2 key, reopening the File/Print menu.
6. Choose option 2. Save Working Copy.
7. If the default directory is correct, type a name for the file and press Enter. If not, press Ctrl-E, type the subdirectory path, type a name for the file, and press Enter. For example, to save the MEMO document to a subdirectory called PUBMAK in the E drive, type e:\pubmak\memo and press Enter.

The document is then saved to the appropriate subdirectory. To get the document, you need to enter the new path.

Combining Documents

Professional Write lets you insert an entire document into the working copy.

We've seen how much work Professional Write can do in editing single documents. But if that was all it could do, you would still be faced with a great deal of retyping. For example, if you created two documents and then later decided to combine them, you would have to open one document and retype the other document inside it. Fortunately, Professional Write makes this work unnecessary by offering features that let you combine documents.

Inserting a Document into the Working Copy

Suppose you need to send several letters that include the same information concerning your product's specifications. You can create a separate file that holds the specifications, then insert that file into the working copy of your letter.

To insert a document into the working copy, perform the following steps:

1. In the working copy, position the cursor where you want the insertion to begin.
2. Press F2, opening the File/Print menu.
3. Select option 4. Insert file, opening the Filename screen.
4. If you have a hard disk and the file you want is in the subdirectory that's displayed, press Enter, opening the directory listing.
   - If the document is in a different subdirectory, press Ctrl-E, type the path leading to the subdirectory, and type the name of the subdirectory. Then press Enter, opening the directory listing.
   - If the document is on a floppy disk, press Ctrl-E, then type the letter of the disk drive you want to access followed by a colon. Press Enter, opening the directory listing.
5. Use the Up and Down Arrow keys to highlight the name of the file you want to insert, and press Enter. The highlighted document is inserted into the working copy at the cursor position.

Inserting a Worksheet File

Insert a worksheet directly into your document.

If you have a project that requires you to support your statements with facts and figures, you'll appreciate Professional Write's ability to import spreadsheet files from Lotus 1-2-3 or Professional Plan into your working copy. Although you may have to tinker with the result a little to get it to look just right, importing the file itself is easy.

The data comes into Professional Write as ASCII text with a hard carriage return at the end of each row. If the worksheet insertion has a right margin smaller than Professional Write's, the worksheet takes on the Professional Write margins.

The insertion capability is very flexible; you can insert the entire worksheet or only a portion of it, depending on your needs. You may even insert a range as specified in the worksheet.

When importing a worksheet, its right margin may not exceed 250 characters—Professional Write's maximum right margin setting. A worksheet cannot be imported if the result pushes the size of your working copy above the available random access memory.

Importing an Entire Worksheet

The process for importing an entire worksheet is much the same as the process for importing a file. Just perform the following steps:

1. In the working copy, position the cursor in the place where you want to insert the worksheet.
2. Press F2, opening the File/Print menu.
3. Choose option 4. Insert file, opening the Filename screen.
4. Type the path of the subdirectory where the worksheet is located, then type the filename and extension of the worksheet.
5. Press Enter. Professional Write responds with the Get/Insert Worksheet Data screen as shown in Figure 4-17.
6. Select option 1. Import entire worksheet. The entire worksheet is imported into the working copy at the cursor.

Importing a Portion of a Worksheet

Follow steps 1-5 above for importing an entire worksheet. This opens the Get/Insert Worksheet Data screen. Then perform the following steps:

1. Select option 2. Import view or range. Professional Write displays a list of named ranges or views from the worksheet.
2. If the range or view you desire is listed, highlight it and press Enter. If it's not listed, type in the desired range of cell coordinates and press Enter; for example, type A1..E15. The selected range or view is inserted into the working copy at the cursor.

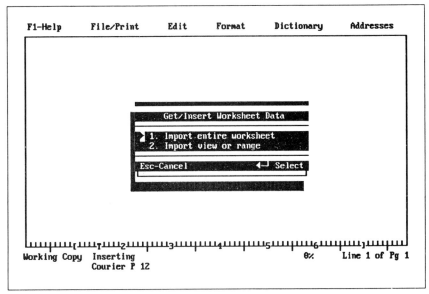

Figure 4-17 The Get/Insert Worksheet Data screen

Summary

In this chapter, you learned to care for and control your files using Professional Write's files directory. You should now be able to save and get files at will and use the files directory listing to access your files.

Don't worry if you haven't mastered the advanced techniques of combining files. As you gain experience, you'll become accustomed to these features, and you'll begin to wonder how you ever wrote without them.

In the next chapter, we'll look at another of these helpful features—the Dictionary and Thesaurus.

F I V E

Using the Professional Write Dictionary and Thesaurus

If checking your spelling and thinking up the perfect word aren't your favorite jobs, Professional Write is here to help with its 77,000-word dictionary and thesaurus. The dictionary will check your entire document for misspellings, stopping at each misspelled word so you can type in the correction. And the thesaurus will help you find that perfect word by offering a list of possibilities.

Even if language *is* your game, you'll find these tools most helpful as both a reference and a second pair of eyes. You can use the thesaurus as a consultant to learn new words and open possibilities for rewordings. If you have a difficult time proofreading on "TV," you can use the dictionary to check those hard-to-find misspellings in which a character is left out or two characters are transposed.

In either case, you'll discover the dictionary's Find and Replace feature most useful. If you create a document then later decide on a more appropriate synonym for a word you used throughout the document, just tell Professional Write to find the old term and replace it with the new one.

The Spell Checking Feature

Create a personal dictionary for each of your projects.

Since the average adult uses approximately 5,000 words on a regular basis, it's a good bet that the words you commonly use will be included in Professional Write's 77,000-word dictionary. If you use several words or terms that are not included, such as terms specific to your business, the dictionary lets you create your own personal dictionary of up to 5,000 words (500 on a floppy disk system).

Professional Write will check the spelling of any document that can be loaded into the workspace. That means that documents in ASCII or in any other format that Professional Write can convert are fair game.

Professional Write offers two spell checking options. You can either check the spelling of a single word or have Professional Write check your entire document. While checking your spelling, Professional Write also looks for words that may be repeated incorrectly, such as "the the." In addition it will look at the capitalization of a word and the format of numbers, such as 1rd or 4st.

Using the Spell Checker

Let's try the spell-checking program on some real text. First, start Professional Write and choose option **1. Create/Edit** from the Main menu. Type the following example as is, typos and all. Your screen should look like the one in Figure 5-1.

```
Dr. Chris Van Lom
145 Paseo Montalban
San Diego, CA. 92129


Dear Sir:
     Thank you for the doubles game of tennis that we
palyed several days ago. My back is still not
recovered from theblow it it recieved when you missed
that overhead.
     I hope to be up and around in several days.
Perhaps we can schedule another match?
```

Checking a Single Word

Let Professional Write look up words for you.

In Figure 5-1, the cursor is resting on the word `Chris`. Now, you may not need to check the spelling of a person's name, but it will serve to illustrate the procedure:

1. Press F5, opening the Dictionary menu as shown in Figure 5-2. If you're working on a floppy disk system, Professional Write will stop for a moment and tell you to insert the Dictionary disk in drive A. Insert the disk, if needed.
2. Choose option **1. Proof word**. Professional Write checks the word in question and responds with the Questionable Word screen as shown in Figure 5-3.

Using the Professional Write Dictionary and Thesaurus

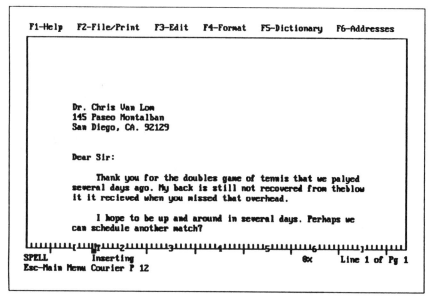

Figure 5-1 A sample document with errors

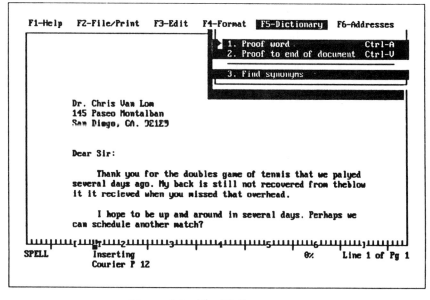

Figure 5-2 The Dictionary menu

Chapter 5

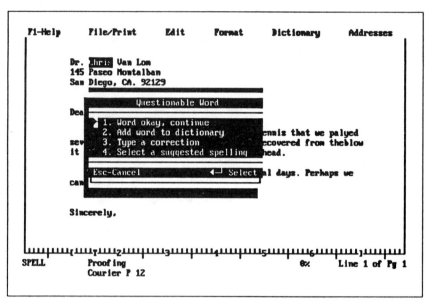

Figure 5-3 The Questionable Word screen

You can use the shortcut keys to bypass the Dictionary menu. Just move the cursor to the word you want to check, and press Ctrl-A.

Since "Chris" is a proper noun, it's not in the Professional Write dictionary, so Professional Write is asking you if "Chris" is spelled correctly and in the proper form. Professional Write also presents four options for you to choose from. Just for kicks, choose option 4 to display a list of what Professional Write thinks may be the correct word. The screen appears, as shown in Figure 5-4.

To choose a word from this list, press the Up or Down Arrow keys to highlight the word, then press Enter. The word is inserted into the document in place of the questionable word.

In this case, the name "Chris" is correct, so press Esc. This closes the list of words and returns you to the Questionable Word screen. If you plan to write several letters to Chris Van Lom, you might want to add the word to your personal dictionary by choosing option 2. Add word to dictionary. If you add a word to the dictionary, Professional Write automatically creates a special file called PERSONAL.SPC to hold your special words.

Choosing option 3. Type a correction opens a correction screen that lets you type in a corrected version of the questionable word. Choose option 1. Word okay, continue to return to the working copy.

Using the Professional Write Dictionary and Thesaurus

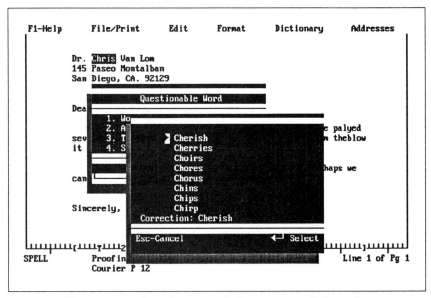

Figure 5-4 A list of suggested alternative words for "Chris"

Checking an Entire Document

Professional Write is a tireless proofreader.

To proof an entire document, perform the following steps:

1. Move the cursor to the beginning of the document.
2. Press F5, opening the Dictionary menu.
3. Choose option 2. Proof to end of document.

If you want Professional Write to proofread a letter of correspondence, move the cursor to the body of the letter and proofread the address yourself. Since most addresses contains several words not listed in any dictionary, Professional Write's dictionary won't help much anyway.

Use the shortcut keys to save time. Position the cursor where you want Professional Write to start proofreading, then press Ctrl-V.

Professional Write begins proofreading the document and stops on the first word it does not recognize, in this case palyed. Professional Write then displays the Questionable Word message box with four menu options.

Since this is just a typo, you know immediately what the correction is. You could just choose option 3. Type a correction, enter the correct spelling, and press Enter. But choose option 4 instead to see a list of suggested spellings, as shown in Figure 5-5.

103

Chapter 5

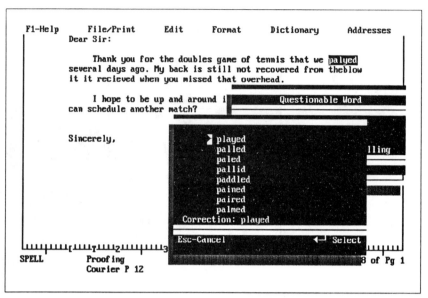

Figure 5-5 The list of possible replacement words

To choose a word, press the Up or Down Arrow key to highlight the correct word, then press Enter.

Professional Write immediately pops the corrected spelling into the document and moves to the next questionable word, `theblow`. In this case, the word is incorrect because it is lacking a space, not because of a misspelling. Because the word is not misspelled, you must type in a correction:

1. Choose option `3. Type a correction`. This opens a correction screen, as shown in Figure 5-6, that lets you enter the correction.
2. Type `the blow`.
3. Press Enter.

Professional Write replaces the incorrect version in the document with the correct version you just typed in, then continues proofreading.

Professional Write even catches repeated words.

The next stop is a repeated word, `it it`. Professional Write is smart enough to distinguish between repeated and questionable words, and displays the Repeated Word menu as shown in Figure 5-7.

In this case, you want to delete the repeated word, so choose option `2. Delete word`. This deletes one of the occurrences of the word and reformats the text to account for the deletion. Professional Write then continues proofreading.

Using the Professional Write Dictionary and Thesaurus

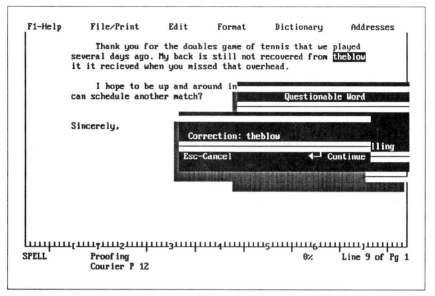

Figure 5-6 The correction screen

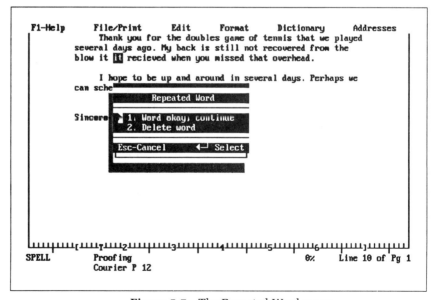

Figure 5-7 The Repeated Word menu

If the two occurrences of the word were separated by a punctuation mark, Professional Write would pass over the repetition, assuming it is correct.

The final problem in this document is a word, `recieved`, that comes under one of those funny spelling rules. If you happen to be an English teacher or copy editor, you probably remember the "i before e" rule and use it without thinking, but for the rest of us, "received" is still a problem word. Fortunately, Professional Write doesn't have to think; it just compares the typed version to the exact spelling in its dictionary. If the typed version doesn't conform, Write questions it and responds with a list of possible corrections as shown in Figure 5-8.

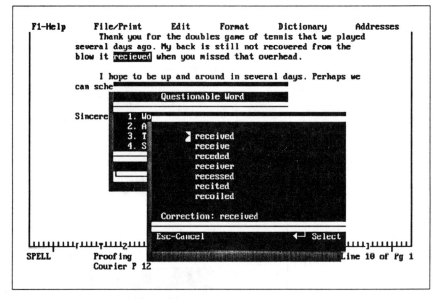

Figure 5-8 Possible corrections for "recieved"

Capitalization

Professional Write considers words that are completely uppercase or completely lowercase to be correct. It will question a word that contains both upper- and lowercase letters if the word is embedded in a sentence. The dictionary includes exceptions for some words that are normally capitalized, such as Minnesota.

Add any words with special capitalization to your personal dictionary, so Professional Write can help you capitalize consistently throughout your document.

The Personal Dictionary

Your personal dictionary is a separate file that can be opened at any time.

When you add your first word to the personal dictionary, Professional Write creates a separate file called PERSONAL.SPC to hold it. Since the personal dictionary is a separate file, you don't have to be working on a document in order to add words to it. Just open the file called PERSONAL.SPC and type in your entries at any point in the list. Professional Write will alphabetize the list of words when you resave the file.

If you're using Professional Write on a floppy disk system and need more room for the personal dictionary, delete the SAMPLE.LTR document from your copy of the dictionary disk. Don't delete anything from the original disks you purchased.

Using Multiple Personal Dictionaries

If you're involved in several projects, you might need to use a separate personal dictionary for each project. For example, suppose you have two aircraft projects underway, each with its own terminology. You can create a specific dictionary for each project and save each dictionary as a separate file.

The catch is that Professional Write will look only in the file named PERSONAL.SPC for special words. That means you'll have to juggle some filenames to keep Professional Write happy.

Back to the aircraft projects. Suppose you're working on one project called Stealth and another project called Pebbles. You could create one file with all the terminology related to the Stealth project and call it STEALTH. Create another file called PEBBLES to hold the terminology specific to the Pebbles project.

Whenever you decide to work on the Stealth project, you need to activate the STEALTH dictionary by renaming it PERSONAL.SPC. However, you don't want to overwrite your personal dictionary file, because it may contain some important words. You need to temporarily swap personal dictionaries:

1. Get the PERSONAL.SPC file.
2. Save the PERSONAL.SPC file under another name, such as PERSONAL.DIC.
3. Get the STEALTH file.
4. Save the STEALTH file as PERSONAL.SPC. This overwrites the PERSONAL.SPC file.

When you're finished, get the new PERSONAL.SPC file and resave it as STEALTH. Then get the PERSONAL.DIC file and save it as PER-

Chapter 5

SONAL.SPC. Resaving the new PERSONAL.SPC file as STEALTH is especially important if you added words to the dictionary. If you didn't resave the file, those new words would be left out of the STEALTH file.

Using the Professional Write Thesaurus

The thesaurus adds color to your writing.

Finding the right word can be a difficult process. It starts with a slight pause at the keyboard, then progresses to typing in a word you know just isn't right. The right word is on the tip of your tongue, but when you finally think of it, it isn't quite right either. Look in the dictionary? Where?!

Well, Professional Write can lend a hand, offering a list of suggestions. Sometimes the list will offer a suggestion that's perfect. Other times, you may have to page through your dictionary to determine the meanings of some of the suggested words. In any case, Professional Write gives you a place to start and a quick reference that will save you some leg work.

When is the thesaurus most useful? That's up to you. Personally, I use the thesaurus when I'm creating the document for the first time. My word choice is pretty final after the first draft. You may like to forge ahead, however, getting it all down first and fine-tuning it later. Professional Write is flexible; use the thesaurus whenever you need it.

Let's try the thesaurus out on a short passage that has more than its share of repetition. Type the following passage, so you'll have some text to work with:

```
It was a relatively dark and stormy night, the wind
howled like a dog at play with an old shoe. The
relative safety of the old run down cellar was
overshadowed by the strange noises emanating from the
bathroom.

Mr. Jones knew that he was relatively safe: He had
just decoded the secret message from the letter his
favorite relative had sent.

The strange noise from the bathroom was Mrs. Jones
getting ready for mahjong, a game she played
relatively well. She always gave it the old college
try, because when the going gets tough, the tough go
and curl their hair in tresses that are relatively
gorgeous.
```

Your screen should look like the one shown in Figure 5-9. Save the document to a file called STORY.

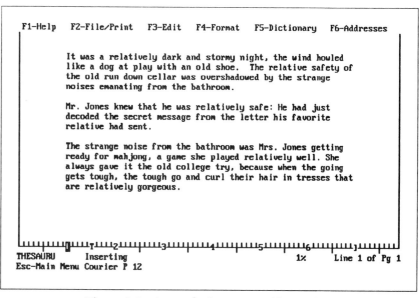

Figure 5-9 A sample document with repetition

Granted, this passage needs a lot more than a few changes in wording here and there; in fact, this file is a good candidate for permanent deletion. But since it has so much repetition and so many overused phrases, it's a perfect model for trying out the thesaurus.

The thesaurus provides a list of synonyms from which to choose.

Almost every bad novel has a dark and stormy night, so let's try to change that phrase to something a little more original:

1. Press the Arrow keys to move the cursor to stormy.
2. Press F5 to open the Dictionary menu, as shown in Figure 5-10.
3. Choose option 3. Find synonyms. This opens a synonym screen, shown in Figure 5-11, that consists of a list of synonyms for "stormy."

There's no right and wrong here, but some choices are better than others depending on how the word is used in context. If you're having a difficult time making a decision, plop one of the synonyms from the list into the document. Just highlight the word you want and press Enter. If the word isn't right, try again.

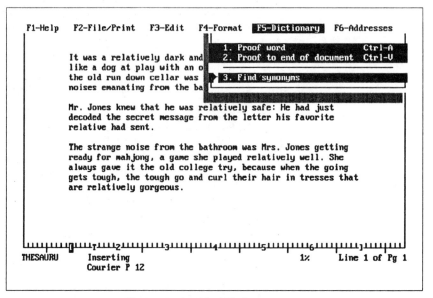

Figure 5-10 The Dictionary menu

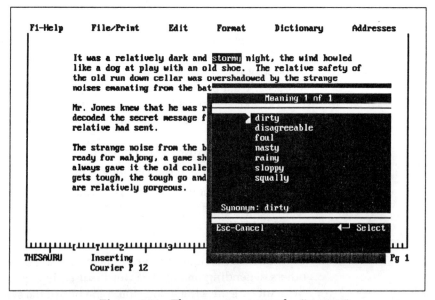

Figure 5-11 The synonym screen for "stormy"

Professional Write always starts with the root form of a word to find a synonym. If you're looking for a synonym and Professional Write comes up blank, remove the word's prefix or suffix and try again. It's a long shot, but it's worth a try.

The Find and Replace Feature

Use Find and Replace to make global changes.

Say you just finished typing a 50-page proposal to produce widgets for the Army's new combat tank, and your proposal is filled with references to widgets. When you're almost done, the Army decides to change its terminology; widgets will now be called gadgets. Going through the entire document, word-by-word, to find every reference to widgets would be both time consuming and frustrating. And in the end there would be no guarantee that you had found them all; at just the wrong moment, the one you missed would appear.

But with Professional Write's Find and Replace feature, such a problem no longer exists. You just tell Write to find every occurrence of "widgets" and replace it with "gadgets," and Write dutifully performs the task. You can even use wild cards to help find words that you forgot how to spell.

Finding Text

Professional Write will search the document from the present cursor position to the end of the document.

Let's see how competent this Find feature is by trying it out on some real text. Get the STORY file, if it's not already displayed on screen, and position the cursor at the beginning of the document. Then:

1. Press F3, opening the Edit menu as shown in Figure 5-12.
2. Choose option **A. Find & Replace**, opening the Find and Replace screen as shown in Figure 5-13.
3. Type **she** to search for the word "she."
4. If you want Professional Write to find only the lowercase versions of "she," not the occurrences that begin a sentence, such as "She," press the Tab key once and type N. Doing this tells Professional Write to consider capitalization in its search.
5. Since you're simply searching for text, you can ignore the last two options that deal with the Find feature. Press Enter. Professional Write begins searching and stops at the first occurrence of the word.

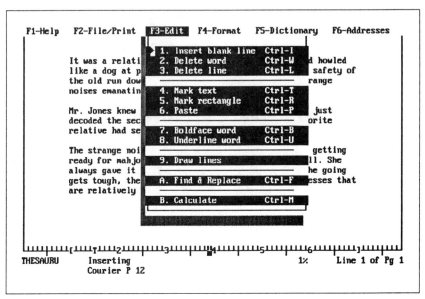

Figure 5-12 The Edit menu

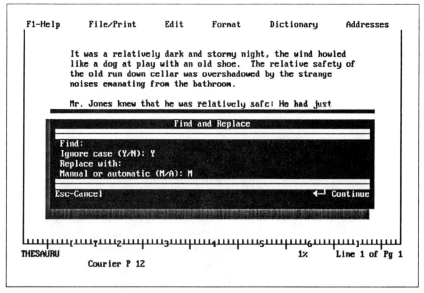

Figure 5-13 The Find and Replace screen

Using the Professional Write Dictionary and Thesaurus

You don't have to go back to the Edit menu to resume the search. Just press Ctrl-F and Enter; Professional Write continues until it finds the next occurrence. If you decide to abort the search and begin searching for another word from this point in the text, type in the new word you want to search for, before pressing Enter.

Find and Replace

We typed a short passage earlier and used the thesaurus a little to revise the "dark and stormy night." During that exercise, you may have noticed that the root word "relative" was repeated several times. Let's clean up that repetition by replacing the occurrences of "relatively" with "somewhat."

Get the STORY file, if it's not displayed on screen, and position the cursor at the beginning of the document. Then:

1. Press F3, opening the Edit menu.
2. Choose option **A. Find & Replace**, opening the Find and Replace screen.
3. Type **relatively**.
4. Press Tab twice, moving the cursor to **Replace with:**.
5. Type **somewhat**.

Professional Write will automatically replace every occurrence of the word or ask for your final OK.

6. Press Tab. This moves the cursor to the final option. If you want Professional Write to automatically replace each and every occurrence of "relatively" with "somewhat" without asking for your final OK, type **a** for Automatic. If you want to check the word before replacing it, press Enter, to accept the default choice, Manual.

If you chose Automatic, Professional Write is probably done with the replacement already. If you chose Manual, Professional Write has stopped on the first occurrence of "relatively" and is waiting for your decision. If that's the case, you'll see the confirmation for Find and Replace screen, as shown in Figure 5-14.

To give the OK, just press Enter, choosing option 1. If you decide not to replace the word, choose option **2. Continue without replacing**.

Use the shortcut keys to bypass the Edit menu. Just press Ctrl-F to open the Find and Replace screen.

113

Chapter 5

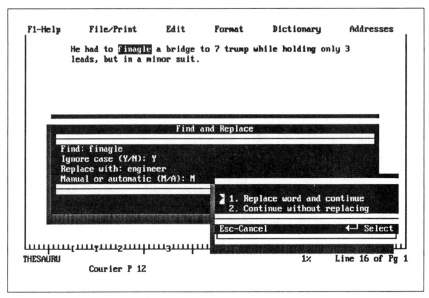

Figure 5-14 The confirmation for Find and Replace screen

Using Wild Cards

Use wild cards to make your computer think.

Professional Write, like most software programs, is normally very literal. If you tell Write to find "relatively" it will find that word but pass over occurrences such as "relative." This isn't all bad; a computer could do a lot of damage to your document by misinterpreting a command. But there are times when you want your computer to act a little more intuitively. That's where wild cards come in.

Wild cards consist of two periods that stand for any and all missing letters. To see how wild cards work, clear the screen without saving the corrections to the STORY file. Just press F2, choose option **7. Erase working copy**, and press Enter when the warning screen appears. Then open the old STORY file. We want to find all occurrences of *relative*, including "relatively," so:

1. Press F3, opening the Edit menu.
2. Choose option **A. Find & Replace**.
3. Type **relative..** and press Enter. Professional Write broadens the scope of its search, and stops on "relatively."

114

Wild cards are not limited to the last characters in a word. You can use wild cards for preceding characters as well. The following examples illustrate the possible uses of wild cards:

Entry	Will Find
age..	aged, agent, agenda
..age	portage, postage, mortgage
..age..	aged, bandages, mortgages

Finding and Erasing All Occurrences of a Word

Ever have that feeling that no word is better than the word you used? If you have, Professional Write is very willing to accommodate your wish and reformat the remaining text to fill in for the deleted word. But be careful. Usually when you find and replace you can go back on your decision by reversing the process. In this case, there's no looking back; you can't tell Write to find nothing. To delete all occurrences of a particular word, perform the following steps:

1. Press F3, opening the Edit menu.
2. Choose option A. Find & Replace.
3. Type the word you want to erase.
4. Press the Tab key twice.
5. Type "" (no space between the quotation marks).
6. Press the Tab key once and choose Automatic or Manual search.
7. Press Enter.

Counting Words

After Professional Write completes its search, it displays a number indicating how many occurrences of the word it has found. You can use this to count how many times you used a particular word in your document. You can even generate an overall word count for your document by using the wild card in conjunction with Find.

Counting Occurrences of a Word

I don't know why you would want to determine the number of times a particular word is used in a document. Maybe you're doing a formal analysis of a Shakespeare play, or maybe you're an English teacher and you want to prove to a student that he's redundant. I'm sure you have your reasons:

1. Get the document and position the cursor at the beginning.
2. Press F3, opening the Edit menu.
3. Choose option **A. Find & Replace**.
4. Type the word you want to count.
5. Press Tab and type **y**, telling Professional Write to ignore case.
6. Press Tab twice and type **a**, putting Find in automatic mode.
7. Press Enter, starting the count.

Professional Write will find every occurrence and display a running total as it does.

Generating an Overall Word Count

Use the Find feature to count your words.

If you're given a limit for the number of words in a report, use the Find feature to generate a word count:

1. Get the document and position the cursor at the beginning.
2. Press F3, opening the Edit menu.
3. Choose option **A. Find & Replace**.
4. Type .. (the wild card entry).
5. Press Tab and type **y**, telling Professional Write to ignore case.
6. Press Tab twice and type **a**, putting Find in automatic mode.
7. Press Enter, starting the count.

Professional Write displays a running tally until it reaches the end of the document.

Summary

In this chapter, you learned to use several of Professional Write's most practical features to improve the quality of your writing. You used the dictionary to double-check your document for misspellings and typos. You took advantange of the thesaurus to access lists of alternative words. And you used the Find and Replace feature to make global substitutions at the touch of a key. All in all, you've had practice using some pretty powerful editing tools.

In the next chapter, we will look at a couple of tools that take us beyond word processing: Professional Write's Drawing and Calculating functions.

S I X

The Drawing and Calculating Functions

Support your text with facts and figures.

Professional Write's Drawing and Calculating functions are the tools you need to go beyond word processing. With the Drawing function, you'll be able to illustrate and enhance your text with simple line drawings. If your work requires you to draw schematics or flow charts, the Drawing function is perfect for the job.

If your reports require you to work with numbers, the Calculator is here to help. Write's Calculating function acts as a useful desktop utility; you no longer have to search for your calculator to perform basic operations. Just bring it up on screen, and you're ready to calculate. After calculating the result, you can insert it right into the text.

Let's see how these two functions work.

Drawing with Professional Write

One program handles both text and graphics.

In the past, you would need two software programs to draw a simple sketch within your text; you would create the drawing with one program and the text with another. Then you would have to cut and paste to form the finished product. To eliminate this juggling act, Professional Write has integrated the drawing and word processing functions.

Suppose you're planning a room addition and want to send the plans to several contractors for their construction bids. With the Drawing function, you can send each of them an identical floor plan, changing only the inside address for each contractor.

Chapter 6

Creating a Drawing

Start by typing the beginning of a letter to the contractors. First, start up Professional Write and choose option 1. Create/Edit from the Main menu. This opens a workspace where you can begin typing. Then, type the following:

```
September 30, 1990


Kelly Construction
300 N. Montgomery
Le Center, Mn. 56000

Dear Sir:
I have enclosed a floor plan for a room addition.
Please look over the plan, and submit a bid by the
first of November 1990 including a timeline for
completion.
```

Your screen should look like the one shown in Figure 6-1. Press Enter four times to create a space between the text and the place where the drawing will start.

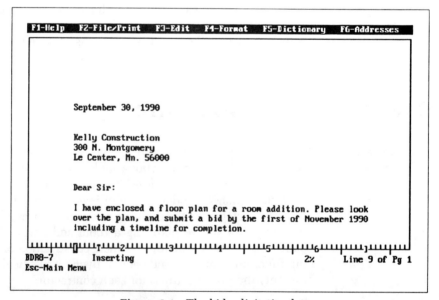

Figure 6-1 The bid solicitation letter

The Drawing and Calculating Functions

Before we start drawing, we need to enter the orientation of the sketch to give us a point of reference. Since the top of most floor plans is North, we'll follow that standard. Type N and press Ctrl-X, centering a capital N at the place where our drawing will start. Press Enter, moving the cursor to line 20. Now we can put Professional Write in the Drawing mode:

1. Press F3, opening the Edit menu.
2. Select option 9. Draw Lines, opening the Drawing submenu as shown in Figure 6-2.

Professional Write lets you draw with any character that your keyboard and printer support.

3. Choose option 2. Select drawing style, opening the Drawing Styles submenu shown in Figure 6-3. This submenu lets you choose between three different line styles. The fourth choice lets you use keyboard characters, such as asterisks or plus signs, instead of a line.
4. Choose option 4. Other, opening a screen where you can type the character you want to use. We'll get clever here. Since we're designing a room addition, we will use the plus sign as our character. The screen should now look like the one in Figure 6-4.
5. To confirm the selection, press Enter. This takes you back to the working copy. At the bottom of the screen, Professional Write indicates that the program is in drawing mode.

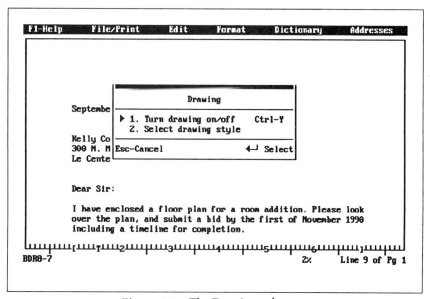

Figure 6-2 The Drawing submenu

Chapter 6

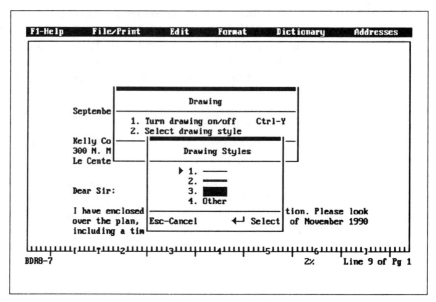

Figure 6-3 The Drawing Styles submenu

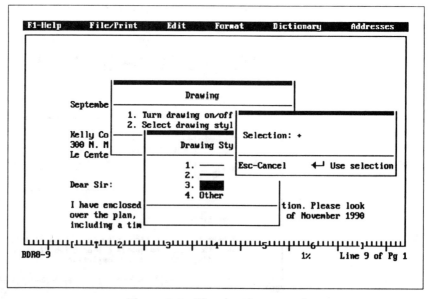

Figure 6-4 The plus sign entered

In drawing mode, you can use the arrow keys to *stretch* a line of characters across the screen. Table 6-1 summarizes the keys and their corresponding directions.

Table 6-1 Cursor Line Drawing Keys

Press	To Stretch Line
Right Arrow Key	To right
Left Arrow Key	To left
Down Arrow Key	Down
Up Arrow Key	Up
Home	Up and to left
PgUp	Up and to right
End	Down and to left
PgDn	Down and to right

In the following example, we will create a floor plan for a room that is 13 by 15 feet. If you want to draw to scale, don't expect too much. Because there is no direct correspondence between the number of characters per inch and the number of lines per inch, you pretty much have to fudge. When you're done drawing, you can type in the exact measurements and draw arrows to indicate dimensions.

1. Press the Right Arrow key until the line of pluses is stretched across the screen to the number 6 in the Ruler line. This represents our 15-foot wall. If you stretch the line too far, hold down the Shift key and press the Left Arrow key to delete the extra pluses.

2. Press the Down Arrow key, stretching the line of pluses down the screen until the line indicator displays **Line 34 of Page 1**. This line represents our 9-foot wall. To erase extra pluses, press Shift-Up Arrow. (Professional Write will automatically square corners for you, but you might have to touch them up on the printout.)

3. At line 34, we need to draw an entrance from the existing house to the new room. Press the Left Arrow key until the cursor is on **5** in the Ruler line. Your drawing should look like the one in Figure 6-5.

4. Press the Down Arrow key, moving the cursor to line 40. This adds 4 feet to our 9-foot wall, making the wall 13 feet long. This also brings us against the house.

   We need to distinguish between the existing wall of the house and the walls that the contractor is to build, so we must use a different character to represent the existing wall.

Chapter 6

5. Press F3, opening the Edit menu.
6. Choose option 9. Draw lines, opening the Drawing submenu.
7. Choose option 2. Select drawing style.
8. Choose option 2, the double line.
9. Press the Left Arrow key, stretching the double line to the left margin, as shown in Figure 6-6.
10. Change the drawing symbol back to the plus sign.
11. Press the Up Arrow key, drawing the last wall. The finished floor plan should look like Figure 6-7.

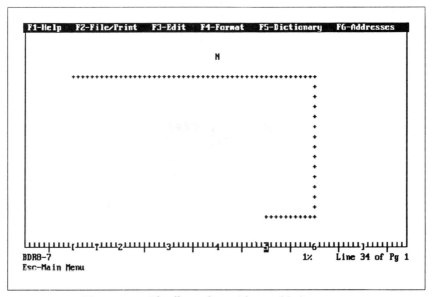

Figure 6-5   The floor plan with an added entrance

Editing the Drawing

After seeing the drawing you might decide to change a few things. For example, you may have originally designed the entrance for a door that swings open, but now you decide that sliding glass doors would look better. Making the change is as easy as editing text:

You can turn the Drawing function on or off at any time by pressing Ctrl-Y.

1. Press Ctrl-Y, turning off the Drawing function.
2. Use the Arrow keys to move the cursor to line 34 and to 5 on the Ruler line. This is the inside corner of the entrance.

The Drawing and Calculating Functions

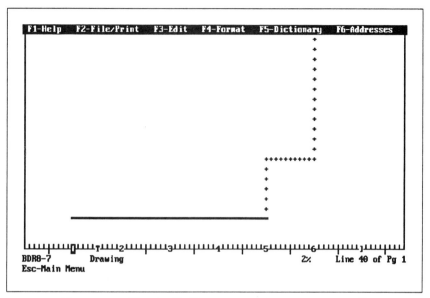

Figure 6-6   The double line representing an existing wall

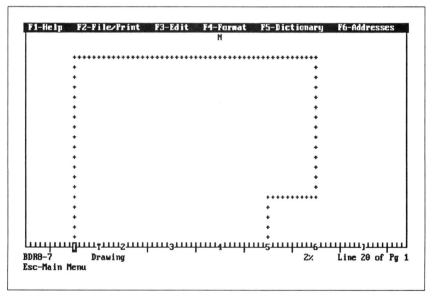

Figure 6-7   The finished floor plan

3. Press Shift-Down Arrow, erasing the vertical line down to line 40. The drawing should now look like the one in Figure 6-8.
4. Now we need to knock out more of the existing wall. Press Shift-Left Arrow, deleting the double line until the cursor is halfway between 4 and 5 on the Ruler line.
5. Press Ctrl-Y, turning the Drawing function on, so we can redraw the entrance.
6. Press the Up Arrow key, inserting pluses up to line 34.
7. Press the Right Arrow key until the cursor is on the 5 in the ruler line, reconnecting the vertical line to the rightmost wall.

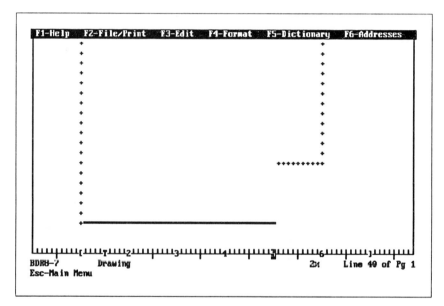

Figure 6-8 The vertical line erased

As shown in Figure 6-9, you can turn the Drawing function off and add notes to indicate where you want the doors and windows. You can even furnish your new room!

Make a file of your most frequently used drawings. That way, you won't have to search through your document files to find the drawing you need. Later, when you learn how to use macros, you'll be able to assign a macro to this file, making it accessible through a keystroke.

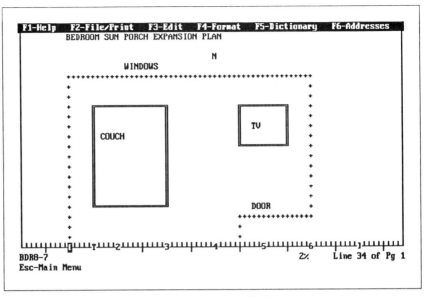

Figure 6-9 The furnished room

Calculating with Professional Write

If you are new to computerized word processing you will probably be surprised to learn that most word processing programs do not include a means of making simple calculations and inserting them into the body of a letter. After all, computers are supposed to compute, aren't they?

Well, don't worry; Professional Write's Calculating function gives your computer back its original identity.

Performing a Calculation

Before we try calculating from within a document, let's try using the Calculator by itself. If you haven't started up Professional Write, do so now, and choose option **1. Create/Edit** from the Main menu. Then:

1. Press F3, opening the Edit menu, as shown in Figure 6-10.
2. Choose option **B. Calculate**, opening the Calculator screen as shown in Figure 6-11. There are two distinct fields in the Calculator. The first is the Expression field; that's where you type the formula. The second is the Result field, where Professional Write displays the answer.

Chapter 6

3. Type 500/5*78, telling the Calculator to divide 500 by 5 and multiply the result by 78: (500/5)*78.
4. Press F9 to calculate the answer. The calculator performs the calculation and displays the answer Result: 7,800.

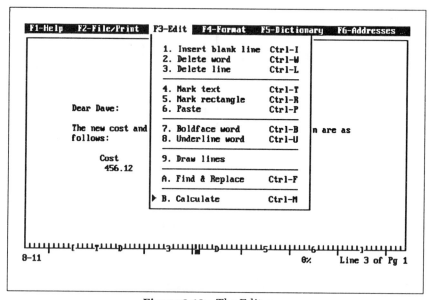

Figure 6-10 The Edit menu

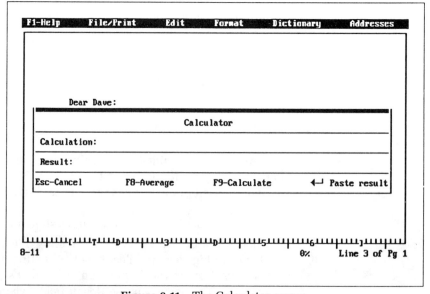

Figure 6-11 The Calculator screen

Using Parentheses

Use parentheses to change the order of calculations.

In the previous example, the mathematical operations were calculated from left to right; the division was done first and then the multiplication. Professional Write calculates in this order: multiplication and division from left to right, then addition and subtraction from left to right.

You can change the order of calculation by using parentheses. Professional Write will calculate the expression within parentheses first, then proceed to calculate from left to right.

To see the result of using parentheses, move the cursor in the calculation field to the 5. The default editing mode in the Calculator is Overstrike, not Insert. Press the Ins key so that the parentheses will be inserted. Type (, press the Right Arrow key until the cursor is to the right of 78, and type). The formula should appear as in Figure 6-12.

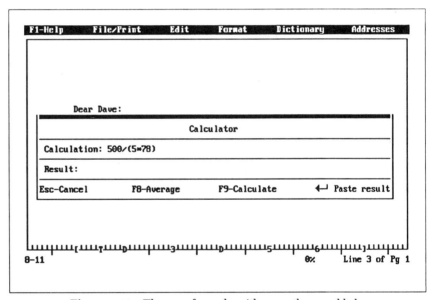

Figure 6-12 The new formula with parentheses added

Press F9 to calculate the formula. The result appears on screen **1.28205128**. As you can see, there's a big difference between (500/5)*78 and 500/(5*78).

You can even use parentheses within parentheses; in such a case, Professional Write works from the innermost pair of parentheses out, then from left to right.

For example, subtract 83 from 78 then multiply the result by 5. Move the cursor to the 7 in 78 and type (. Move the cursor to the rightmost parenthesis and type -83). The entire expression is **500/(5*(78-83))**. Press F9 to see the result, as shown in Figure 6-13.

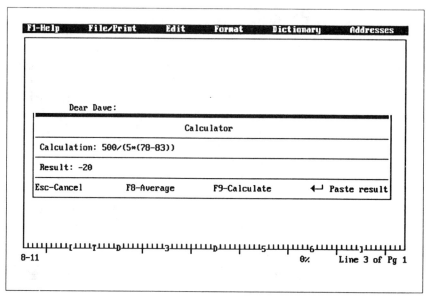

Figure 6-13 The embedded calculation

Inserting Numbers into the Calculator

The Calculator lets you perform calculations on existing numbers.

If you already have the numbers you need to work with somewhere in your document, you don't need to retype them in the Calculator. You can just copy them right from the text into the Calculator.

Let's try it out on our COST document. Press Esc, closing the Calculator. Get the COST file. Before we begin calculating, we need to add headings to our columns to give us some idea of what we're going to do:

1. Press the Down Arrow key until the cursor is in the blank line above the numbers.
2. Press the Tab key moving the cursor over the first number, and type Cost. (Even though we're going to enter text, the decimal tab stops still serve to align the entries.)
3. Press the Tab key, moving the cursor over the second number, and type Sale.
4. Move the cursor so the cursor in the Ruler line is over 5, and type Markup. The document should now look like the one in Figure 6-14. Why did we add the Markup column? Simply because we'll need a place to enter our result.

The Drawing and Calculating Functions

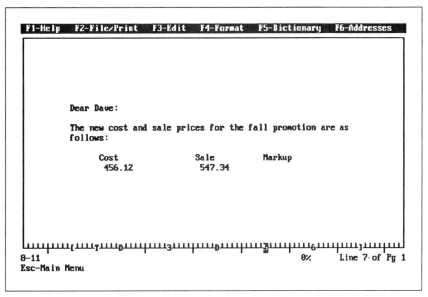

Figure 6-14 The revised COST document

If you don't tell it otherwise, the Calculator assumes you want to add.

Our next task is to use our cost and sale numbers to calculate the percentage markup:

1. Move the cursor to the left of the first number, 456.12.
2. Press Ctrl-T, putting the Calculator in Mark Text mode.
3. Press the Right Arrow key, stretching the highlight until it covers both numbers.
4. Press Ctrl-M, activating the Calculator. Professional Write assumes that we wanted to add the two numbers highlighted in the marked text, so it calculates the sum.

To determine the percentage markup, however, a mere sum won't do. We need to divide the cost by the sale price and subtract 1. In order to do that, we need to edit the formula:

1. Move the cursor over the plus sign, press the Ins key, and type /.
2. Press the Ins key again, returning Professional Write to the Insert mode.
3. Type (to the left of the first number, and type) to the right of the second number.
4. Type −1 to the right of the closing parentheses. The entire expression is (456.12/547.34)−1.

5. Press F9, calculating the result. Your screen should now look like the one shown in Figure 6-15.

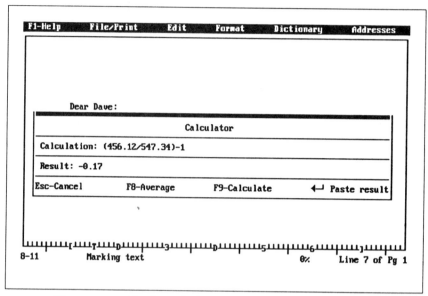

Figure 6-15 The formula for calculating percentage markup

Now we're ready to insert the result from the Calculator into the text:

1. Press Enter, closing the Calculator and returning to the working copy. A message appears, telling you to Move cursor to where you want the result and press Enter.
2. Move the cursor to the line under the Markup heading and press Enter.
3. Delete the negative sign that precedes the number, and add a percent sign after it. The markup should now read 17%.

Calculating Averages

One of the most helpful features of the Calculator is its ability to calculate the average of several numbers. You don't even have to supply the formula! To calculate an average, perform the following steps:

1. Enter the numbers you want to average, separated by plus signs, into the Calculation field. (If you already have the numbers in your

document, just mark the block and choose option C from the Text Block Operations menu. You don't need to enter the plus signs.)

2. Press F8 to calculate the average.

Rounding Off Your Results

Professional Write includes up to 15 significant digits after the decimal point. If you want to round off the result before you paste it in, just press the Tab key to move to the Result field, use the arrow keys to move the cursor, and press Del to delete the extra digits.

Summary

In this chapter, you learned to use two of Professional Write's more powerful functions. You can now draw simple diagrams to illustrate your ideas and enhance the appearance of your reports and memos. With the Calculating function, you can perform calculations on the fly and insert the results in your text.

Now that you've learned to get our documents up and running with facts and figures, you can go on to fine-tune its appearance with the use of fonts.

S E V E N

Using the Write Fonts

Adding fonts to your document can enhance its appearance and improve its readability considerably. You can use fonts to enlarge headings that introduce important points, to shrink footnotes so they'll be less distracting, and to vary the style of print to set off a section of text. Used correctly, fonts can be one of your most powerful desktop publishing tools.

This chapter assumes that your printer supports at least a few different fonts. If you're not sure, refer to the printer booklet that came with Professional Write. If your printer does not support fonts, you can use different type style, such as boldface and underline, to emphasize or set off text.

What Are Fonts?

A font is any set of characters that share a common typeface and point size. For example, Helvetica 12-point is a font; Helvetica is the typeface, and 12-point is the size. Just for reference, there are 72 points in one inch.

Don't confuse typefaces with Professional Write's type styles, such as bold and italic. Type styles simply enhance whatever font you choose.

Fixed-Pitch and Proportional Fonts

The term "pitch" refers to the number of characters per inch. You can vary the font's pitch to suit your taste. You can also vary the spacing between letters by choosing either fixed-pitch or proportional. Fixed-pitch simply means that every letter is given the same amount of room; a skinny "i" and a squat "m" are allotted the same space. Proportional fonts take each character's girth into consideration. Personally, I find the proportional font more appealing, but there are important uses for fixed-pitch as well—for example, in setting up text that needs to be aligned vertically.

Portrait and Landscape

Portrait and *landscape* refer to the orientation of text on the page. In portrait orientation, the text is printed along the short edge of the page as in a letter of correspondence. In landscape orientation, the text is printed along the wide edge.

Consider the Source

You must tell Professional Write the location of the fonts.

Many printers that are capable of printing fonts have them built in. Such fonts are appropriately called *internal fonts*. Other printers require outside help to access a wider variety of fonts. For example, you may have to plug a special cartridge into your printer. You may even have to transfer fonts (*soft fonts*) from special software packages to your printer, a process referred to as *downloading*.

In any case, you need to tell Professional Write where the fonts are located, so Write can pass the information on to your printer. This saves you the time and trouble of entering special commands each time you try to change a font.

Setting Up Fonts

Setting up fonts consists of feeding Professional Write the information it needs concerning the printer you're using and the location of the fonts. To set up fonts, first specify the printer you're using:

1. Choose option 2. Setup from the Main menu, opening the Setup menu.
2. Choose option 1. Select printer 1, opening the Printer 1 Selection screen. (Option 2. Select printer 2 does not support fonts.)
3. Highlight the printer you're using.

4. If you did not select a printer port during setup, press Tab, moving to the Printer Port column, and highlight the port you're using.
5. Press Enter.

Your next step depends on the printer you just chose. If you chose a Hewlett-Packard laser printer, Professional Write displays a source submenu. Skip ahead to the section on setting up an HP laser printer to determine what to do.

If you chose Unlisted printer, Professional Write displays a screen that lets you type in codes for type styles, such as boldface and underline, that your printer probably can handle. You can use these type styles as you would use fonts. If you're at this screen, jump to the following section on setting up an unlisted printer.

If the printer you chose cannot handle fonts, or if Professional Write already has the setup information it needs for your particular printer, it returns you to the Setup menu.

If your printer does handle fonts and is not a Hewlett-Packard LaserJet, a list of fonts is displayed as shown in Figure 7-1. Just highlight the font you decide to use, and press Enter.

```
                    Printer 1 Selection
                    Select Regular Font

   Font          Orientation   Point   Pitch   Styles

   Courier       Portrait      12      10      N,B,I,BI
   Courier       Portrait      8       15      N,B,I,BI
 ▶ Courier       Portrait      10      12      N,B,I,BI
   Courier       Portrait      14      8.5     N,B,I,BI
   Courier       Portrait      18      6.6     N,B,I,BI
   Courier       Landscape     8       15      N,B,I,BI
   Courier       Landscape     10      12      N,B,I,BI
   Courier       Landscape     12      10      N,B,I,BI

   Selection: Courier

   Esc-Cancel            PgDn-More            ⏎ Select

Printer: PostScript Printer
Printer port: PRN:
```

Figure 7-1   A list of available fonts

Setting Up Fonts on an HP Laser Printer

Professional Write requires more information for complex printers.

Because the HP laser printer is capable of accessing fonts on cartridges and disks, Professional Write requires more setup information than it does for other printers. When you select one of these printers, Professional Write displays a Source submenu as shown in Figure 7-2. This submenu asks you to specify the source of your fonts. As you can see, the setup procedure varies depending on whether you're using soft fonts from a disk or fonts from a cartridge.

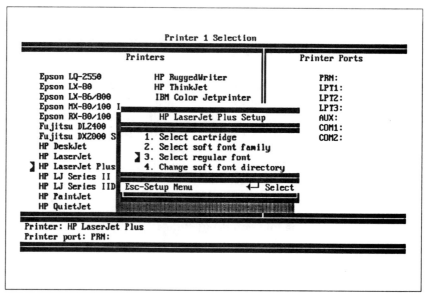

Figure 7-2   The Source submenu

Cartridge Setup

1. Choose option 1. Select cartridge from the Source submenu, displaying a list of cartridges.
2. Choose the type of cartridge that's plugged into your printer. This returns you to the Source submenu.
3. If you're setting up a DeskJet or LaserJet, skip to step 5. If not, choose option 2. Select soft font family, opening a list of soft font families as shown in Figure 7-3.
4. Choose the soft font family you want to use. This returns you to the Source submenu.
5. Choose option 3. Select regular font to view a list of available fonts as shown in Figure 7-1.
6. Highlight the font you intend to use, and press Enter.
7. Press Esc to return to the Setup menu. (If you're using a serial printer, pressing Esc opens the Serial Port Settings screen. Refer to the Appendix for a detailed explanation.)

Using the Write Fonts

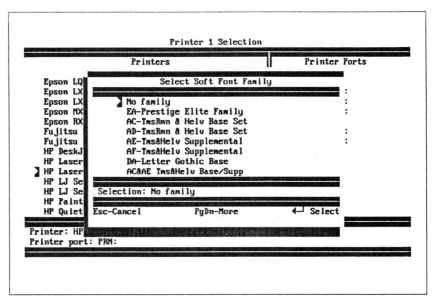

Figure 7-3 The Select Soft Font Family menu

Soft Fonts

1. Choose option 2. Select soft font family from the Source submenu. This displays a list of soft font families as shown in Figure 7-2.

2. Choose the family you want. This returns you to the Source submenu.

3. Choose option 4. Change soft font directory.

4. At the directory prompt, type the complete path and subdirectory of your soft font files. For example, type d:\soft.

5. Press Enter.

6. Choose option 3. Select regular font. Professional Write displays a list of the soft fonts available as shown in Figure 7-1.

7. Highlight the font you intend to use, and press Enter, returning you to the Source submenu.

8. Press Esc to return to the Setup menu. (If you're using a serial printer, pressing Esc opens the Serial Port Settings screen. Refer to the Appendix for a detailed explanation.)

Whenever you begin to work on a document, Professional Write assumes that you want to use the font most recently selected.

Approximating Fonts with an Unlisted Printer

After choosing Unlisted Printer from the Printer 1 Selection screen, you'll see a screen that lets you type in codes for various type styles.

1. Refer to the manual that came with your printer to determine the type styles it supports and the ASCII control codes required to turn the type styles on and off.
2. Type the ASCII decimal equivalents next to the code listed on screen. If the code consists of more than one number, separate the numbers with a space or a comma. For example, next to `Boldface on:`, type `27,69`. Press Tab to move to the next type style on the list. If your printer does not support a type style on the list, skip that type style.
3. Press Enter to store the codes.
4. If you selected a parallel printer port, the Setup menu appears. If you selected a serial port, the Serial Port Settings screen appears. Refer to the Appendix for instructions on setting up a serial printer.

Changing Fonts

Normally, you will change fonts in a pre-existing document. You'll type the document in the regular font and then go back and change the fonts of specific elements to set them off. Or, you may get a document that someone else has created containing fonts that your printer does not support. In either case, Professional Write simplifies the process of changing fonts.

Changing to Fonts That Your Printer Supports

You can change the font for an entire document.

Whenever you create and save a document, Professional Write saves the fonts too. If you ever need to print the document on a different printer, or if you need to print a document that someone gave you, you must change the fonts to those that your printer supports. To change the font for an entire document, perform the following steps:

1. Get the file that has the font you want to change.
2. Press Esc, returning to the Main menu.
3. Choose option `2. Setup`, opening the Setup menu.

Using the Write Fonts

4. Choose option **1. Select printer 1**, displaying a list of available fonts as shown in Figure 7-1. Printer 2 does not support fonts.
5. Highlight the font you want to use and press Enter.
6. Press Esc, returning to the Main menu.
7. Select option **1. Create/Edit**, returning to the working copy of the file. The new font will now be in effect for all text in the document, old and new.

Changing the regular font has no effect on any text that has been formatted in other font for special effect. It's easier to change these fonts when you're in the Preview mode, which we'll look at more in the next chapter.

Changing Fonts with a Block Command

You can change the font in an entire block of text, leaving surrounding text unchanged.

To go back and change the default font every time you wanted to set off some text from the regular font would require a great deal of work, all of it unnecessary. With Professional Write, you can change fonts simply by using a block command.

Let's try it out. Letterhead is always a good candidate for changes in font, and since we already have the letterhead from Dave's Appliance Service, let's use that. Suppose Dave wants to set off the name of his shop so his customers will remember him the next time their toasters go on the blink. Just perform the following steps:

1. Get the LHEAD file from the EXAMPLES subdirectory.
2. Position the cursor over **D** in **Dave's**.
3. Press F3, opening the Edit menu.
4. Choose option **4. Mark text**.
5. Press End, highlighting the rest of the line.
6. Press F10, opening the Text Block Operations menu.
7. Choose option **4. Change font or size**. Professional Write displays a list of the available fonts. This list varies depending on the choices you made when setting up your fonts.
8. Highlight a font that's larger than the regular font, and press Enter.

Your font selection also specifies the orientation. Be careful when selecting this orientation. Fonts can only be printed in one orientation on a single page; that is, you cannot print in portrait and landscape orientation on the same page. If you try, Professional Write will print in one orientation on the first page, form feed to the second page, and print the next orientation on that page.

Seeing Fonts on Screen

Professional Write indicates the new font by displaying it in a different color or brightness.

Now that you've changed a font, you can see how the font appears on screen. If you're working on a monochrome monitor, the new font appears brighter, like boldfaced text. If you have a color monitor, the text is a different color. Not very revealing, is it? Don't worry, you'll get to see how it actually looks before you print it out.

For now, you can determine the font by referring to the bottom of the screen. Just as with type styles, whenever you move the cursor to the line with the special font, the special font is indicated at the bottom of the screen. In Figure 7-4, for example, Courier P 10 is displayed. This indicates that the typeface is Courier, it's in portrait orientation, and the type size is 10-point.

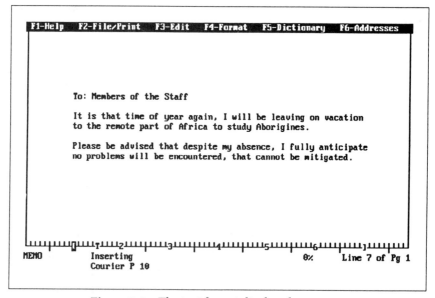

Figure 7-4 The text format displayed on screen

If an asterisk (*) is displayed to the left of the typeface, your printer does not support the font you chose.

Preventing Problems with Fonts

Head off the common problems now.

Because Fonts are not displayed in the working copy as they will appear on the printed page, they can cause some unforeseen problems, wreaking havoc on surrounding text or graphics. As you gain experience with fonts, you'll get a feel for handling them, and you'll be able to anticipate the problems they'll cause. Until you reach that point, you can use Professional Write's Preview feature, which lets you see the fonts as they will appear (see Chapter 8), and you can try to head off some of the more common problems listed in the following sections.

Accommodating a Large Font

If you use a font larger than 14 points in a single-spaced document, the large font will overlap the text above and below it. You can prevent this problem in any of the following ways:

- Choose a slightly smaller font.
- Try a different enhancement, such as bold.
- Add a blank line above and below the line with the large font.
- Double-space the entire document or the section with the large font.

Adjusting Tables and Tab Settings

A table is a logical place to include different font sizes. Column and row headings can be enhanced to set them off from the actual table data, for example. A font can even be used in the data to stress certain numbers or results. In any case, Professional Write uses the tab settings to correctly print the table. You may need to shift those settings to accommodate a change in font.

You should also be aware of hard carriage returns when typing a table. Make sure you enter a hard carriage return at the end of a row (the horizontal line) so that Professional Write will not automatically wrap that row to the next row. If you're typing a column of numbers, however, do not use a hard return at the end of each element in the column.

Accommodating Fonts in Graphics Elements

Fonts can help you get the most out of your graphics, but they may cause problems with your line drawings.

Using a variety of fonts in boxed text can create magnificent effects. For example, if you use flow charts in your projects, you may want to use the regular font for most of the text and highlight general categories with a larger font. When you attempt to do this, however, you'll find that the lines of your boxes begin to break up.

The solution: Don't use a larger font. Use a fixed-pitch font with the same point size as that used for the line drawing characters. Try boldfacing or underlining the text you want to emphasize.

Summary

In this chapter, you learned how to use fonts to enhance the look and improve the readability of your documents. If you want to learn more about techniques, try flipping through books or reports lying around your home or office to see how the pros lay out their work. You may even experiment a little by typing passages that you find particularly attractive and effective.

Don't hesitate to go back and practice some of what you learned here. Although this is a brief chapter, it contains some dense material. If you have a printer that doesn't support fonts, try setting up for a complex printer, such as the Hewlett-Packard (we can all dream, can't we?), and play around with the examples using that setup.

In the next chapter, you'll get to see what some of those fonts really look like, and what, if any, damage they've done to your document.

E I G H T

Previewing a Document

Professional Write lets you print your document to screen before printing it on paper.

Wouldn't it be great to see what your masterpiece looks like on screen before it's printed out on paper? The designers of Professional Write apparently thought so, because they included a feature that makes it possible. This Preview feature lets you "print" the document to your screen, so you can see what your special formatting enhancements look like before you waste time, paper, and ribbon printing your document. You can even print two pages to the screen to see how facing pages will appear in the final product. Here is a list of what the Preview displays:

- Embedded commands, such as *NEW PAGE*, show you the effects of your page breaks.
- Fonts, both the typeface and point size. Point sizes of 8, 10, 12, 14, 18, 24, and 30 are shown as they will actually print. Characters of other sizes are represented by one of the 8–30 point sizes.
- The embedded *GRAPH* command is displayed. If you specify the graph file to be used, Professional Write displays a gray box the size of the graph to be printed. This helps you determine if the placement of the graph is correct. We'll look at inserting graphs in Chapter 9.
- Justified or compressed text appears as it will print. Type styles such as boldface and italic are displayed as they will appear.
- Wrapped lines are displayed as they will print, helping you see the effects of Professional Write's automatic wordwrap and the effects of your hard returns.

If you need to change a particular enhancement, you can make the change right on the Preview screen. There's no need to go back to the working copy. If you need to edit some text, however, you must return to the working copy. Let's explore this wonderful feature in greater depth.

Before You Begin

Before you begin, you need to look at a few important points, such as whether your computer hardware is capable of running the Preview feature, and what limitations you'll encounter.

Hardware Requirements

To run Preview, your computer must have graphics capabilities.

Professional Write's Preview feature requires that your computer be equipped with a Color Graphics Adapter (CGA), an Enhanced Graphics Adapter (EGA), a Hercules graphics card, or a graphics card that's 100% compatible. The folks at Software Publishing Corporation also recommend an 80286 CPU machine because of the time required to process Preview. The Preview feature works fine on an 8088, but it's considerably slower.

If you don't have the equipment needed to run the Preview feature, you can still use the fonts and special enhancements. You'll just need to use your imagination to determine what the enhancements will look like on paper.

Preview's Page Limitation

You can use the Preview feature to preview documents up to 30 pages long. If you want to preview a longer document, you must break the document into sections consisting of fewer than 30 pages each.

The Printer Setup

Professional Write uses the information you entered during the printer setup to create the Preview screen. If you haven't performed the setup steps as detailed in the Appendix and Chapter 7, perform the steps now. Otherwise, Professional Write cannot create an accurate representation of what your particular printer can produce.

Getting Started

As you know from setting up your printer, Professional Write lets you perform the setup for two different printers. Since the Preview feature lets you see the document as either printer would print it, you need to specify which printer you intend to use. (Normally, you'll use printer 1 since it's the one that supports fonts.) To select the printer you want, perform the following steps:

1. Get the document you want to preview. We'll use the MEMO document as an example.
2. Press F2, opening the File/Print menu.
3. Choose option 5. Print working copy, opening the Print Options menu as shown in Figure 8-1.
4. Press Tab repeatedly until the cursor is at the Print to: entry.
5. If the entry indicates the printer you intend to use, press Esc. Otherwise, type the number representing the correct printer.

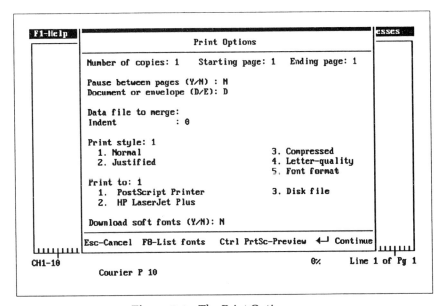

Figure 8-1 The Print Options menu

If you have a second printer, switch the Preview from one to the other by returning to the Print Options screen and repeating the steps.

Chapter 8

Starting the Preview

Once you're sure you've specified the correct printer, you can preview a document at any time; you don't have to save the document first. Assuming you retrieved the MEMO document earlier, let's preview it to see how the fonts appear on screen. If the Print Options menu is still displayed, press Ctrl-PrtSc, closing the menu and starting Preview. If the menu is not displayed:

1. Press F2, opening the File/Print menu.
2. Choose option 6. Preview working copy.

You can use the shortcut keys to bypass the File/Print menu. When you decide to preview the document, press Ctrl-PrtSc, telling Professional Write to print the document to screen.

Professional Write displays a screen message Preparing Page, which tells you that it is in fact carrying out your command. Depending on the hardware installed, it may be take several moments for Professional Write to complete the task.

Use the full-page view to determine the big problems.

Don't be shocked by what you see next. The miniature memo you see on screen, but probably can't read, is a full-page view. It's no mistake; your screen should resemble Figure 8-2. Although this view doesn't help much in previewing fonts, it does let you see the overall layout of text on the page—a sort of aerial view.

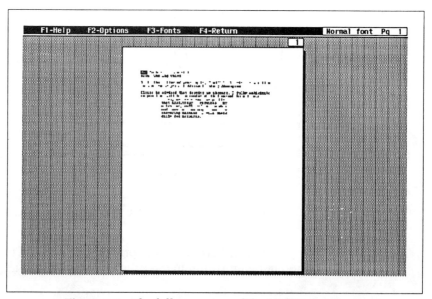

Figure 8-2 The full-page view of the MEMO document

Using the Full-Page View

Since the MEMO document doesn't have much fancy formatting, you may not see the purpose of the full-page view. To illustrate how this view can help, I added a footer to the MEMO document, as shown in Figure 8-3. Notice all the blank space between the footer and the rest of the document. This is the sort of problem that the full-page view is most adept at revealing.

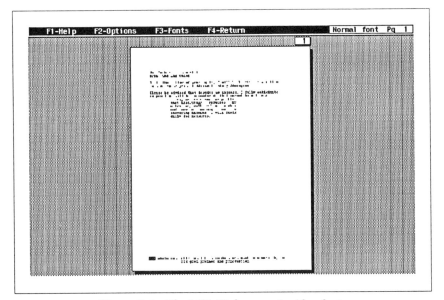

Figure 8-3 The MEMO document with a footer

Once you see the problem, it's easy to fix. Just return to the working copy and make your adjustments. In this case, you could choose to double-space the text to use more of the white space, or move the footer up and move the rest of the document down slightly. You may even decide to use a header instead of a footer.

Moving the Word Cursor in Full-Page View

The word cursor is not designed for editing.

Unlike the cursor you usually use to edit your document, the word cursor doesn't let you type new characters or use editing commands such as Ctrl-T to mark text. Instead, it is designed to help you move through the document to evaluate the layout of the pages and the effectiveness of the page breaks.

To do this more efficiently, the word cursor leaps through the document, jumping from word to word or page to page. Table 8-1 provides a list of cursor movement keys for the word cursor.

Table 8-1 Cursor Movement Keys for the Full-Page View

Key	Cursor Movement
Right Arrow Key	One word to right
Left Arrow Key	One word to left
Down Arrow Key	One line down
Up Arrow Key	One line up
Home	Beginning of line
End	End of line
Ctrl-Home	Top of page
Ctrl-End	Bottom of page
Ctrl-PgDn	Top of next page
Ctrl-PgUp	Bottom of previous page

Practice using the cursor movement keys to move around the MEMO document until you feel comfortable moving the cursor. Move the cursor to one of the words that's in a different font, then look at the upper right corner of the Preview screen. The font, orientation, and point size of the word are displayed. The page number of the page being previewed is also displayed.

The Split Screen

The split screen lets you see two pages at a time, to give you a clear idea of what the facing pages will look like.

When you start to preview a document, only the first page is displayed, in the center of the screen. When you move the cursor to the second page, the first page is shifted to the left, and both the first page and second page are displayed on screen. When you go to the third page, the first page is shifted off the screen to the left, and pages two and three are displayed.

Previewing a document in this manner makes it easy to see the effects of your page break commands and Professional Write's automatic page breaks.

Starting Preview at a Selected Page

If your document is long and you want to preview only a specific page, moving through the document page by page can take some time. To speed the process along, you can specify the page that Professional Write will display first, thereby eliminating the need for Professional Write to format the preceding pages. To start Preview at a specific page, perform the following steps:

1. Press F2, opening the File/Print menu.
2. Choose option 5. Print working copy, opening the Print Options screen.
3. Type the page you want to preview next to Starting page:.
4. Type the page you want to preview last next to Ending page:. If you want to preview a single page, type the same number you typed at step 3.
5. Press Ctrl-PrtSc, starting Preview at the selected page.

Page numbers in the Preview screen may not coincide with those in the working copy. If you changed page numbers in the header or footer, or if your document contains embedded commands, the numbers will differ.

You can bypass the File/Print menu by using the shortcut keys. When you decide to preview your document, press Ctrl-O, opening the Print Options menu, and continue from there.

Using the Preview Menus

At the top of the Preview screen is a menu bar that lists four pull-down menus:

F1-Help
F2-Options
F3-Fonts
F4-Return

To access these menus, press the corresponding function key. Just as in the Create/Edit screen, pressing the function key pulls down a menu that lists several options. The menus and the options that each menu presents are listed below.

F1-Help

Consistent with all other modes of Professional Write, pressing the F1 key opens a context-sensitive Help screen. Context-sensitive means that Professional Write knows what you're doing and presents a Help screen that addresses the task you're trying to perform.

F2-Options

The Options menu lets you change the three following elements:

View   Change from full-page to close-up view
Print styles   Change the print style of the entire document
Paper size   Change the size of paper on which you intend to print

Changing Views

So far, we've worked only with the full-page view. The Options menu lets you change to a close-up view to see a more detailed version of your document. To change views, perform the following steps:

1. Press F2, opening the Options menu.
2. Choose option 1. Change views.

To bypass the Options menu, use the shortcut keys Alt-V to change the view.

We'll work with the MEMO document in close-up view later, but for now, return to the full-page view.

Changing Print Styles

Change print styles from within Preview using the Options menu.

The Options menu also lets you change the print style of the entire document without leaving the Preview screen. To change the print style, perform the following steps:

1. Press F2, opening the Options menu.
2. Choose option 2. Set print styles, opening the Print Styles submenu, as shown in Figure 8-4.
3. Highlight the print style you want and press the spacebar. The print style options are listed below with a brief explanation of each.
4. Press Enter. Professional Write displays the document with the new print styles.

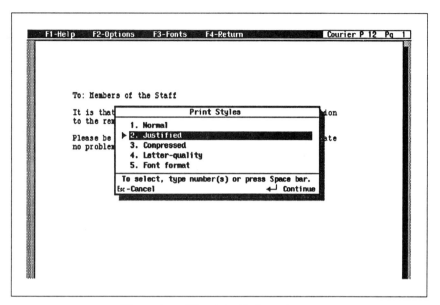

Figure 8-4 The Print Styles submenu

Normal: This is the default option. When you initially create your document, the document has no special formatting elements. It appears the same as if you had created it on a typewriter.

Justified: Selecting this option formats the text in the style that newspapers use. The text is spread out to make it flush with both the left and right margins. Professional Write juggles the text to make it fit. Figure 8-5 shows how the MEMO document looks after being right-justified.

Compressed: Some printers let you print more characters per inch than normal. If you choose this option, you'll see an approximate representation of the document, but point sizes and margins may not be accurate.

Letter-quality: Some printers have separate settings for draft-quality and letter-quality printing. Choosing this option has no effect on how the document is displayed.

Font format: You can use this choice to see how your font changes affect the wordwrap and vertical character alignment. You can also make the necessary corrections to accommodate the change.

   To bypass the Options menu, use the shortcut keys Alt-S to open the Print Styles submenu.

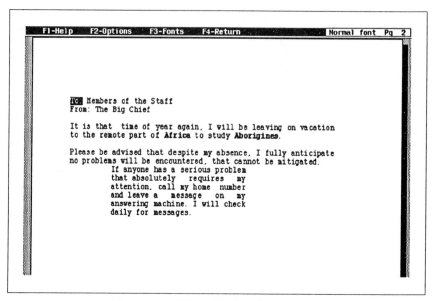

Figure 8-5 The MEMO right-justified

Changing Paper Size

Preview displays your document as it will print, on whatever paper size you choose.

For Professional Write to display the page breaks and wordwrap correctly, it must know what size paper you intend to use. The default paper size is the standard 8½ by 11 inches. Professional Write also provides for legal size—8½ by 14 inches—and for two larger sizes. To select a paper size, perform the following steps:

1. Press F2, opening the Options menu.
2. Choose option 3. Change paper size, accessing a list of possible paper sizes.
3. Highlight the paper size you intend to print on, and press Enter.

To bypass the Options menu, use the shortcut keys Alt-P to access the list of paper sizes.

Changing the paper size when in Preview, does not change the paper size on the Print Options menu. To be consistent, you must enter the change in both the Preview screen and in the Print Options menu in the working copy.

F3-Fonts

We looked at fonts in detail in Chapter 7, so you're already aware of which fonts your printer can handle. With the Preview feature, you can see how the fonts look in the document. If you don't like a particular font, you can change it in the Preview screen without returning to the working copy. Professional Write makes the change both in Preview and in the working copy.

Changing Fonts

Change the font of an entire document or of a single word.

Professional Write offers several options for changing fonts. You can change a document's regular font, change the font of one word or of a continuous line of text, or even change every occurrence of a particular font. To make these font changes, perform the following steps:

1. Press Alt-V, changing to the close-up view.
2. Move the cursor to the word that has the font you want to change. Professional Write displays the name of the font in the upper right corner of the screen.
3. Press F3, displaying the Fonts menu as shown in Figure 8-6.
4. Select option 1. Change a font. Professional Write highlights the word containing the cursor. If several words to the left or right of the highlighted word have the same font, those words are highlighted, too. If a sentence or paragraph is formatted as a specific font, the entire sentence or paragraph is highlighted. After highlighting the text, Professional Write displays a menu listing the available fonts.
5. Highlight the font you want to use and press Enter. Professional Write responds by asking if you wish to change all occurrences of the font. The default answer is No.
6. If you wish to change all occurrences of the font, type y and press Enter. Otherwise, just press Enter. Professional Write carries out your command.

You can bypass the Fonts menu. After highlighting the word with the font you want to change, press Alt-F to access the list of available fonts.

Listing Fonts Used in a Document

You can view a list of all the fonts used in a document.

The Fonts menu also lets you view a list of all the fonts you used in the document. To view this list, perform the following steps:

Chapter 8

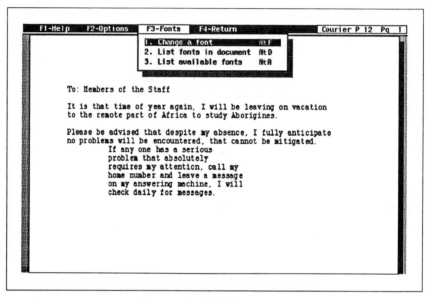

Figure 8-6 The Fonts menu

1. Press F3, opening the Fonts menu.
2. Choose option 2. List fonts in document. Professional Write displays an overlay like the one in Figure 8-7.

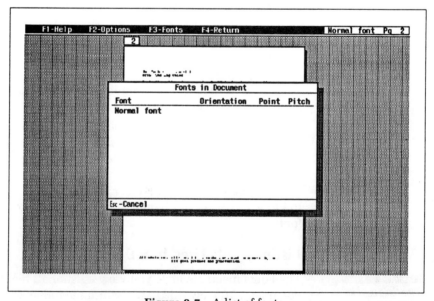

Figure 8-7 A list of fonts

To list the fonts using the shortcut keys, press Alt-D.

Listing Available Fonts

If you want to change a font, but you're not sure what you want to change it to, you can refer quickly back to a list of the fonts available on your printer. Just perform the following steps:

1. Press F3, opening the Fonts menu.
2. Choose option **3. List available fonts**. Professional Write displays a list of the available fonts.

To bypass the Fonts menu, press Alt-A, displaying a list of available fonts.

F4-Return

You can move back and forth between working copy and Preview to make all necessary changes.

The F4 key takes you from the Preview screen back to the working copy. Since you may have moved the word cursor on the Preview screen, Professional Write gives you the option of returning to the working copy in either of two locations: the starting cursor location (the original location in the working copy) or the current location (the location in the Preview screen). The option of returning to the current cursor location is especially helpful; if you find a problem while you're previewing, you can return to the exact same spot in the working copy to fix it. To return to the working copy, perform the following steps:

1. Press F4, opening the Return menu as shown in Figure 8-8.
2. If you want to return to the original location of the cursor, type **2**. If you want to return to the current location, press Enter or type **1**.

Use the shortcut keys to return to the working copy more quickly. To return to the present position, press Esc. To return to the original position, press Alt-X.

The Close-Up View

Zoom in on your document.

We've seen how the Preview feature gives us an overall view of the page so we can evaluate its layout and make the necessary changes. Because

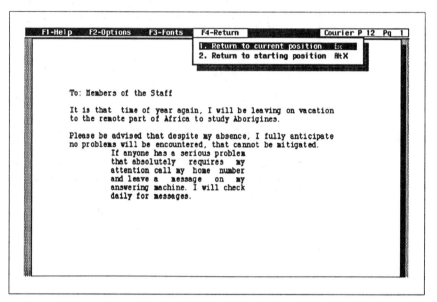

Figure 8-8 The Return menu

this view shrinks the document so drastically, it prevents us from seeing the fonts and print styles in more detail. To help us evaluate these detailed format elements, the Preview feature lets us change from the full-page to the close-up view whenever necessary. You still won't be able to edit for spelling and punctuation, but you will be able to see how your fonts will look, and you'll be able to change them without returning to the working copy.

Since the close-up view enlarges the page, you won't be able to see the entire page on screen. The amount you will see depends on the graphics capability of your system.

Let's change the view of the MEMO document to see what our font changes look like on screen:

1. Get the MEMO document.
2. Press Ctrl-PrtSc, starting the Preview feature.
3. Press Alt-V, changing the view from full-page to close-up. In a few moments, Professional Write displays the document, as shown in Figure 8-9.

As you can readily see, the formatting of the characters in this document are easy to identifiy. `Africa` is bold and `Aborigines` is in italics.

Previewing a Document

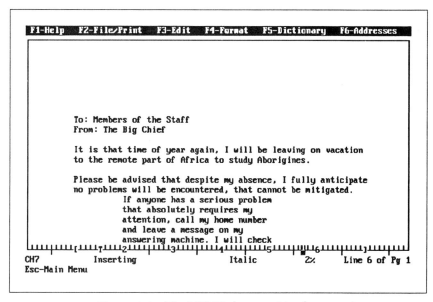

Figure 8-9 The MEMO document in close-up view

Moving the Word Cursor in Close-Up View

The word cursor lets you advance the screen so you can view the rest of the page.

The word cursor moves a little differently in the close-up view than it does in the full-page view. Table 8-2 summarizes the cursor movement keys and what they do.

Table 8-2 Cursor Movement Keys for the Close-Up View

Key	Cursor Movement
Right Arrow Key	One word to right
Left Arrow Key	One word to left
Down Arrow Key	One line down
Up Arrow Key	One line up
Home	Beginning of line
End	End of line
Ctrl-Home	Top of page
Ctrl-End	Bottom of page
PgDn	Next screen of text for same page
PgUp	Previous screen of text for same page
Ctrl-PgDn	Top of next page
Ctrl-PgUp	Bottom of previous page

In this mode, the word cursor cannot move to an area that has no text, such as a large blank space. Blanks can only be seen in the full-page view. As you move the word cursor through the document, the font of each word is displayed in the upper right corner of the screen.

Correcting Problems

You may need to return to the working copy to fix a problem.

The Preview feature lets you find problems before you print the document. Depending on the nature of the correction needed, you may be able to perform the necessary steps in the Preview mode. If you need to return to the working copy to make the fix, don't worry; with Professional Write's Return feature you can jump back and forth between Preview and the working copy quickly and easily.

The following sections present a list of common corrections you may need to perform.

Correcting Wordwrap Problems

Now that you don't have to press Enter at the end of each line, you may find yourself omitting necessary hard returns or adding extra returns by mistake.

Although these wordwrap problems may be difficult to find, even in Preview, they are easy to fix.

Deleting a Carriage Return

If a line comes up short, you probably have an extra carriage return.

Professional Write inserts soft carriage returns at the end of every line of text as it fits the text from margin to margin. A hard carriage return overrides the Wordwrap feature and forces Professional Write to begin a new line. If a line comes up short in the middle of a paragraph, chances are you have an extra carriage return. To remove a hard carriage return, perform the following steps:

1. Press Esc, returning to the working copy.
2. Move the cursor to the end of the short line.
3. Press Del.
4. Press Ctrl-PrtSc to return to the Preview screen. The line should now be reformatted to fit correctly.

Inserting a Carriage Return

Two lines that run together indicate a missing carriage return.

If you notice a line that's joined to the previous line when you intended it to start at the left margin on the next line, a hard carriage return is probably missing. Here's how to fix it:

1. Move the word cursor to the first word of the sentence that should start a new line.
2. Press Esc, returning to the working copy.
3. Press Enter, inserting a hard return. The lines separate in the working copy, and Professional Write rewraps the lines to accommodate the change.
4. Press Ctrl-PrtSc to return to the Preview screen.

Inserting a Hard Space

Sometimes, when you're typing your document, you may not realize that a particular phrase would look better on one line. While previewing the document, you notice that Professional Write has divided the phrase between two lines. You can insert hard spaces between words in the phrase to trick Professional Write into viewing the phrase as a single word. Here's how:

1. Move the cursor to the space at the end of the first word.
2. Press Esc, returning to the working copy.
3. Press Ins, putting Professional Write in the Overstrike mode.
4. Press Ctrl-spacebar, inserting a hard space.
5. Move the cursor to the next space where you want to insert a hard space, and repeat step 4. Continue repeating steps 4 and 5 until all the hard spaces you need are inserted.
6. Press Ctrl-PrtSc to return to the Preview screen.

Correcting Page Breaks

Widows and orphans are isolated lines of text.

If you're not familiar with the terms "widows" and "orphans," don't worry. As soon as you begin to preview your document, they will be the first to introduce themselves.

Widows

A widow is a single line of text that has been chopped off the end of a paragraph on one page and is isolated at the top of the next page. The line probably looked okay in the working copy, but when you saw what the page breaks did to that line, you realize that there's a problem.

There are a couple of ways to solve the problem. One is to go back in the text prior to the widow and delete any unnecessary blank lines. This essentially tightens up the page before the widow and pulls the widow up to the previous page. This is a fairly safe way to correct the problem.

The second technique is to enter a *NEW PAGE* command in the widow's paragraph to send the entire paragraph or part of it to the next page. This technique is especially effective with charts or tables that you don't want to split between two pages. You need to be careful with the *NEW PAGE* command, however. Don't send too many lines to the next page, because you'll end up with a short page. Also, use some foresight; the *NEW PAGE* command may create more widows and orphans in subsequent pages.

Orphans

Like a widow, an orphan is an isolated line of text. In this case, the first line of the paragraph is isolated on the bottom of the page, and the rest of the paragraph is printed on the next page.

The easiest way to solve this problem is to insert a *NEW PAGE* command in front of the orphan line. This forces the line to the next page. Since it's only one line, you don't have to worry as much about creating widows and orphans on subsequent pages, but you should still use a little caution.

Correcting Unjustified or Uncentered Lines

If you notice that justification or centering did not work on a particular line, the problem may be that there is a hard carriage return at the end of the line. If you notice a problem, follow the steps detailed above for deleting a hard carriage return.

If that doesn't work, the problem is probably caused by a font change. Changes in font often create a variance in the number of characters per line of text. Proportional fonts are especially tricky, since the size of the space taken by the individual character depends on the width of the character. If fonts are causing the problem, you need to reformat individual lines, as described in the following section.

Reformatting Individual Lines

Use embedded commands to reformat individual lines.

If a centered or justified line does not appear as it should, and a hard carriage return is not causing the problem, you can use an embedded command to correct the formatting. Here's how:

1. Position the cursor at the beginning of the line you want to format.
2. Press Esc, returning to the working copy.
3. To center the line, type *CENTER* or *c*. To right-justify the line, type *RIGHT* or *r*. (Do not type spaces between the asterisks and the characters.)
4. Press Ctrl-PrtSc to return to the Preview screen.

Adjusting Tables, Lists, and Outlines

For tables to look right, the columns must line up vertically. If you used a different font within a table or as a column head, you may notice that the alignment is slightly off. For example, a smaller font may not have reached as far to the right as you had expected, or a larger font may reach too far right. Depending on the nature of the problem, you may try any of the following solutions.

Aligning Numbers in a Table

If you have a column of numbers with decimal points, and the numbers don't align properly, make sure you used decimal tab stops in the table.

Adjusting Tab Settings to Align Columns

If you move a column, you need to move the tab stop as well.

If you moved a column in the working copy, but the column is not in its new position in Preview, you may need to reposition your tab stops. Professional Write uses the tab settings when it prints a table to align the columns. If you moved a column while you were editing, you must move the tab stop to align with the new position of the column.

If you're using larger fonts in column headings or in data entries, make sure you set the tab stops far enough apart to accommodate the larger font. Otherwise, you may see overlapping characters in Preview. Another way to prevent this problem is to use a smaller font in column headings.

If the text in a bulleted list or in an outline is not aligning as it should, try placing a tab stop directly after the bullet or number. This should correct the problem.

Using Font Format to Adjust for Different Fonts

Font Format automatically compensates for fonts.

If you notice a line with a different font that is too short or too long, you can add the Font Format print option to compensate for the fonts. You can use Font Format for an entire document. Here's how:

1. Press F2, opening the Options menu.
2. Choose option `2. Set print styles`, opening the Print Styles submenu.
3. Type `5` and press Enter, selecting option `5. Font format`. The effects of the Font Format are immediately displayed on the Preview screen.

Choosing Font Format for the entire document may cause problems with other sections of text. If that happens, try turning Font Format on and off with commands embedded in the working copy. To add the commands, perform the following steps:

1. Return to the working copy.
2. Position the cursor in the blank line before the text that's to be affected.
3. If you have chosen Font Format for the entire document and you want to turn it off for this section, type `*FORMAT NO*`. If you want to turn Font Format on for this section, type `*FORMAT YES*`.
4. Move the cursor to the blank line after the text that's to be affected.
5. If you want to turn Font Format back on, type `*FORMAT YES*`. To turn Font Format off again, type `*FORMAT NO*`.
6. Press Ctrl-PrtSc to see the results of your changes on the Preview screen.

If adding Font Format doesn't work, try turning off Font Format and choosing a fixed-pitch font rather than a proportional font for the problem word or phrase.

Overlapping Lines

Professional Write lets you add a blank line above and below large fonts to compensate for overlapping lines.

If you have a single-spaced document that includes a font larger than 14 points, chances are that font will extend into the lines above and below. You have two options for accommodating this large font. You can either double-space the entire document or insert a blank line above and below the line with the large font.

Fortunately, Professional Write includes an editing command to insert blank lines. To insert a blank line, perform the following steps:

1. Move the cursor to the line above the line with the large font.
2. Press F3, opening the Edit menu.

3. Select option `1. Insert blank line`.
4. Move the cursor to the line below the line with the large font and repeat the insertion.

The shortcut keys offer an even quicker alternative. Move the cursor to the line above the line with the large font and press Ctrl-I.

Summary

The Preview feature gives us the foresight we always wanted. By printing documents to screen before printing them on paper, we get to view the effects of the printing process before it's too late. And if a problem reveals itself, we can fix it immediately in Preview or return quickly to the working copy.

Now that we've worked out all the bugs on screen, let's print our perfected document on paper.

N I N E

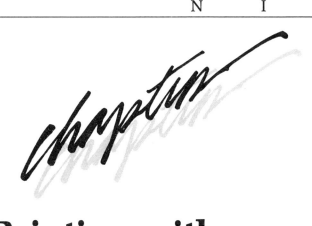

Printing with Professional Write

So far, you've seen how Professional Write gives you the power to manipulate your documents. Its features enable you to perform just about any word processing task you may encounter. Printing with Professional Write is no different. Write's Print Options screen gives you control over your printing jobs by letting you send detailed instructions to your printer.

> If you haven't set up your printer, refer to the section on customizing Professional Write in the Appendix. Then, if you intend to print with fonts, refer to the section on setting up fonts in Chapter 7.

Setting Print Options

The document must be on screen for Professional Write to print it.

When you're ready to print, get your document. Then, open the Print Options screen:

1. Press F2 to open the File/Print menu.
2. Choose option **5. Print working copy**, opening the Print Options screen, as shown in Figure 9-1.

After you get the document you want to print, use the shortcut keys Ctrl-O to go directly to the Print Options screen.

Chapter 9

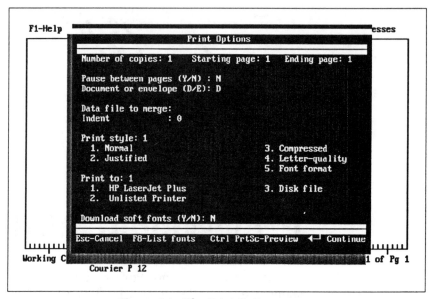

Figure 9-1 The Print Options screen

As you can see, the screen consists of a variety of print options, each with a setting typed next to it. To change a setting, press the Tab key until the cursor is at the setting you want to change, then type in the new setting. (Press Shift-Tab to move the cursor back to a previous setting.) When the settings are correct, press Enter to start printing. The options are explained in the following sections.

Number of Copies

The default setting is 1, for a single copy. If you want more than one copy, simply type the number of copies you want. If you're printing a multipage document, Professional Write prints one copy of the entire document before starting on the next copy.

Starting Page, Ending Page

You can stop printing at any time by pressing Esc.

This option lets you specify where you want the printing to start and stop. You can use this option to print a single page or a range of pages within a multipage document. Enter the page number of the first page to be printed, next to `Starting page:`. Enter the page number of the last page to be printed, next to `Ending page:`. To print a single page, enter the same number at both options.

Pause Between Pages

Professional Write gives you the choice to print continuously or to pause between pages. If you're using continuous form feeds, keep this option's default setting of N (No). If you're printing on a single piece of paper, change the setting to Y (Yes). Professional Write prints the first page, then waits for you to insert a piece of paper. Press Enter to continue printing.

If your printer has a built-in feeder that feeds individual sheets, you don't have to pause between pages. In this case, the printer driver automatically sends your printer the proper instructions.

Printing an Envelope

If the envelope is not legal size, you may need to reposition it in the printer.

In the past, you may have had to retype an address in a separate file in order to print it out on an envelope. With Professional Write, that's no longer necessary. Write will lift the address right out of your letter and print it on a legal size envelope.

For Professional Write to accomplish this feat, the letter must fulfill the following format requirements:

- The inside address must be flush with the left margin.
- The first line must be a date line or the first line of the inside address.
- A blank line must follow the inside address.

If the first line is a date and ends in two digits, Professional Write skips that line and starts printing the following lines until it reaches a blank line. If the first line is the beginning of the inside address, Professional Write begins printing the first line. To print the envelope, perform the following steps:

1. Get the letter that has the address you want to print; make sure the letter fulfills the format requirements.
2. Insert the envelope in the printer, aligning the top of the envelope with the print head.
3. Press Ctrl-O, opening the Print Options menu.
4. Press Tab four times, moving the cursor to the Document or envelope: option.
5. Type E, choosing Envelope.
6. Press Enter. Professional Write prints the address 10 lines down and 3.5 inches in from the left margin.

Data File to Merge

Professional Write can merge files, but you need to tell Write where the files are located.

With Professional Write, you can create a form letter, leaving a space for the inside address. When you print the letter, you can have Professional Write retrieve an address from an address file and insert it into the space.

To do this, Write needs to know where the address file is located. You can specify the location by moving the cursor to the `Data file to merge:` option and typing the complete path and filename of the address file. For example, if the address file were called CLIENTS and were in the MAIL directory in drive C, you would type `c:\mail\clients`. Chapter 10 describes the procedure for creating and using form letters.

Indent

If your left margin looks correct on screen but prints too close to the left edge of the page, use the Indent option to make your adjustment. To change the setting:

1. Move the cursor to the `Indent:` option.
2. Type the number of spaces you want the text to be shifted right.
3. Print out a single page of the document with the new setting so you can check the results.

If you save the working copy after changing the indent option, the new setting is saved as part of the document file.

Print Style

The Print Style option lets you choose a print style for the entire document.

Choose any of the settings listed to print the entire document in that style. You can even combine styles—for example, justify and compress. To select a style, type the number of the style you want to use, next to `Print style:`. To combine styles, separate the numbers by a comma; for example, to print justified and compressed, type **2,3**. The print style options are discussed in the following sections.

Normal

Choose `Normal` to print the document in your printer's regular style. The Normal setting does not eliminate any font changes or type styles you may have inserted in your working copy.

Justified

The Justified setting spreads out your text, making it flush left and flush right with the margins—like text in newspaper columns. On printers that microjustify, Write gives each character a little more space. On printers that do not microjustify, Write inserts spaces between the words. Since justification of a short line at the end of a paragraph looks odd, the hard return at the end of the line overrides the justification setting.

If you want to justify only a portion of the text, use embedded commands. In the blank line above the text you want justified, move the cursor to the left margin and type *JUSTIFY YES*. Move the cursor to the blank line following the text you want to justify (make sure the cursor is at the left margin) and type *JUSTIFY NO*.

Don't overuse justification. The extra spaces between characters and words may have a negative effect on the document's appearance and often hurts the readability of a piece.

Compressed

If your printer has the capability to print in compressed style, you can choose this option to reduce the size of the characters. This smaller print makes your characters look like those in a book.

Letter-Quality

Some dot matrix printers offer the option of printing in draft-quality or letter-quality mode, letter-quality being the better of the two. The Letter-Quality option is activated either by a switch on the printer itself or by a command from your computer.

If your printer offers these quality options and does not have a manually operated switch, you can switch modes here. Just type 4 after Print style:.

Print to

To preserve formatting elements in an ASCII file, print the file to a disk.

The Print to option lets you print your document to a variety of destinations. The first two settings send the document to either of two printers. The third setting presents an interesting feature. You may remember that in saving an ASCII file, you normally have to sacrifice the document's formatting elements. This print setting lets you preserve those elements in the conversion process. You can then send the file via modem with all its formatting intact.

Download Soft Fonts

If you set up your printer to download soft fonts, you may remember that you had to enter a path and filename so Professional Write could locate the fonts. Answering Yes here tells Write to look for the file that contains the soft fonts.

Once the soft fonts are downloaded, they remain in the printer's memory until the printer is turned off or reset.

Inserting Printer Control Codes

Type printer control codes in your document to use special type styles.

Although Professional Write covers most fonts and type styles, your printer may offer a style that Write does not include in any of its setup screens. To cover these missing styles, Write includes an embedded *PRINTER* command that lets you specify a type style from within your document. To use the *PRINTER* command, perform the following steps:

1. Move the cursor to the place in the document where you want the special style to begin.
2. Type *PRINTER <ASCII decimal equivalent>*. These codes are in the manual that came with your printer. For example, to turn enlarged character mode on for the brother M-1109, type

    PRINTER 27,87,1

    (27,87 is the actual command for enlarged character mode; 1 represents "On.")
3. Move the cursor to the place where you want the style to end.
4. Type

    PRINTER 27,87,0

    (The first two numbers specify the enlarged character mode; the 0 represents "Off.")

If the command consists of several numbers, type commas between each number. You can use up to 20 numbers in a single *PRINTER* command.

Joining Files

Professional Write uses the header or footer from DOC1 for all joined DOC files, ensuring consistent page numbering.

Because the size of your files is limited by your computer's RAM, you may find that you have to break a large document into several pieces and save each piece as a separate file. For example, you may divide a document into five files named DOC1, DOC2, DOC3, DOC4, and DOC5. If you were to print these files separately, you'd have to fiddle with the page numbering to get it just right, and even then your page breaks would suffer.

To prevent this problem, you can join the separate DOC files, to print them as a single document. First, get the DOC1 file and move the cursor to the end of the text. Then, type the following *JOIN* commands at the left margin:

```
*JOIN DOC2*
*JOIN DOC3*
*JOIN DOC4*
*JOIN DOC5*
```

You can also print out several separate documents, starting each document on a new page. For example, you may want to print several chapters in a book, but you don't want the chapters to run into each other. To accomplish this, simply insert a *NEW PAGE* command between the *JOIN* commands:

```
*NEW PAGE*
*JOIN DOC2*
*NEW PAGE*
*JOIN DOC3*
*NEW PAGE*
*JOIN DOC4*
*NEW PAGE*
*JOIN DOC5*
```

Adhere to the following guidelines when using the *JOIN* command:

- Type the *JOIN* commands at the end of the first document. (Embedded commands, including *JOIN*, will not work in subsequent, joined documents.)
- Type the *JOIN* commands at the left margin.

- If you use fonts, make sure all of the joined documents are set up identically for Printer 1.
- Avoid using Font Format with joined documents.

Use the *JOIN* command to import a file at the printing stage without making that file part of the working copy.

Inserting a Graph During Printing

Professional Write includes an embedded command, *GRAPH*, for inserting graphs into a document. The graphs that it will accept are listed below:

- Harvard Graphics, when the graph is exported as a picture file.
- PFS:Graph Version B, when the graph is printed as a disk file.
- PFS:First Graphics, when the file is exported in the Professional Write format.
- PFS:First Choice, when the file is exported in the Professional Write format.
- Professional Plan, when the file is exported in the Professional Write format.

If you want your graph to look the same as when you created it, be sure to print it out on the same printer.

To import a graph at the printing stage, type the *GRAPH* command at the place where you want the graph inserted. The *GRAPH* command tells Professional Write both to insert a graph and where to find it. For example,

```
*GRAPH C:\HARVARD\GRAPH1.PIC*
```

tells Write to insert a graph, then gives the location of the graph: drive C, the HARVARD directory, the GRAPH1.PIC file.

Professional Write takes over from there. You don't have to insert blank lines to make room for the graph, because Write calculates the space required. If you do insert blank lines, Write prints the graph in the available space. If there's not enough room, Professional Write starts printing the graph on the next page.

Summary

The Print Options screen gives you convenient access to the more common adjustments required for specific printing jobs. For those printing jobs that require special treatment, Professional Write offers a range of embedded commands that go beyond the listed options. By using the Print Options screen and embedded commands and by learning a few ASCII printing codes, you should be well on your way to mastering your printer.

In the next chapter, you will learn how to turn your printer into a form letter assembly line.

T E N

The Address Book and Form Letters

In the previous chapter, you briefly encountered a feature called *merge*, which lets you combine files at the printing stage. You learned how to insert files and graphs while printing and how to create a composite document without changing the working copy. Although merge is useful in performing such tasks on documents, it really shines when you use it to write and send letters of correspondence.

Write features the Address Book, which can store the names and addresses of up to 2,000 people (1,000 if you're using a system with two 5.25-inch floppy disks). With the Address Book, you no longer have to flip pages or search through your Rolodex to find an address. Simply type the name you want to find; Professional Write displays the name, address, phone number, and other pieces of information that you may want to know. By merging the Address Book with a form letter, you can print out personalized letters to everyone on your mailing list.

Creating the Address Book

The Address Book is a special kind of file, called a database file, that stores a list of information. The file is filled with *records*— the names and addresses that make up the list. To create the Address Book, you need to perform two operations:

- Create an Address Book file.
- Enter records into the file.

Creating an Address Book File

Professional Write leads you through the process of creating a file for your Address Book. To create a file, perform the following steps:

1. Start with a blank screen.
2. Press F6, opening the Addresses menu, as shown in Figure 10-1.
3. Choose option 1. Select Address Book. Professional Write displays a window that shows the default directory for the Address Book.
4. Press Ctrl-E, then type the path of the drive or directory you want to use and the filename. For example, type c:\wdata\tennis.
5. Press F7, opening the Description box, as shown in Figure 10-2. This box lets you type the name of the file to be created.
6. Type the name you want to use for your Address Book. For example, type tennis.
7. Press Enter. Professional Write responds with the Address Book screen, as shown in Figure 10-3.

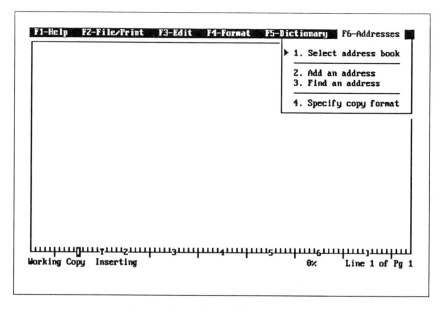

Figure 10-1 The Addresses menu

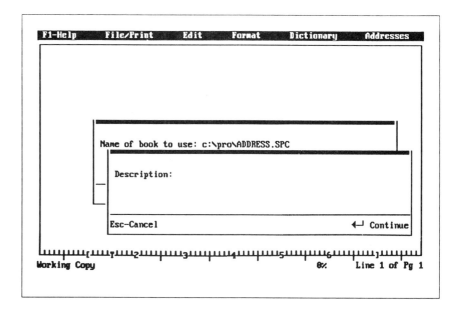

Figure 10-2 The Address Book description screen

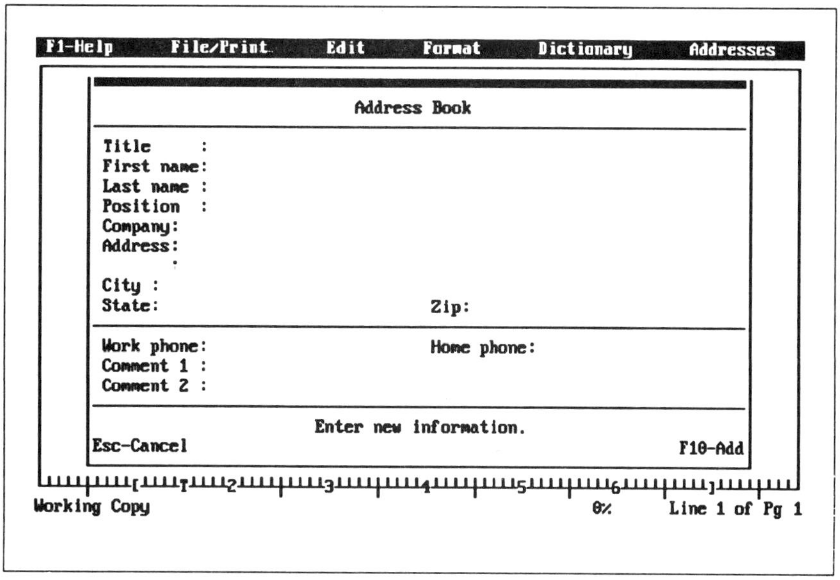

Figure 10-3 The Address Book screen

Entering Records

The screen you see now is the one you'll use for entering records. On the left side of the screen is a list of attributes: first name, last name, and so on. About two-thirds of the way down is a horizontal line that divides the screen. The top part of the screen lists all the attributes required for an inside address; this is the address of the person who is to receive the letter. The bottom part of the screen lets you add additional information such as phone numbers.

The attributes are also known as *field names*; the space after each field name is the field, where you type in the specific information. Keep the following information in mind when entering records:

- Records are typed in the Overstrike mode. To change to the Insert mode, press the Ins key.
- Press Tab to move from one field to the next.
- Press Shift-Tab to move to the previous field.
- You do not have to enter information in every field. Professional Write automatically skips over blank fields.
- The Address Book automatically sorts the records in alphabetical order based on the name in the Last name field.

When entering records, use a consistent format; that is, don't use California in one place and CA in another.

To give yourself some records to work with, enter the following information. (You can delete the information later.)

```
Title: Mr.
First name: Michael
Last name: Kelly
Position: President, Rancho Tennis Club
Company: Rancho Tennis Club
Address: 1700 Palm Dale Drive
       : P.O. Box 3
City: Indian Wells
State: CA                    Zip: 92007
Work phone: (619)555-1200    Home phone: (619)484-0745
Comment 1: Wife's name, Guy
Comment 2: Mike
```

Check the record for spelling and accuracy, then press F10, saving the record to the Address Book. This clears the record from the screen and returns you to a clear Address Book screen so you can enter your next record:

```
Title: Mr.
First name: Gope
Last name: Kissel
Position: Teaching Pro, Rancho Tennis Club
Company: Rancho Tennis Club
Address: 1700 Palm Dale Drive
       : P.O. Box 3
City: Indian Wells
State: CA                          Zip: 92007
Work phone: (312)234-1200          Home phone: (312)678-4950
Comment 1: Wife's name, Farsi
Comment 2: Paco
```

Edit the record, press F10, and continue typing:

```
Title: Mrs.
First name: Gloria
Last name: Kilroy
Position: Membership Secretary, Rancho Tennis Club
Company: Rancho Tennis Club
Address: 1700 Palm Dale Drive
       : P.O. Box 3
City: Indian Wells
State: CA                          Zip: 92007
Work phone: (617)123-2760          Home phone: (617)546-5897
Comment 1: Husband's name, Mack
Comment 2: Ms. Kilroy
```

Adding Records

You can add records to your Address Book at any time. To add a record, perform the following steps:

1. Press F6, reopening the Addresses menu.
2. Choose option `2. Add an address`, reopening the Address Book screen.
3. Enter your record as described in the previous section.

Chapter 10

Finding a Record

When you need to use one of the records you entered, for reference or to insert into a letter, you must find the first record. You can perform the search in any of the following ways:

- Page through the Address Book.
- Specify a field entry for Write to search for.
- Use a wild card entry.
- Specify several field entries to narrow the search.

Flipping Pages

If you like flipping pages and searching for the record yourself, Professional Write makes that option available. To search manually, begin from the working copy. Then,

1. Press F6, opening the Addresses menu.
2. Select option 3. Find an address. This opens a screen that looks similar to the screen used to enter records. The only difference is the message at the bottom of the screen. Here, the message tells you to Enter search instructions. To search for the record manually, leave the screen blank.
3. Press F10. Professional Write searches the last names in the Address Book alphabetically and displays the first name it finds. In this case it's the record of Michael Kelly.
4. Press F10 again, and the Mrs. Kilroy record appears.
5. Press F10 again to see the last record, Mr. Kissel.

Adding Search Criteria

Every database uses one or more fields to index information; that is, to keep the information in order. The Address book indexes the records you entered according to the various field entries. You can use these entries to have Professional Write find a record or at least narrow your search.

If you know the exact spelling of the last name of the person to whom the letter is directed, using the Find feature is the best way to get the record. Suppose you want to send a letter to Mr. Kilroy:

1. From the working copy, press F6, opening the Addresses menu.

2. Select option **3. Find an address**, opening the Address Book search screen.
3. Press the Tab key until the cursor is in the Last name field.
4. Type `Kilroy`. Professional Write ignores capitalization and any spaces before or after the search entry.
5. Press F10, starting the search. The Kilroy record appears.
6. Press F10 again. Professional Write beeps and displays a screen message, `This is the last matching record`. Had there been another Kilroy record, it would have appeared.

Using Wild Cards

If you don't know the exact spelling of a person's name and you don't have the time to flip pages, you can use wild cards to search for the record.

Wild cards consist of two periods that represent any and all characters you're unsure of. For example, if you're not sure whether the person's name is spelled Smith or Smyth, you can use the wild card Sm..th to find the record. The following is a list of examples that show how wild cards may be used.

Entry	**Will Find**
sm..	Smith, Smothers, Smyth
..th	Booth, Smith, Smyth
..it..	Kittel, Smith, Vitale

In the three example records, each last name began with the letter "K." You could use the wild card Ki.. to narrow the search:

1. Press Esc to clear the Search screen.
2. Press the Tab key to move the cursor to the Last name field.
3. Type `Ki..`
4. Press F10 to start the search. The Kilroy record appears.
5. Press F10 again, and the Kissel record appears.

Adding Criteria to Narrow the Search

Suppose you want to find a woman's address and all you know is the state where she lives and the first letter of her last name. To find the address, enter the exact spelling of the state (or its abbreviation) in the

State field. Then, type a wild card—for example W..—in the Last name field. The search screen shown in Figure 10-4 will find only those records that have CA in the State field and a last name that begins with W.

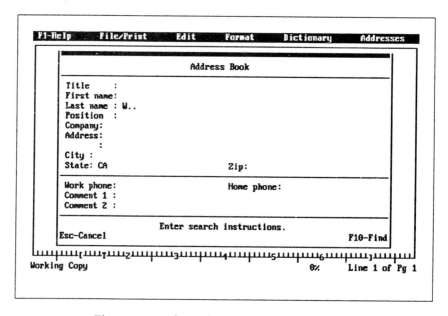

Figure 10-4   The Multiple Criteria Search screen

You can narrow the search even further by entering additional wild cards or exact matches in other fields.

Copying an Address into a Letter

Now that you have some records in your Address Book, and you're able to find them, you can begin inserting information from those records into your letters. All you need to do is specify which information you want inserted and where in the letter you want it inserted. For example, if you want to personalize a form letter to send to several people, you might type Dear *Title* *Last name*. Professional Write then lifts that information from whatever records you have chosen and inserts it into the letter.

With other word processing programs, you need to set up the inside address and salutation as above, whenever you want to insert information from your database. Professional Write, however, gives you a predesigned format to save you the time and trouble.

Let's insert one of the addresses from our Address Book into a blank screen, using Write's format.

1. Choose option **1. Create/Edit** from the Main menu, opening a blank working copy screen.
2. Move the cursor to the place where you want to insert the address.
3. Press F6 to open the Addresses menu.
4. Choose option **3. Find an address**.
5. Press F10 to find the first address in the Address Book. Professional Write displays the Kelly record. At the bottom left of the screen is the **F8-Copy to working copy** message.
6. Press F8 now. The title, name, position, and address, are entered into the working copy at the cursor position.

Modifying the Address Copy Format

Inserting the inside address is great, but you really shouldn't start your letter with "Dear Sir" or "Dear Madam," so let's modify the format to include a more personal salutation. First, you need to access the predesigned format:

1. Press F6, opening the Addresses menu.
2. Choose option **4. Specify copy format**. Professional Write displays the Copy Format screen.

Professional Write provides for nine lines of entries, each of which can contain more than one piece of information. Notice that the entries here look like embedded commands; each field is bracketed by asterisks. The entries function in much the same way as embedded commands, too. They lift information from somewhere else and insert it into the working copy.

To add a personal salutation, press the Tab key until the cursor is at Line 7. This leaves one blank line between the inside address and the salutation. Type **Dear *Comment 2*** and press F10 to save the revised copy format.

To see if it works as planned, return to the working copy and press F2 to open the File/Print menu. Choose option **7. Erase working copy**, to remove the Kelly address. Then,

1. Press F6 to open the Address menu.
2. Choose option **3. Find an address**.

3. Press F10 to display the first record in the Address Book.
4. Press F8, inserting the inside address and salutation into the working copy, as shown in Figure 10-5.

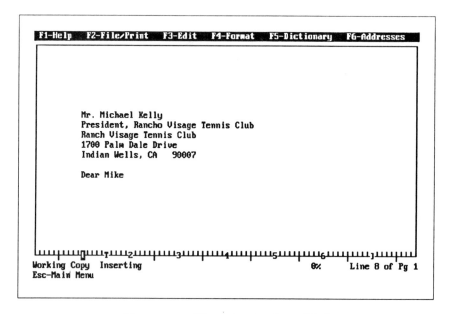

Figure 10-5 The salutation line added

As you can see, we forgot to enter punctuation after the name. Changing the entry is easy. First, go back to the Copy Format screen. Press the Tab key to move the cursor to Line 7. Press the Right Arrow key until the cursor is in the space after the rightmost asterisk. Type the punctuation you want to use in your letter.

Updating Your Address Book

After some time, you will inevitably need to change the records in your Address Book. A contact person may get promoted, or one of your customers may change the name of her company. In any case, you'll need to know how to enter such changes to your records.

Editing Records

If you need to change some information in a record, first find the record. With the record displayed on screen, use the Tab key to move the cursor from one field to the next. Press Ctrl-E to delete an entire field, then type the new information, or use the arrow keys to move the cursor within the field, and then make your correction.

The default mode for the cursor is Overstrike; if you want to change to the Insert mode, press Ins.

Deleting Records

A record can be deleted only when it is displayed on screen. You cannot delete a group of records with a single action, but you can search for and delete related records one at a time. Suppose one of your outside vendors has gone out of business. You can search for all records with that company's name and delete them one at a time.

1. Find the record you want to delete.
2. Press F9 to delete the record on screen. Professional Write displays the warning screen shown in Figure 10-6.
3. If you're sure you want to delete the record, press Enter. Otherwise, press Esc. If you delete the record, Professional Write begins searching for the next record that matches the search criteria.

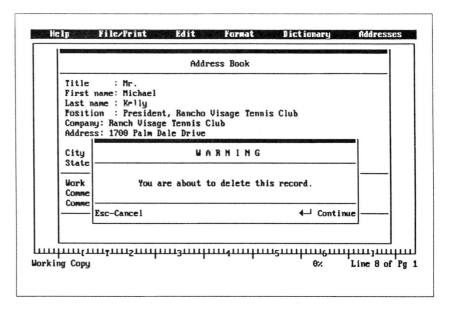

Figure 10-6   The Record Deletion warning screen

Creating and Using Several Address Books

Besides the default Address Book file, ADDRESS.SPC, you can create any number of Address Books with unique filenames. For instance, the tennis club membership could be named TENNIS.SPC or CLUB.SPC. (The extension .SPC is only for identification purposes; Professional Write does not need it to open the Address Book.) To open a different Address Book, perform the following steps:

1. Press F6, opening the Addresses menu.
2. Choose option `1. Select address book`. A screen appears that shows the default directory for the Address Book.
3. Press Ctrl-E to clear the default path.
4. Type the path of the drive or directory you want to use and the filename. For example, type `c:\wdata\tennis`. If you've forgotten the filename, type the path and press Enter. This displays the file directory. Highlight the filename of the Address Book you want to use and press Enter.

Form Letters

You can set up more detailed form letters to use information from other databases.

Inserting an inside address and salutation from your Address Book can give even the driest of form letters a personal touch, but a form letter really needs specific details to give it life. With Professional Write you can pull information from several other databases to add those personal details to your letters. Professional Write can access information from any of four databases:

- The Professional Write Address Book
- Professional File
- dBASE
- Any delimited ASCII data file

Composing the Letter

The form letter acts as a template for entering information from the database.

The first step in creating a form letter is to compose the standard text, including the names of the fields you want inserted. For example, if you're a real estate agent and you want to inform the residents in a particular subdivision that their real estate values have risen 20%, you can create the letter shown in Figure 10-7.

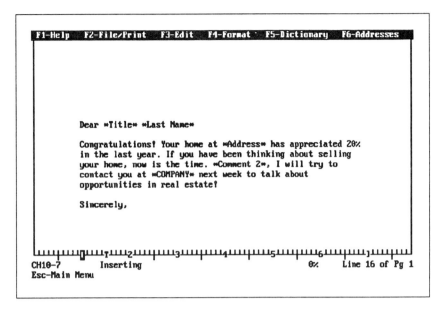

Figure 10-7 A real estate form letter

As Figure 10-7 illustrates, a field name can be inserted anywhere within the text. This letter is designed to insert the person's address and place of employment. The person will be addressed less formally in the body of the letter, due to the entry we added in the Comment 2 field.

Follow the proper syntax for entering field names in your letter:

- The field name must be inside asterisks with no spaces between the asterisks and the name.
- The field name must be typed exactly as it appears in the database.
- If the field name consists of two or more words, there must be a space between the two words.

Merging Letter and Database

Professional Write will automatically merge the letter and the database during printing to print the personalized version of the form letter. First, make sure the form letter is displayed on screen. Then, tell Professional Write which database to use and where it is located:

1. Press F2, opening the File/Print menu.
2. Choose option 5. Print working copy. The Print Options screen appears.

Chapter 10

3. Press Tab to move the cursor to Data file to merge:.
4. Enter the path and filename of the database you want to access. For example, type c:\wdata\tennis.
5. Press Enter. Professional Write responds with the Search screen from the Address Book. Here you have two options:
   - To print the letter for all records in this Address Book, press F10. The records will be printed in alphabetical order based on the entries in the Last Name field.
   - To print only a few records or one particular record, use the directions for Finding a Record earlier in this chapter. Then press F10 to begin printing.

After printing the letters, Professional Write displays a message screen that indicates the number of records found.

If you use field names within the body of your letter, you cannot use the Copy Format to insert an inside address. You must insert the field names, as shown in Figure 10-8.

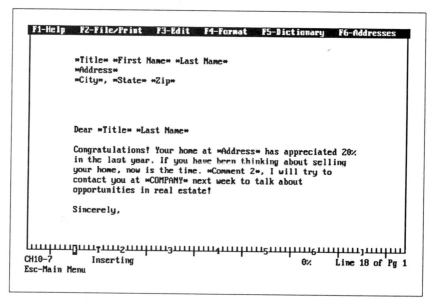

Figure 10-8 The form letter with inside address fields

Using Data from Professional File or dBASE

The predesigned format that Professional Write offers for the inside address and salutation is convenient for those specific tasks, but it does have its limitations. You can't change field names, add or delete fields, or create reports. To perform such tasks, you need a more flexible database, such as the one offered by Professional File or dBASE.

Refer to Chapter 12 for instructions on creating a Professional File database.

Professional File and dBASE are fully featured databases that are much more flexible than the Address Book when it comes to sorting, searching, and inserting information into form letters. For example, if you want to sort your letters by zip code to take advantage of the bulk rate, you can use Professional File or dBASE to do the sorting. Professional File and dBASE also let you use abbreviations for the field names. To use dBASE or Professional File, perform the following steps:

1. Create the form letter.
2. Press Ctrl-O, opening the Print Options screen.
3. Press the Tab key to move the cursor to Data file to merge.
4. Type the path and filename of the database you want to access. If your path is a floppy disk drive, make sure the disk containing that file is in the drive. Make sure you enter the filename extension.
5. Press Enter. Professional Write displays a Search screen.
6. To print a letter for each record in the database, press Enter. To print a letter for only a few records, type search criteria next to the field names. Professional Write will search for records with the matching criteria. Table 10-1 provides a summary of the search criteria.
7. Press F10, opening the Sort Order screen. Professional Write allows for a two-level sort; that is, Professional Write sorts according to one field first, then uses the secondary sort as a tie-breaker. By default, Professional Write sorts the records in alphabetical ascending order, unless you specify otherwise.
8. Use the Tab key to move the cursor to the field you want to use as the primary sort field.
9. Type 1, telling Write to sort according to this field first.
    - To sort in numerical order, type n after 1.
    - To sort in descending order, type d.
    - To sort according to a secondary field, use the Tab key to move to that field, and type 2.
10. If you used an abbreviated field name in your letter, you need to specify that in the Sort Order screen. Move the cursor to the field you abbreviated, and type the abbreviation you used. For example, if you used *LN* for *Last name*, type LN in the Last name field. If a sort instruction is already entered, separate the instruction from the abbreviation with a semicolon—for example, Last name: 1nd;LN.

Chapter 10

11. Press F10, opening the Format screen. This screen lets you specify how to format the information in your records.
12. Use the Tab key to move the cursor to the field you want to format.
13. Type the formatting instructions, as shown in Table 10-2. For example, if you want the month of a billing date spelled out, type **January dd, yyyy**. Professional Write will format the date in your database to correspond to this format.

Table 10-1 Search Criteria

Field Entry	Records Selected
MAN	Man only, capital letters not considered
17	Any value equal to 17
..dd	Any text ending with dd
dd..	Any text starting with dd
?ddd	Any four letter word ending in ddd
..dd..	Any text containing the letters dd
..	All entries, except blank fields
dd;ee	dd or ee only
=15;=78	Any value equal to 15 or 78
/dd;ee	Any entry *not* dd or ee
〈7;〉21	Any number less than 7 or greater than 21
〈7;dd	Any value less than 7 or text equals dd
/..	Every blank entry
/=5	All values *not* equal to 5
/dd..	Any *text* *not* starting with dd
/a-〉z	Any entry *not* starting with a letter
/=7-〉10	Any value *not* 7 to 10
a-〉z	Any text starting with a letter
=7-〉10	Any value 7 to 10, including 7 and 10
〉=10	Any value greater than or equal to 10
〈10	Any value less than 10
=〈10	Any value equal to or less than 10

Table 10-2 Format Instructions

Code	To Print
Date formats	
0m	The month as a two-digit number
mm	The month as a one- or two-digit number
Jan	The month abbreviated
January	The month spelled out
0d	The day as a two-digit number
dd	The day as a one- or two-digit number
0y	The year as a two-digit number
yy	The year as a one- or two-digit number
yyyy	The date as a four-digit number
Time formats	
0h	The hour as a two-digit number
hh	The hour as a one- or two-digit number
0m	The minute as a two-digit number
mm	The minute as a one- or two-digit number
0s	The second as a two-digit number
ss	The second as a one- or two-digit number
c0	1/100 of a second as a two-digit number
cc	1/100 of a second as a one- or two-digit number
Text formats	
A	An uppercase letter
a	A lowercase letter
E or e	Same case as used in record
N or n	A number
X	An uppercase letter or a number
x	A lowercase letter or a number
¦	Left-justified when used as leftmost character; Right-justified when used as rightmost character
~!@#$%^&*()-_=+[]{}\\|;:'",<.>/?spacebar	Punctuation marks, symbols, and spaces used as is

(continued)

Table 10-2 *(continued)*

Code	To Print
Numeric formats	
9	The number (a space if the position is not used)
0	The number (a 0 if the position is not used)
#	The number (nothing if the position is not used)
*	The number (an asterisk if the position is not used)
.	A decimal point
,	A comma
spacebar	A space
+	A plus sign if the number is positive; A minus sign if the number is negative
−	A minus sign if the number is negative; Blank if the number is positive
() or ⟨⟩	Enclose negative number
$	Dollar sign

Exporting Address Book Data to Professional File

Transferring data consists of merging data from the Address Book into a special form letter and then printing the form letter to a Professional File disk file.

If you have Professional File, you can export the data from your Address Book to Professional File, to save the time and effort of retyping the information. The procedure can be performed in two steps:

- Export the data from the Address Book to a delimited ASCII file, called EXPORT.PF
- Import the EXPORT.PF file into Professional File

Exporting Data from the Address Book

1. Start with a clear screen.
2. Type "*Title*", and press Enter.
3. Repeat step 2 for all the fields you want to transfer. For the last field, do not type the comma after the closing parenthesis.
4. Save the working copy, so you won't have to retype this template later.
5. Press F2, opening the File/Print menu.
6. Choose option 5. Print working copy.

The Address Book and Form Letters

7. Press the Tab key to move the cursor to the `Data file to merge` option.
8. Type the path and filename of the Address Book you want to transfer.
9. Press the Tab key to move the cursor to the `Print to` option.
10. Type 3 to print the file to disk.
11. Press Enter. Professional Write displays a screen that asks you where you want to send the file.
12. Press Ctrl-E, then type `export.pf` (add a description for the file, if you want to).
13. Press Enter. Professional Write displays the Search screen.
14. If you want to transfer all the records, press F10. If you only want to transfer selected records, enter the search criteria in the Search screen, then press F10. Professional Write prints the database to the EXPORT.PF file.
15. Press Enter to return to the working copy.

Importing Data into Professional File

1. Create a database form, as explained in Chapter 12. Use field names that are identical to the fieldnames used in your Address Book.
2. Return to the Professional File Main menu.
3. Choose option `4. Copy`, opening the Copy menu.
4. Choose option `5. Import records`, opening the Import Records menu.
5. Choose option `3. Import from delimited ASCII`, displaying a screen that lets you specify the file you want to import.
6. Press Tab three times, moving the cursor to `Filename:`.
7. Type the path and filename of the EXPORT.PF file. For example, type `c:\pro\export.pf`.
8. Press Enter, displaying a screen that lets you specify which Professional File database you want to use.
9. Type the path and filename of the form you created to import the data.
10. Press Enter. Professional File displays a message, telling you how many files were imported.

Chapter 10

Printing Mailing Labels or Envelopes

If you sorted your letters during printing, sort your envelopes in the same order.

Earlier in this chapter, you learned how to print an address from the Address Book to an envelope. If you had to follow the same procedure for mass mailings, it would take forever.

Luckily, you don't. Just access the Print Options menu once and then feed your envelopes continuously or one at a time. The steps required are similar to those used for printing letters.

To print using manual feed:

1. Make sure the form letter you want to use is on screen.
2. Press F2, opening the File/Print menu.
3. Choose option `5. Print working copy`.
4. Press the Tab key to move the cursor to the `Pause between page` option, and type `y`, telling Professional Write to pause before printing the next envelope.
5. Move the cursor to the `Document or envelope` option and type `e`, choosing Envelope.
6. Move the cursor to the `Data File to merge` option.
7. Press Ctrl-E, and then type the path and filename of the database file that contains the addresses.
8. Change any other options on the Print Options screen as needed.
9. Insert the envelope in the printer, aligning the top of the envelope with the print head.
10. Press Enter, opening a Search screen.
11. Enter search criteria in the Search screen, and press F10. Professional Write prints the first address it finds and then pauses.
12. Continue the process until all your envelopes are printed.

Printing with continuous feed consists of convincing Professional Write that each envelope or label is a page.

To print using continous feed:

1. Begin with a clear screen.
2. Type the field names that will be used to send the letter; that is, name, address, city, state, and zip code as you want them to be printed. If you use abbreviations for the field names, make sure you match them in the Sort Order screen.
3. Press F4, opening the Format menu, and choose option `1. Set left/right margins`.
4. Set the left margin where you want to start printing. Set the right margin far enough right so it doesn't restrict your address.
5. Press Enter.

6. Press F4, reopening the Format menu; then choose option 2. Set top/bottom margins & length.
7. Set the top margin according to how far down you want the first line to print. Set the bottom margin to 0.
8. Now, you need to reset the page length so the length will match that of the label or envelope.
   - Measure the height of the envelope or label in inches.
   - Multiply the measurement by 6. (Professional Write prints 6 lines per inch.)
   - Enter the result as the new page length
9. Press Enter.
10. Press Ctrl-O, opening the Print Options screen.
11. Press the Tab key to move the cursor to the Pause between pages option, and type N.
12. Press the Tab key to move the cursor to the Document or envelope option and type d.
13. Move the cursor to the Data File to merge option.
14. Press Ctrl-E, and then type the path and filename of the database file that contains the addresses.
15. Change any other options on the Print Options screen as needed.
16. Insert the envelopes or mailing labels in the printer, aligning the top of the first envelope or mailing label with the print head.
17. Press Enter, opening a Search screen.
18. Enter search criteria in the Search screen, and press F10. Professional Write begins printing.

Before beginning contiuous feed, select a small group of records to test the settings.

Summary

With Professional Write's built-in Address Book, you can personalize a standard letter to send to several people on your list. By accessing broader, more flexible databases such as Professional File and dBASE, you can create complex form letters and insert information that is specifically directed to each individual recipient. When the time comes to mail these letters, you can save additional time through the automated mailing address system.

In the next chapter, you will learn to use macros to take a few more shortcuts.

E L E V E N

Macros

The only restriction for using macros is that you cannot run one macro from inside another one.

A macro is simply a record of keystrokes that performs a given task. You have already seen several macros disguised as shortcut keys. Ctrl-B, for example, is a macro. Without this macro, you would have to press F3 and choose option 7. Boldface word from the Edit menu every time you wanted to boldface text. Professional Write offers macros for the more common tasks required in word processing. For those not-so-common tasks, Professional Write lets you customize your system by creating up to thirty-five macros (fifteen on a floppy disk system). Each macro can contain up to forty different keystrokes.

Creating a Macro

Creating a macro is a two-step operation:

- Record the keystrokes required to perform a task.
- Assign a two-key combination to the macro.

Before you begin creating a macro, position the cursor in the document at the place where you want Professional Write to begin recording your keystrokes. In the following example, you will create a macro for inserting your name and address into a document:

1. Choose option 8. Use macros from the File/Print menu, or press Alt-0 (that's a zero). The Macros menu appears, as shown in Figure 11-1.

Chapter 11

2. Choose option 2. Record a macro. Professional Write displays a message screen, as in Figure 11-2, telling you that recording is in progress.

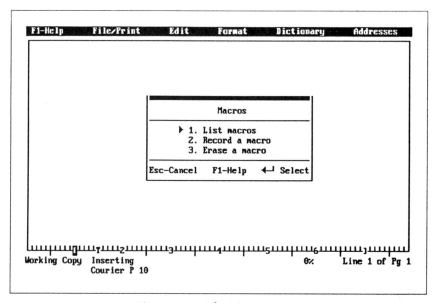

Figure 11-1 The Macros menu

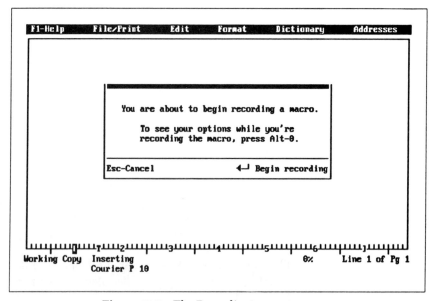

Figure 11-2 The Recording message screen

3. Press Enter, to return to the working copy. From this point on, Professional Write records your keystrokes to create the macro.
4. Type your name and address in the following format:

   ```
   First name Last name
   Street address
   City, State  Zip code
   ```

5. Press Alt-0, opening the Recording Options screen, as shown in Figure 11-3.
6. Choose option 2. End and save recorded keystrokes. Professional Write responds with the Save Recorded Keystrokes menu, as shown in Figure 11-4. This menu lists all of the keystrokes available for your macros. The keystrokes consist of Alt and a letter, or Alt and a number from 1 to 9.
7. Use the PgDn key to see more of the menu.

If you choose a keystroke that is already in use, Professional Write overwrites the previous macro.

8. Press the Up or Down Arrow key to highlight the keystroke you want to use. It's a good idea to choose a keystroke that reminds you of the task you want the macro to perform. Alt-N may be a good choice for the macro you just created, because the macro inserts your name.
9. Type a brief description of the macro (up to twenty characters); for example, type Insert my name. The discription serves a dual purpose; it helps you remember what the keystroke is used for, and it shows you that the keystroke is assigned to a macro.
10. Press Enter, assigning the keystroke combination to your macro.

Alt-N is now assigned to your new macro. Move the cursor to a blank line in the working copy and press Alt-N. Your name and address are inserted at the cursor position.

If you're in the process of recording a macro and a step in your macro requires you to choose an item from a menu, type the number of the item or use the shortcut keys. Do not select the item by highlighting it.

The File Print Macro

After you've printed a few documents, you have a pretty good idea of what printer setup you will be using most often. The required steps begin to seem like busy work. This is a sign that you need a macro. Begin with a blank screen. Then,

Chapter 11

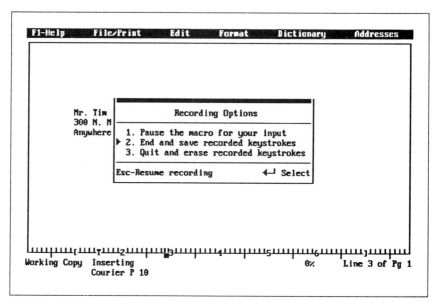

Figure 11-3 The Recording Options screen

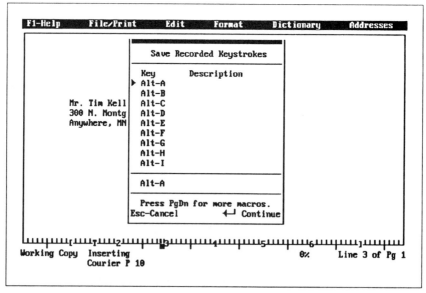

Figure 11-4 The Save Recorded Keystrokes menu

1. Choose option 8. Use macros from the File/Print menu or press Alt-0, opening the Macros menu.

2. Choose option 2. Record a macro. Professional Write displays a message screen telling you that recording is in progress.
3. Press Enter to return to the working copy.
4. Press F2 to open the File/Print menu.
5. Type 5, choosing option 5. Print working copy. This opens the Print Options screen.
6. Enter any changes to the options as required.
7. Press Enter. Professional Write form feeds one sheet of paper but prints nothing, because the screen is blank.
8. Press Alt-0, opening the Recording Options screen.
9. Choose option 2. End and save recorded keystrokes, opening the Save Recorded Keystrokes menu.
10. Use the PgDn key to see more of the menu.
11. Press the Up or Down Arrow key to highlight the keystroke you want to use; Alt-P would be a wise choice.
12. Type a brief description of the macro (up to twenty characters); for example, type Print working copy.
13. Press Enter, assigning the keystroke combination to your macro.

Try it out. Get a file and then press Alt-P.

The Pause Macro

The pause macro waits for you to enter information before it completes its task. Suppose you're a real estate agent and you're sending prospective clients information about constantly fluctuating interest rates. You can create a form letter and have Professional Write get the letter, wait for you to enter the most current interest rate, and then print the letter for all your clients. To create this macro, perform the following steps:

1. Choose option 8. Use macros from the File/Print menu, or press Alt-0, opening the Macros menu.
2. Choose option 2. Record a macro. Professional Write displays a message screen telling you that recording is in progress.
3. Press Enter, to return to the working copy.
4. Press F2 to open the File/Print menu.
5. Type 1, choosing option 1. Get file.
6. Press Ctrl-E and type the path and filename of the form letter.
7. Press Enter to get the form letter.

8. Move the cursor to the place where you want to insert the interest rate.
9. Press Alt-0, reopening the Recording Options menu.
10. Type 1, choosing option `1. Pause macro for your input`, and press Enter.
11. Type the current interest rate.
12. Press F9 to continue recording your keystrokes.
13. Press F2, reopening the File/Print menu.
14. Type 5, choosing the `Print working copy` option. Professional Write displays the Print Options screen.
15. Press the Tab key to move the cursor to `Data file to merge:`.
16. Type the path and filename of the Address Book you're using for clients.
17. Press Enter. Professional Write displays the Search screen.
18. Enter your search criteria and press F10. Professional Write prints the letters, inserting the current interest rate. Wait for Write to stop printing.
19. Press Alt-0, opening the Recording Options screen.
20. Choose option `2. End and save recorded keystrokes`, opening the Save Recorded Keystrokes menu.
21. Use the PgDn key to see more of the menu.
22. Press the Up or Down Arrow key to highlight the keystroke you want to use; Alt-I may be a good one.
23. Type a brief description of the macro (up to twenty characters); for example, type `Interest rate`.
24. Press Enter, assigning the keystroke combination to your macro.

You can pause a macro as many times as necessary and at whatever step you wish. For example, you could have it pause at the Search screen, so you can send the letter to a certain group of clients.

Starting Over

If you make a mistake during the recording process, Professional Write lets you start over. Press Alt-0 and choose option `3. Quit and erase recorded keystrokes`. Professional Write stops the recording process and lets you start from scratch.

Listing Macros

If you can't remember which macro you used to perform a particular task, press Alt-0 and choose option `1. List macros`. Professional Write displays a list of macros complete with descriptions. To activate a macro on the list, highlight the macro and press Enter.

Deleting a Macro

There's really not much need to delete a macro. As you saw earlier, you can simply write over a macro if you need to use that keystroke. If you do decide to delete a macro, however, just perform the following steps:

1. Press Alt-0, opening the Macros menu.
2. Choose option `3. Erase a macro`. Professional Write displays a list of macros.
3. Use the Up and Down Arrow keys to move the highlight to the macro you want to delete, and press Enter. Professional Write displays a warning screen telling you that you are about to erase a macro.
4. Press Enter to erase the macro.

Editing a Macro

To edit a macro, simply recreate it. If you try to save the revised macro to the same keystroke as the old version, Professional Write will warn you that you are about to overwrite the old version. Simply press Enter to complete the deed.

Summary

As you gain experience, you will begin to notice yourself performing several word processing tasks on a regular basis. Now that you know how to create macros, you can start using them to take over these daily chores, leaving you with the more creative work.

TWELVE

Creating a Professional File Database Form

Professional File is a database program that keeps track of names, addresses, invoices, part numbers, accounts payable, and any other information that must be filed. When combined with Professional Write, it can be used to insert a wide variety of information into word processed documents.

This chapter is designed to help you understand and set up your Professional File database so that you can access the information most efficiently. Later chapters will show you how to create reports and records that let you pull the raw data out of your database and insert it in a more meaningful context.

Understanding Databases

A database is a collection of records that contain individual entries. A doctor, for example, may create a database by having her patients fill out standard forms during the first visit.

The doctor could use this database to perform any of several tasks. For example, she could page through the stack to find all the patients with high blood pressure and send them pamphlets on how to treat their condition.

A computerized database, such as Professional File, works the same way. You begin by creating a *form*—a template that lets you fill in the blanks with information. The blanks in this case are referred to as *fields*. By entering information into the fields, you generate a *record*. A record is merely a collection of information; it may contain the specifications for a single part or the name and address of a client. A collection of such records is called a *database*.

With this computerized database, you can find records with the touch of a key, sort them however you wish, and insert any piece of information from the database into your Professional Write documents.

Starting Professional File

> If you have not yet installed Professional File, follow the instructions in the Appendix for installing and customizing your system.

Create a separate directory, FDATA, to store your Professional File data files, as discussed in the Appendix.

To run Professional File, you first need to activate the drive that holds the Professional File program files. If the program files are in drive C and `C:>` is displayed on screen, you're ready to begin. If the program files are in drive D, however, you need to type `d:` and press Enter. DOS will activate drive D and display `D:>`.

Once you're in the correct drive, you're ready to start Professional File. First, you must tell DOS the name of the directory that contains the program files. To do this, type `cd\pro`, telling DOS, "Change Directory to PRO." DOS responds as before with the prompt `C:\PRO>`, indicating that the PRO directory is active. You can now run the files in that directory. Type `pf` and press Enter to launch Professional File. Your screen should resemble Figure 12-1.

Designing a Form

The first step in creating a database is to design a form to generate records. Designing a form requires a great deal of foresight. You need to anticipate what information you will need and how that information will be used, and you need to determine the most effective wording for your field names. If your business already uses paper forms that contain the required fields, use those forms to guide you. If not, write down a few ideas before you start.

As you're designing the form, keep the following guidelines in mind:

- Include a field that will give each record generated by the form a unique number. This lets you spot duplicate records easily. For example, in an invoice form, include an invoice number field.

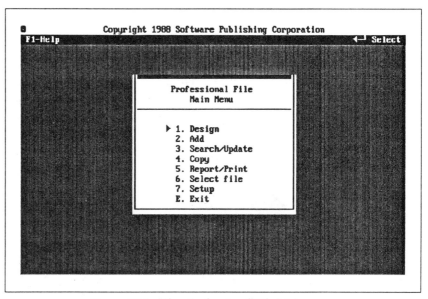

Figure 12-1 The Professional File Main menu

- Type the most important information, such as an invoice number or part number, in the upper left corner of the screen. That way, you won't have to search the entire screen to find it.
- Be logical. Your form should present information in a natural flow, from left to right and top to bottom.
- Leave the blank space for entering data to the right of the field name, not below it. Leave sufficient space for your entries.
- Keep field names just long enough to explain the data that follows. Long field names take space away from your entries and may cause problems when you need to use them in form letters.
- If an entry can be typed in a number of ways, include an example of how you want it entered—for example, `DATE(MM/DD/YY):`.

Creating the Form

When you have a fair idea of how you want to set up the form, you're ready to open the Form Design screen and begin:

1. Choose option `1. Design` from the Main menu, opening the Design menu, as shown in Figure 12-2.

2. Choose option 1. Create new design. Professional Write displays a Filename screen, prompting you to name a file for the form.
3. Press Ctrl-E to erase the default path, and type the path and filename you want to use for your form. For example, type c:\wdata\invoice.
4. Press Enter. Professional File displays the Form Design screen shown in Figure 12-3.

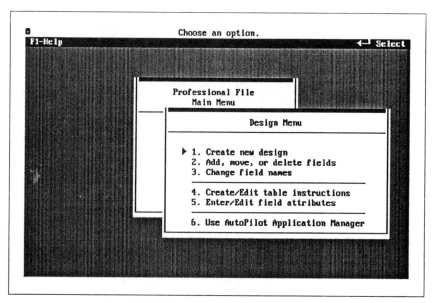

Figure 12-2 The Design menu

You can enter up to 100 fields per page, and use up to 32 pages per form.

Let's examine the Form Design screen. At the top left corner is the name of the file, in this case, INVOICE. The next item is the screen message Design the form by typing field names. In the top right corner is the page indicator, which shows that this is page 1 of a 1-page form. To see the next page of a multipage form, simply press PgDn; the page indicator reflects the change.

The next line down is the menu line. This line contains a list of the keys you need to press to open the corresponding pull-down menus or screens. Press F1 now to view the Help screen shown in Figure 12-4.

As you can see, Professional File "knows" what you're working on and gives you the information you need. Since you haven't typed any entries, the Help screen is concerned with getting you started. This is know as context-sensitive help. To close the Help screen, press Esc.

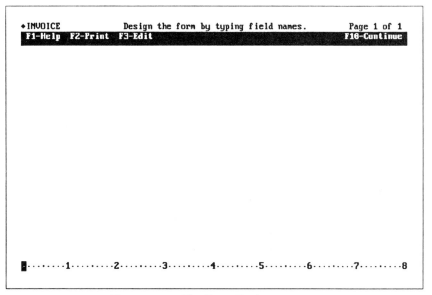

Figure 12-3 The Form Design screen

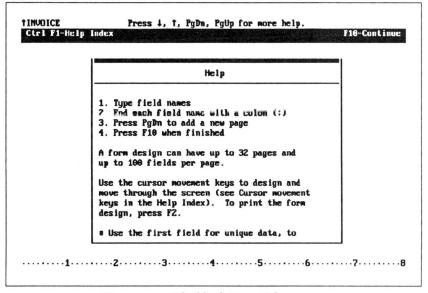

Figure 12-4 The blank Form Help screen

Entering Field Names

Use the cursor in the ruler line to align the field names.

Now that the Form Design screen is displayed, you can begin entering field names to create your form. The following example shows how to create an INVOICE form.

Begin by entering the field name for the INVOICE number. Position the cursor so that it is as far to the left as it can go, and as close to the top of the screen as possible. Then type `INVOICE NUMBER:`. The colon after the field name is absolutely essential to the form. Without it, Professional File has no idea where the field name ends and the entry begins. Your screen should resemble Figure 12-5.

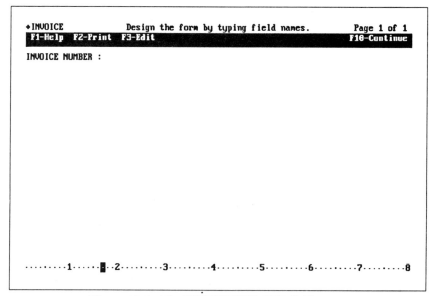

Figure 12-5 The INVOICE NUMBER field name

Press the Tab key twice moving the cursor to the number 3 on the ruler line. The next most important piece of information is the date, so type `date(MM/DD/YY):`. Press the Tab key until the cursor is positioned at 6 on the ruler line, and type `PO#:`. This field will be used for the purchase order number.

Press Enter twice, leaving a blank line and moving the cursor to the left margin. Type `CUSTOMER NAME:`. Since the customer's name could be long, press Enter, leaving the rest of the line blank.

Next, type the billing address: `BILL TO ADDRESS:`. Press the Tab key, moving the cursor to 4 on the ruler line. Then type `CITY:` and press Enter.

Next, type the field name for the state STATE:. Press the Tab key, moving the cursor to 4 in the ruler line, and type ZIP:. After this last entry, your screen should resemble Figure 12-6.

Enter the fields for the shipping address, as shown in Figure 12-7.

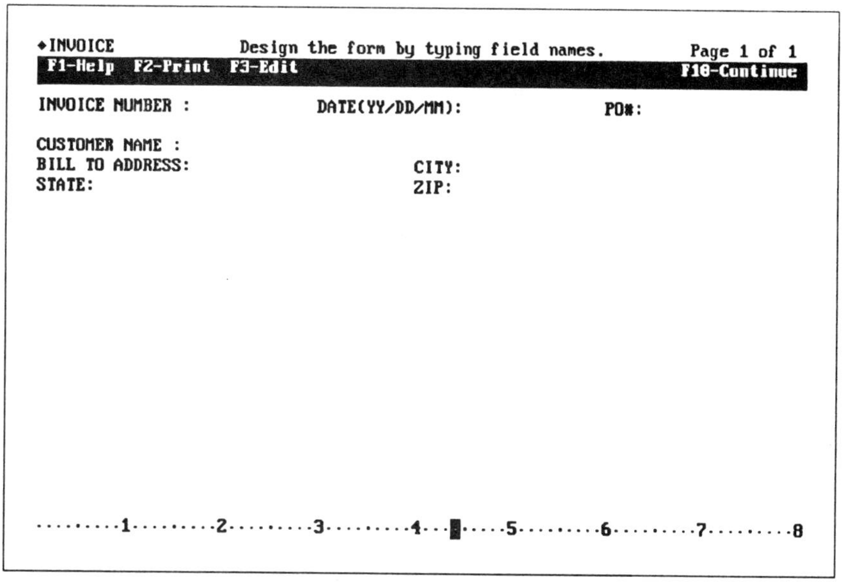

```
◆INVOICE              Design the form by typing field names.        Page 1 of 1
 F1-Help  F2-Print  F3-Edit                                          F10-Continue
  INVOICE NUMBER :            DATE(YY/DD/MM):              PO#:

  CUSTOMER NAME :
  BILL TO ADDRESS:             CITY:
  STATE:                       ZIP:




      ........1........2........3........4..▮....5........6........7........8
```

Figure 12-6 The INVOICE form with several fields

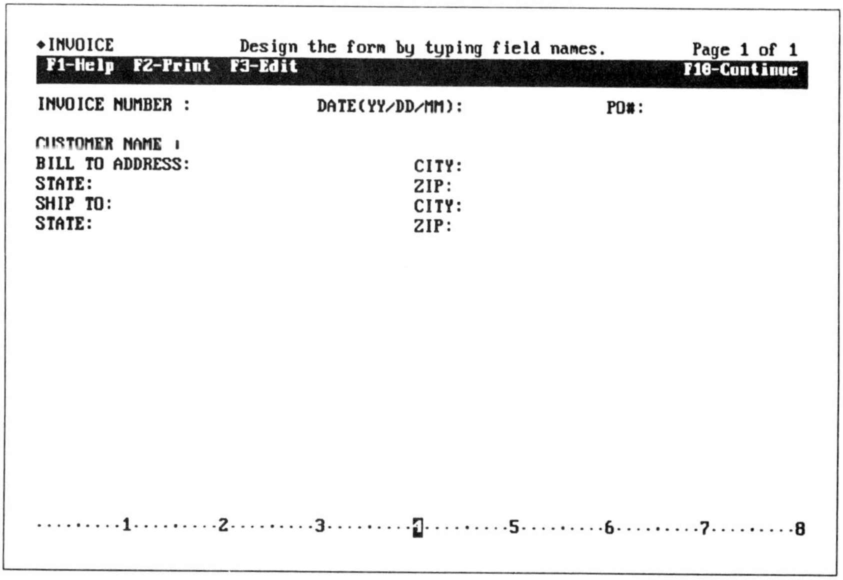

```
◆INVOICE              Design the form by typing field names.        Page 1 of 1
 F1-Help  F2-Print  F3-Edit                                          F10-Continue
  INVOICE NUMBER :            DATE(YY/DD/MM):              PO#:

  CUSTOMER NAME :
  BILL TO ADDRESS:             CITY:
  STATE:                       ZIP:
  SHIP TO:                     CITY:
  STATE:                       ZIP:



      ........1........2........3........▮........5........6........7........8
```

Figure 12-7 The shipping address fields added to the form

You may have noticed that the billing and shipping addresses run together. You can fix that problem and improve the readability of the form by adding a blank line between the two addresses:

1. Move the cursor to the S in SHIP TO:.
2. Press F3, opening the Edit menu shown in Figure 12-8. (The Edit menu is explained in greater detail in the next section of this chapter.)
3. Choose option 1. Insert blank line.

You can bypass the Edit menu by using shortcut keys. After you position the cursor, press Ctrl-I to insert the blank line.

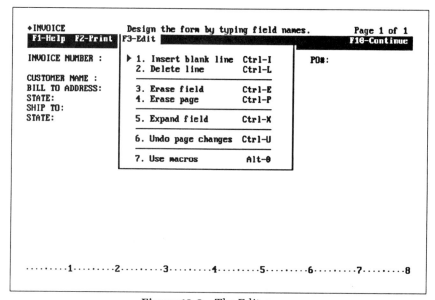

Figure 12-8 The Edit menu

The remainder of the invoice is for the items ordered. To keep these items separate from the billing and shipping information, press and hold the = (equal sign) key until the signs are entered all the way across the screen. Press Enter, moving the cursor to the next line. Now, you can start entering the field names for the items ordered:

1. Type PRODUCT: (don't forget the colon).
2. Press the Right Arrow key until the cursor is halfway between 2 and 3 in the ruler line; then type QUANTITY:.

3. Move the cursor to halfway between 4 and 5 in the ruler line, and type PRICE: to allow for a price per unit entry.
4. Next, move the cursor to 6 in the ruler line, and type EXTPRICE:. Later, when you begin entering data, you can use Professional File to calculate the extended price and insert the result directly in this field.
5. Finally, you need a field name to indicate if the item is on back order. Postion the cursor between 7 and 8 on the ruler line, and type BO:. Your form should now resemble the one shown in Figure 12-9.
6. Press Enter.
7. Repeat steps 1-6 until you have 3 lines for items ordered.

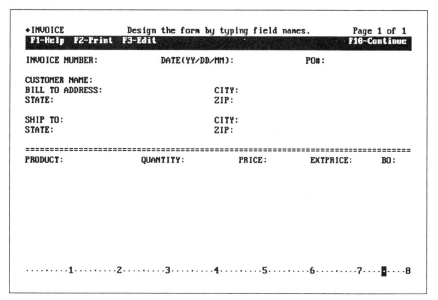

Figure 12-9 The INVOICE form with a product line added

If you need to repeat a line on your form several times, consider using a macro. Move the cursor to the place where you want the macro to start, and Press Alt-0. Then type the line. When you're finished typing, press Alt-0 again. Then choose a keystroke combination from the Macros menu (Alt-R for Repeat) and add a description for your macro (Repeat line). You can then move the cursor to the next blank line and press Alt-R.

The last fields in an invoice are those that calculate the dollar total including sales taxes. Enter those field names as shown in Figure 12-10.

```
 ♦INVOICE            Design the form by typing field names.       Page 1 of 1
 F1-Help  F2-Print  F3-Edit                                       F10-Continue
 INVOICE NUMBER:         DATE(YY/DD/MM):            PO#:

 CUSTOMER NAME:
 BILL TO ADDRESS:                       CITY:
 STATE:                                 ZIP:

 SHIP TO:                               CITY:
 STATE:                                 ZIP:
 ================================================================================
 PRODUCT:            QUANTITY:          PRICE:     EXTPRICE:      BO:
 PRODUCT:            QUANTITY:          PRICE:     EXTPRICE:      BO:
 PRODUCT:            QUANTITY:          PRICE:     EXTPRICE:      BO:



                                                   SUBTOTAL:
                                                        TAX:
                                                      TOTAL:

 .........1.........2.........3.........4.........5.........6.......▮7.........8
```

Figure 12-10   The completed INVOICE form

Saving the Form

Now that you have the basic structure of your form laid out, you should save the form. Press F10, saving the form to disk. This protects your work in case anything goes wrong during the editing stage.

Editing the Form

Change your form before entering information into the fields to avoid headaches later.

If you want to edit a form, you first need to get the form on screen. To do that, perform the following steps:

1. Choose option 1. Design from the Main menu. Professional File displays the Design menu.
2. Choose option 2. Add, move, or delete field names. Professional File displays a filename screen asking you which file you want to edit.
3. Press Ctrl-E, erasing the default directory.
4. Type the path and filename of the file you want to edit. For example, type c:\fdata\invoice.

5. Press Enter. Professional File displays the form with a warning message, letting you know that any changes you make are permanent, and suggesting that you create a backup copy of the database. Because you haven't entered data in any of the fields, this is not a concern. If you had entered information, you should make a backup copy of the form. Making changes to the form does not destroy the data, but it can make it inaccessible.
6. Press Enter to continue.

The Edit Menu

Press F3 to access the Edit menu. You will use this menu most frequently when creating and perfecting your form. It lets you insert blank lines, erase fields, and even undo your editing changes.

To the right of each option is a corresponding shortcut key that lets you bypass the Edit menu. Thus, instead of pressing F3 to open the Edit menu and then selecting option 2 or option 3, you can simply move the cursor to the field you want to change and press the corresponding shortcut key.

To make these combinations easier to remember, most of them are abbreviations for the option's name: Ctrl-I for Insert, Ctrl-L for Delete Line, and Ctrl-U for Undo. You may have to stop and think at first, but these shortcuts soon become as natural as pressing the Shift key to capitalize. The following sections explain each item on the Edit menu.

Insert Blank Line

To insert a blank line, position the cursor at the beginning of the second line, and choose this option. Inserting a blank line is useful for separating sections of your form.

Delete Line

To erase an entire line of field names, or to delete a blank line, move the cursor to the line you want delete, and choose option 2 from the Edit menu.

Erase Field

This option does not remove a field name; it merely deletes information entered in the field. To delete an entry, move the cursor to the field that contains the entry, and choose the Erase field option.

Erase Page

Erase page performs different functions depending on what you're doing. If you are in the process of creating a form, choosing Erase page removes all field names from the page. If you are typing entries in the fields, this option deletes all entries, leaving the field names intact.

Choose this option with caution.

Expand Field

When entering data, you may discover that one of your entries is too long to fit in the field. Professional File overcomes this problem by automatically expanding the field length temporarily, so that more information can be entered.

When a field has an entry that is longer than the allotted length, > is displayed after the last character that fits. To see the entire entry, position the cursor in the field containing the > symbol and select this option.

Undo Page Changes

If you're entering data in your form and decide that you want to begin with a blank form, select this option. All entries are erased from the fields, leaving you a blank form.

If you are editing a record that had been previously saved and want to restore the record to the pre-edit condition, select this option.

If you are designing a new form and want to begin again with a clear screen, select this option.

Use Macros

A macro repeats keystrokes that you have recorded. If you frequently perform a task that requires several keystrokes, you can use a two-key combination to replay the series of steps. Refer to Chapters 11 and 15 for more information on using macros.

Adding a Field

A good piece of information to include on an invoice is the date shipped. This date indicates whether or not an order has been shipped and lets the managers keep track of the time it takes an order to get to the customer.

To add the DATE SHIPPED field name, move the cursor to the line directly above the the line of equal signs, and type `date shipped:`.

Press F10 to save the change. When you save the new version, Professional File will insert the new field into every record created with the old version.

Moving a Field Name

To move a field, you need to delete the field from its old location and retype it in the new location. If you generated records with this form already, make sure you retype the field name exactly as it appeared in the old version. Otherwise, Professional File will not know what to do with the data.
Press F10 to save the change.

Deleting a Field Name

Deleting a field name is as easy as deleting a word in the Overstrike mode. Simply move the cursor to the first letter of the field name you wish to delete and press the spacebar until all of the characters are erased, including the colon.
Press F10 to save the new version.

Changing Field Names

Professional File matches data to field names by the order in which the names appear. That is, the first piece of information is matched to the first field name found in the form. So as long as you keep the name in the same place, changing it does not confuse Professional File.

Suppose you want to change RECORD NUMBER to RECORD#. Simply move the cursor to the first letter in NUMBER and press the spacebar until the word is deleted. Then type #.

To move and rename a field without losing data, move the field name first and save the change. Professional File reorganizes the database to accommodate the change. Then rename the field.
Press F10 to save any changes.

Reordering Records after Editing

After you change your form, the records in your database are rearranged in reverse order. The record that was last is now first. This is no big problem, but if you want to return the records to their original order, perform the following steps:

1. Choose option 2. Add, move, or delete fields from the Design menu. Make no changes to the form.

2. When the form appears, press F10. Because you made no changes, the records are quickly "redesigned" and the first record is now in its proper place.

Field Attributes

Add field attributes after designing your form but before entering any data.

Field attributes tell Professional File what to do with certain pieces of information. You can assign any of the following attributes to a field to help Professional File work with your database:

- Index
- Unique Data Entry
- Default

The following sections explore field attributes in greater depth.

Indexed Fields

You can create up to eight separate indexes, but don't get carried away; indexes tend to slow down the program.

In order to accelerate sorting and searching of a database, Professional File uses a process called indexing. For every field you index, Professional file creates a separate ordered list specifically for the data in that field. File uses this list to search and sort the data more quickly.

Suppose you're in advertising and you decide to run a special promotion through the mail. To take advantage of the bulk rates at the post office, you need to sort your mailing labels by zip code. You can tell Professional File to index the zip code entries. Then, when you decide to print the labels, Professional File can use the index to sort the records, rather than searching each record.

Unique Data Entry Field

The Unique Data Entry field ensures that information in a field is different for every record. For example, if you want to use a unique invoice number for each invoice you send out, you can assign a unique data entry attribute to check the number.

When you enter an invoice number, Professional File checks the same field in all other records to make sure that the number is not already in use. If the same number is used elsewhere, Professional File does not let you reenter it.

To perform this check, Professional Write automatically indexes the field, using up one of the eight available index fields.

Default Entries

If you find that you frequently enter identical data in the same field, consider using a default entry. For example, if you deal exclusively with customers in Iowa, you can have Professional File automatically enter IA in the STATE field, so you don't have to type it every time.

Adding Field Attributes to the Form

To add field attributes to your form, perform the following steps:

1. Choose option 1. Design from the Main menu, opening the Design menu.
2. Choose option 5. Enter/edit field attributes. Professional File displays a Filename screen asking you which file you want to edit.
3. Press Ctrl-E, erasing the default directory.
4. Type the path and filename of the file you want to edit. For example, type c:\fdata\invoice.
5. Press Enter.

Notice that the cursor is positioned in the INVOICE NUMBER field, not in the area of the field name. This is important to notice, because you will be adding attributes to the field itself, not to the field name.

Every invoice number should be unique, and the invoices should be indexed according to their numbers. Therefore, you need to assign two attributes to the invoice number:

1. Press F2, opening the Attributes menu, as shown in Figure 12-11.
2. Select option 7. Edit indices.
3. The cursor is already in position, so type u ("u" is the code for "unique"). The "u" will be displayed as bold or as a different color, depending on your hardware. Professional File does not automatically begin processing the new attribute; instead, it allows you to move the cursor to another field.
4. Press F10. The Design menu reappears, and Professional File automatically indexes the invoice numbers. Professional File will not allow a duplicate invoice number to be entered.

Since the Unique Data Attribute automatically indexes the field, there is no need to type i for the index attribute.

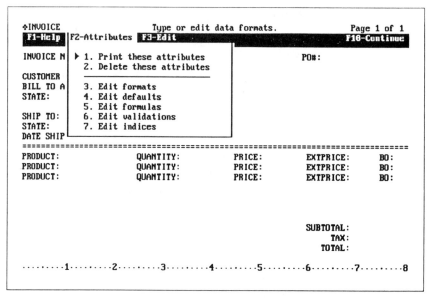

Figure 12-11 The Attributes menu

While you're add it, add a default entry to the STATE field:

1. Press F2, opening the Attributes menu.
2. Choose option **4. Edit defaults**. The Form screen appears with no attribute entries in any fields.
3. Press the Tab key to move the cursor to the first STATE field.
4. Assuming most of your customers are in Iowa, type **IA**.
5. Press F10 to save the default entry.

The new default entry will only be entered in records created from this point on.

Format Attributes

Format attributes ensure that information is entered consistently, to help Professional File find and interpret the data more efficiently. Formatting also saves you some work by entering some of the symbols that may be required by the format. For example, if you use the format nnn-nn-nnnn, simply type the entry, 555555555, and Professional File enters it according to the specified format, 555-55-5555.

Professional File lets you specify the format for any of four types of data:

- Dates
- Time
- Numbers
- Text

Date Format

Let's use a date format for the DATE field on the INVOICE form:

1. Press F2, to open the Attributes menu.
2. Choose option `3. Edit formats`.
3. Press the Tab key to move the cursor to the DATE field.
4. Type `yy/dd/mm`.

The date field is now formatted to accept entries only in the specified format. When you begin to enter dates, simply type the six digits that make up the date; Professional File will insert the slashes. Table 12-1 provides a list of possible date formats.

Table 12-1 Date Formats

Code	To Print
0m	The month as a two-digit number
mm	The month as a one- or two-digit number
Jan	The month abbreviated
January	The month spelled out
0d	The day as a two-digit number
dd	The day as a one- or two-digit number
0y	The year as a two-digit number
yy	The year as a one- or two-digit number
yyyy	The date as a four-digit number
~!@#$%^&*()-__=+ []{}|;:' ",<.>/? spacebar	Punctuation marks, symbols, and spaces used as is

Time Format

If you need to enter the time on your form, use any of the time formats listed in Table 12-2.

Table 12-2 Time Formats

Code	To Print
0h	The hour as a two-digit number
hh	The hour as a one- or two-digit number
0m	The minute as a two-digit number
mm	The minute as a one- or two-digit number
0s	The second as a two-digit number
ss	The second as a one- or two-digit number
c0	1/100 of a second as a two-digit number
cc	1/100 of a second as a one- or two-digit number
AM or a.m.	As is
PM or p.m.	As is
~!@#$%^&*()-_=+[]|;:'",<.>/? spacebar	Punctuation marks, symbols, and spaces used as is

Numeric Format

With the INVOICE form on screen, enter a format attribute for the INVOICE NUMBER field:

1. Press Shift-Tab to move the cursor back to the INVOICE NUMBER field.
2. Type **999999**. The INVOICE form should now look like the one in Figure 12-12.

The series of 9s entered in the field causes Professional File to accept any numbers entered. If no number is entered, Professional File leaves a space in place of the 9. By entering six 9s, the largest number that can be entered is six digits. This not only ensures a correct format, but it also provides a quick check for typos.

The numeric format allows only numbers to be entered, so don't use the format if you think you may need to enter a letter in this field at some future date. For example, Canadians use a postal code that combines numbers and letters. If the field were formatted as numeric, the postal code could not be entered. Instead, use the text format discussed later. Table 12-3 provides a complete list of numeric formats.

Creating a Professional File Database Form

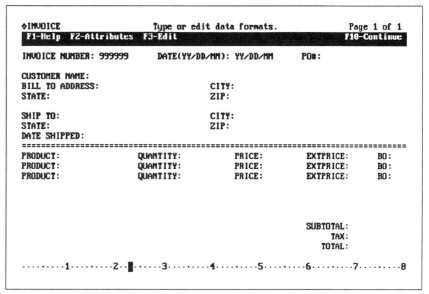

Figure 12-12 The form with two formatted entries

Table 12-3 Numeric Formats

Code	To Print
9	The number (a space if position is not used)
0	The number (a 0 if the position is not used)
#	The number (nothing if the position is not used); Data is left-justified in the field
*	The number (an asterisk if the position is not used)
.	A decimal point
,	A comma
spacebar	A space
+	A plus sign if the number is positive; A minus sign if the number is negative
−	A minus sign if the number is negative; Blank if the number is positive
() or ⟨⟩	Enclose negative number
$	Dollar sign

When using any of the characters above, type in as many characters as there will be numbers and spaces. For instance, if the normal entry is six numbers in a field, type six zeros in the field.

The Text Format

If you need to enter information that requires consistent capitalization and formatting, use the text format. For example, if the field must be typed in all capital letters, specify a text format, and you won't have to worry about pressing Shift or Caps Lock. Just type the entry in lowercase, and Professional File will take care of the rest. Table 12-4 lists the text formats available.

Table 12-4   Text Formats

Code	To Print
A	An uppercase letter
a	A lowercase letter
E or e	Same case as used in record
N or n	A number
X	An uppercase letter or a number
x	A lowercase letter or a number
¦	Left justify when used as leftmost character; Right justify when used as rightmost character
~!@#$%^&*( )-_=+[]\\;:'",<.>/? spacebar	Punctuation marks, symbols, and spaces used as is

Because the N can stand for any number, it can represent common patterns used in entering numbers:

NNN-NN-NNNN	Social Security numbers
(NNN)-NNN-NNNN	Telephone numbers with area code
¦NNNNN-NNNN	Zip codes
NNNNN-NNN	Postal codes

When you're done entering all of your format attributes, press F10 to save them.

Using Formulas

Add formulas to your form before you begin entering data.

If you need to perform a calculation on the numbers in your form, let Professional File do it. Not only will it save you work, but it will also minimize errors that can be introduced by keying the numbers into a calculator and retyping the results. The procedure for creating formulas requires two simple steps:

Creating a Professional File Database Form

- Type an *identifier* in the field that contains the information to be used.
- Type the formula, using the identifiers, in the field where the result of the calculation is to appear.

You may remember that you created a field on the INVOICE form for the extended price. You can add a formula to the form that multiplies the quantity of parts by the price per part and inserts the result directly into the EXTPRICE field:

1. Press F2, opening the Attributes menu.
2. Choose option **5. Edit formulas**. Professional File responds by displaying the Form screen with no attributes.
3. Press the Tab key, moving the cursor to the first QUANTITY field.
4. Type **#Q1** (for quantity 1). The identifier must be preceded by the pound sign (#).
5. Press the Tab key again, positioning the cursor in the first PRICE field.
6. Type **#P1** (for price 1). Your Form screen should resemble Figure 12-13.
7. Press the Tab key to move the cursor to the first EXTPRICE field.
8. Press Ctrl-X to expand the field.
9. Type **#EX1 = #Q1 * #P1** (extended price equals quantity times price). Professional File starts to beep because there is not enough room in the field for the entry.

If you wish, the formula can be in lowercase letters, Professional File makes no distinction as to case. The spaces are important; without them Professional File will not recognize the field identifiers properly. You do not have to extend the field, as there is no field name restricting the entry.

When you have an entry that's too long, you need to expand the field. Here's how:

1. Press F3, to open the Edit menu.
2. Select option **5. Expand field**, opening a screen where you can type the rest of the formula.
3. Finish typing the formula.
4. Press the Tab key to close the window.

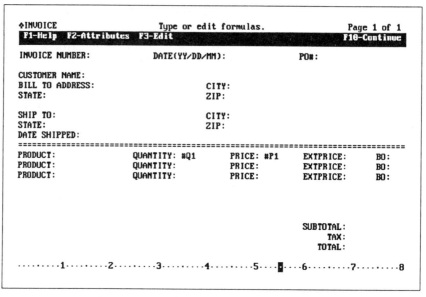

Figure 12-13 The two field identifiers entered

 To expand a field in a hurry, press Ctrl-X.

Now that the beeping is stopped, you can enter the identifiers and formulas for the next two lines:

1. Press the Tab key to move the cursor to the second QUANTITY field.
2. Type #Q2.
3. Press the Tab key.
4. Type #P2.
5. Press the Tab key again, moving to the EXTPRICE field.
6. Before entering the formula, expand the field.
7. Type the formula #EX2 = #Q2 * #P2.

Repeat the identifiers and formula for the third product line, using Q3, P3, and EX3.

Subtotal Formula

Now that you have a total for each part, you need to add the totals and enter the result in the SUBTOTAL field:

1. Press the Tab key to move the cursor to the SUBTOTAL field.
2. Type #ST = #EX1 + #EX2 + #EX3.

This formula will calculate the total of the extended prices.

Using a Conditional Formula

The sales tax calculation is a simple one, except that the state sales tax cannot be charged if the products are to be shipped out of state.

What is needed here is a formula that identifies the destination of the product, and then decides whether the sales tax is to be added to the total. This is called a conditional, or If...Then...Else... formula. The formula says, "If the products in the order are being shipped to Iowa, then calculate and add the sales tax to the subtotal; else, do not. To make it work, you must enter an identifier in the SHIP TO field:

1. Move the cursor to the second STATE field.
2. Type the identifer, #SHIP.
3. Move the cursor to the TAX field.
4. Type the formula: #TX = IF (#SHIP="IA"; #ST*.07; 0)

Here's the model:

    =IF (condition; true expresssion; false expression)

Our formula basically says, "If the entry in the field identified as #SHIP is IA; then the sales tax is equal to #ST (subtotal) times .07 (7%); if the entry in the field is not IA, the sales tax is 0."

A Final Formula

Finally, you need to calculate the total of the invoice. To do so, you need to add the tax to the subtotal. That's easy enough:

1. Move the cursor to the TOTAL field.
2. Type =#ST + #TX.

In this formula, you did not have to create an identifier for the TOTAL field, because the TOTAL is not going to be used as a value for other formulas.

Press F10 to save your work.

Using Field Validations

A validation restricts an entry to a range of values or to a specific value. For example, if you created a form that included a PETTY CASH field, you could use a validation, such as PETTY CASH:<=200, to prevent an entry of over 200 dollars.

You could also specify a range of entries. Suppose you create a job application and your company can hire people only between the ages of 18 and 70. You can enter the following validation in the AGE field to help you check the entry:

```
AGE: NOT(#AGE<18 OR #AGE>70)
```

You can also combine a conditional formula with a validation:

```
AGE: IF(#AGE<18;"NO";"YES")
```

The statement essentially says, "If the entry in the AGE field is less than 18, display "NO" in the AGE field; else, display "YES."

Including Validation Messages

If you type an entry that does not match the validation criteria, Professional File tells you to retype the entry but does not tell you what's wrong with it. To receive more specific feedback from Professional File, you can add a message to your validation. Then, if you type an entry that the validation vetos, the message will appear at the top of the screen telling you why the entry is unacceptable.

For example, you could type a message next to the validation NOT(#AGE<18 OR #AGE>70) to tell you that the entry must be between 18 and 70:

```
AGE: NOT(#AGE<18 OR #AGE>70); "Age must be 18 to 70"
```

Note the addition of the semicolon after the formula, separating the validation and the message, and notice the quotes around the message. Now, if you enter 17 into the AGE field, Professional File automatically displays Age must be 18 to 70 at the top of the screen.

Validation Comments

You can also add comments to your validation to help you remember specific formatting requirements or other information. The comments appear only when you are editing a form and are in the Enter Validation mode. Comments must be enclosed in brackets, as shown in the following example:

```
AGE: NOT(#AGE<18 OR #AGE>70); "Age must be 18 to 70"
{This is the new age range}
```

Remember to press F10 to save any changes.

Summary

Building a form for entering data takes time and requires you to think ahead in order to design a form that works now and *will* work in the future.

Of course, you don't really know that the INVOICE form you created here works. In the next chapter, you will begin entering data, to test the form.

T H I R T E E N

Working with Records

In Chapter 12, you created a form, leaving blanks so data could be entered. In this chapter, you will fill in the blanks to generate a few records, making sure you created a field for every piece of information you need to enter. You will also test the field attributes and formulas you entered, to make sure they function properly. Once you have a few records to work with, you'll get to see how Professional File searches and sorts the records.

Before you use your form to generate hundreds or thousands of records, test it.

Getting the Form

Professional File holds up to 59,000 single-page records, or up to 8 megabytes.

Before you begin entering information, you need to get the form you just created. In order to practice with the examples in this chapter, get the INVOICE form:

1. Choose option **2. Add** from the Main menu shown in Figure 13-1. Professional File displays a screen that lets you specify the file you want to open.
2. If the default path is correct, type the filename and press Enter. For example, type `invoice` and press Enter. If the default path is not correct, press Ctrl-E; then type the path and filename, and press Enter—for example,

    `c:\fdata\invoice`

    In either case, the INVOICE form appears, as shown in Figure 13-2.

Chapter 13

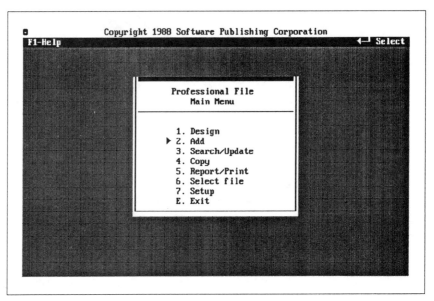

Figure 13-1 The Main menu

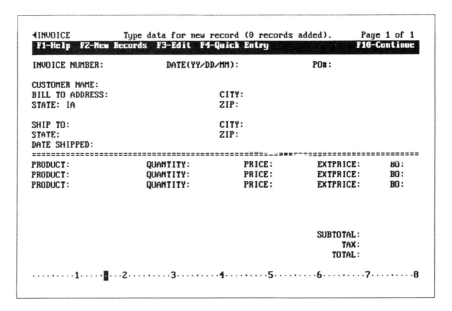

Figure 13-2 The INVOICE form

This screen differs a little from the screen you used to create the form. The screen still has a menu bar, but the menus are different:

Working with Records

Press	To Open
F1	A context-sensitive help screen
F2	The New Records menu, which includes options for searching, printing, and deleting records
F3	The Edit menu, for editing entries
F4	The Quick Entry menu, which offers keystroke savers

Entering Information

Check the entry in the STATE field to make sure it defaulted to IA.

The cursor is positioned in the INVOICE NUMBER field. Remember that we entered a numeric format in this field. Let's see what happens if we try to enter information that does not conform to that format. Type FFFF and press the Tab key. Professional File responds with a screen message above the menu bar, informing you that the entry is incorrectly formatted. See Figure 13-3. The cursor stays where it is, waiting for you to correct the entry.

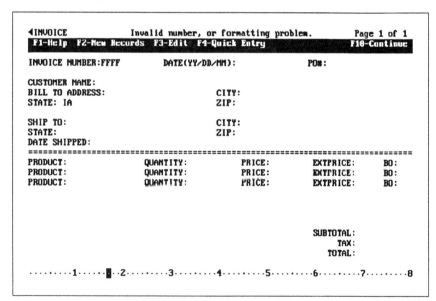

Figure 13-3 The Invalid Entry message screen

Erasing a Field

Since this entire entry is incorrect, erase it and start over. You can erase a field in any of three ways:

Chapter 13

- Press the Backspace key, erasing all of the characters.
- Position the cursor in the field you want to erase, open the Edit menu, and choose option 3. Erase Field.
- Position the cursor in the field you want to erase, and press Ctrl-E.

Erase the entry, using one of the procedures above, then type 1000 and press the Tab key. Professional File accepts this entry and moves the cursor to the DATE field.

Entering a Date

The DATE field also requires a special format, but this format is a little more flexible. As long as you enter something that resembles a date, Professional File accepts the entry and translates it into the required format.

Type Sept 12 1990 and press the Tab key. Professional File accepts the entry and puts it in the specified format: 90/12/9, as shown in Figure 13-4.

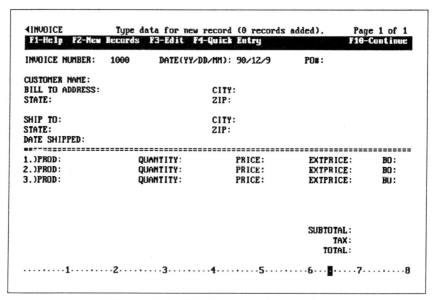

Figure 13-4 The Date entry formatted

Using Quick Entry to Enter Date and Time

If your computer is equipped with a clock, or if you entered the date at startup, Professional File lets you copy the date directly into the DATE field:

Working with Records

1. Press Shift-Tab, moving the cursor back to the DATE field.
2. Press F4, opening the Quick Entry menu.
3. Choose option **5. Enter Date**. Professional File automatically inserts the date into the DATE field in the required format.

To save even more time, move the cursor to the DATE field, and press Ctrl-D to insert the date. To insert the time, press Ctrl-T.

Testing Formulas

Use simple numbers to check your formulas.

In Chapter 12, you entered formulas to calculate total cost. Before you begin entering numbers, test the formulas to make sure they perform the calculations as you intended. Sometimes, you'll notice a problem with the formula simply by looking at the result it determines.

Check the formulas in the INVOICE form:

1. Press the Tab key to move the cursor to the QUANTITY field.
2. Type 10.
3. Press the Tab key, moving the cursor to the PRICE field.
4. Type 20.
5. Press the Tab key, moving the cursor to the EXTPRICE field. The result is displayed, as shown in Figure 13-5.

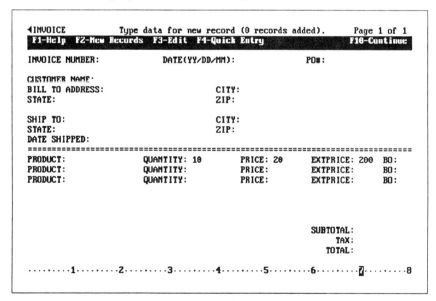

Figure 13-5   The result inserted in the EXTPRICE field

If the answer did not appear as expected, there is probably a flaw in your formula. Check the other fields that have calculations; then return to the Design menu to correct the problem.

Repeat the entries for quantity and price in the next two product lines. When you press Tab after typing a number in the third Price field, Professional File automatically calculates the extended price, subtotal, tax, and total, as shown in Figure 13-6.

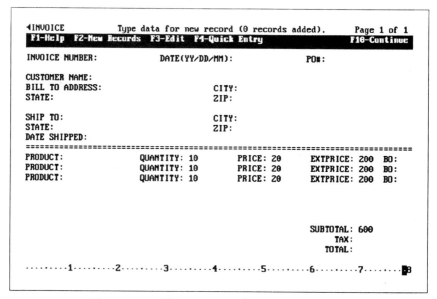

Figure 13-6   The answer in the SUBTOTAL field

Using the Formula Entries to Play What-If

Since the formula fields are interconnected, you can play with the entries to determine the net effect of a change. Say one of your vendors offers a 10% discount on an order of 50 parts or more, and you're filling out an order form for 40 parts. To find out if you would save money ordering more parts, you can change the quantity ordered and have Professional File recalculate the total according to the new entry. To recalculate a single field, perform the following steps:

1. Make the change you want to test.
2. Move the cursor to the field you want to recalculate.
3. Press F2, opening the New Records menu.
4. Choose option 7. Recalculate field. Professional File recalculates using the new entry, and inserts the result.

Working with Records

To recalculate an entire page:

1. Make the change you want to test.
2. Press F2, opening the New Records menu.
3. Choose option **8. Recalculate page**. Professional File recalculates the entire page using the new entry, and inserts the results.

You can bypass the New Records menu. To recalculate a single field, type the change, move the cursor to the field you want to recalculate, and press Ctrl-K. To recalculate a page, type the change and press Ctrl-C. Press Ctrl-C now to complete the calculations for the form.

Checking the Conditional Formula

To make sure the conditional state sales tax formula worked as planned, look at the number in the TAX field. Since you used IA as the default entry in the STATE field, 7% sales tax should have been figured for the subtotal of $600.00; that is, **42.00** should be displayed in the TAX field, as shown in Figure 13-7.

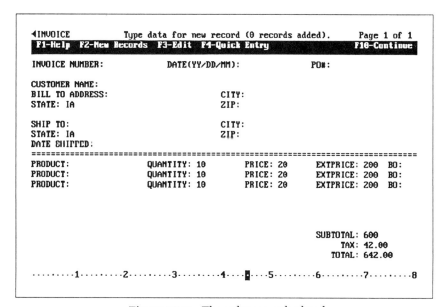

Figure 13-7 The sales tax calculated

To determine if the formula leaves out the state sales tax for other states, move the cursor to the STATE field and type **CA**. Press Ctrl-C,

237

recalculating the page. The TAX field should display 0.00, and nothing should be added to the subtotal. See Figure 13-8.

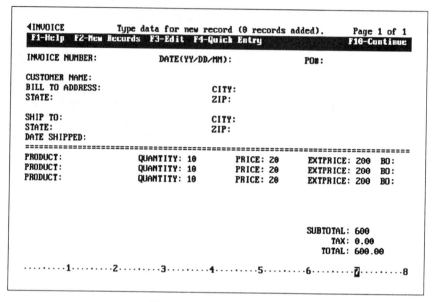

Figure 13-8 No sales tax

Adding Comments

The Attachment screen does not offer fancy formatting or editing features, just a basic means for adding comments.

You may want to add specific comments to a record, such as the name of a contact person or a phone number you can call for service. Such information is not part of the form, but it helps to have the information in a convenient place. With Professional File, you can add these comments to an *Attachment* page at the end of your form:

1. Press the PgDn key until you pass the last page that has field names. The Attachment screen appears, as in Figure 13-9.

2. Type a comment; for example, type Promised customer 10% discount on all orders over 50 parts.

Any information entered in the Attachment screen cannot be used to sort records or to search for a record.

Working with Records

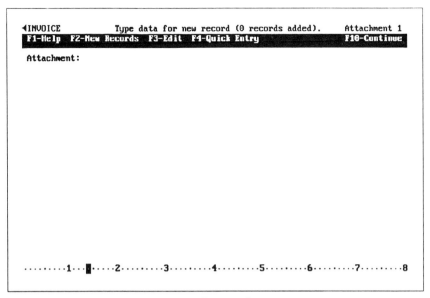

Figure 13-9 The Attachment screen

Modifying the INVOICE Form

After seeing the form, you realize that several changes would make the form more readable. For example, you could format the fields that contain dollar amounts so the dollar sign is displayed. You could also number the product line for each item ordered to keep the items separate. To format the fields, perform the following steps:

1. Press Esc to exit the record. Professional File warns you that the record has not been saved.
2. Press Enter, deleting the entries. This returns you to the Main menu.
3. Choose option 1. Design, opening the Design menu.
4. Choose option 5. Enter/Edit field attributes. Professional File displays a blank INVOICE form.
5. Press the Tab key to move the cursor to the SUBTOTAL field.
6. Type $99999.99 formatting the subtotal entry to display a dollar sign.
7. Press Tab, moving the cursor to the TAX field.
8. Type $9999.99

9. Press Tab, moving the cursor to the TOTAL field.
10. Type **$99999.99**
11. Press F10 to save the new formats.
12. Press Esc, returning to the Design menu.

To add numbers to the product lines:

1. Choose option **3. Change field names**. Professional File displays a warning screen that tells you to make a backup copy of the database before changing a field name.

   Because no records have been entered, this is unnecessary. If you had entered records, you would need to copy them to a floppy disk to keep them safe.

2. Move the cursor to the first PRODUCT field name.
3. Type **1.)PROD** adding a number to this line.
4. Press the Home key and then the Down Arrow key, moving the cursor to the next PRODUCT field name.
5. Type **2.)PROD**
6. Press the Home key and then the Down Arrow key.
7. Type **3.)PROD**. Your form should now look like the one in Figure 13-10.
8. Press F10 to save the changes. Professional File redesigns the database, incorporating the changes.

If you intend to change a field name, copy the database file to a floppy disk. That way, you can restore the original format and information if problems occur.

Creating More Records

After all of the formulas, formats, and validations have been checked, you need to create a few records to see how Professional File works with the database. If the INVOICE form is not on screen, get it:

1. Choose option **2. Add** from the Main menu. Professional File displays a screen that lets you specify the file you want to open.

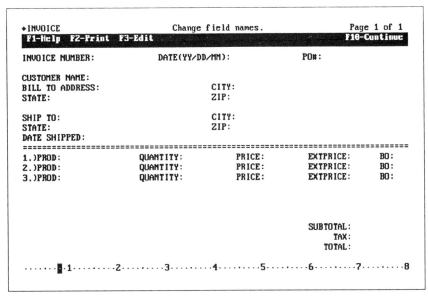

Figure 13-10 The numbered product lines

2. If the default path is correct, type the filename and press Enter. For example, type invoice and press Enter. If not, press Ctrl-E; then type the path and filename, and press Enter—for example,

   c:\fdata\invoice

   In either case, the INVOICE form appears.

Use the Tab key to move the cursor to the next field; press Shift-Tab to move it back.

Now that the INVOICE form is on screen, type the entries as shown in Figure 13-11.

After typing the entries, press F10 to save the record. Professional File presents an empty form, ready to accept entries for the next record. At the top of the screen, Professional File displays the number of records entered, 1.

Quick Entry

One way of saving time during data entry is to copy identical information from previous records. Try it; press Ctrl-F to copy the previous invoice number to this form. 1000 is copied from the previous record into the INVOICE NUMBER field on this form.

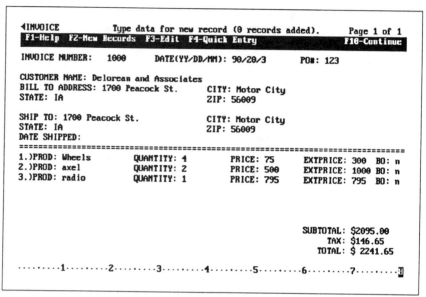

Figure 13-11 Entries for Invoice number 1000

Since you added a unique data entry attribute to this field, Professional File will not let the number be entered. Press Tab to enter the number; Professional File responds with the message, `Another record contains this unique value`. Press Ctrl-E to erase the entry, and type **1001**. Press the Tab key, entering the new number and moving the cursor to the DATE field.

Since there is no unique data entry attribute in the DATE field, press Ctrl-F to copy today's date from the previous record. Press Tab to enter the date and move the cursor to the PO# field.

Referring to the Previous Record

After you refer to a previous record, you can no longer copy entries from the previous record using Quick Entry.

Suppose you want to make sure the purchase order number in this record differs from the one in the previous record. You can refer to the previous record through the New Records menu. Press F2, opening the menu, as shown in Figure 13-12.

Choose option **1. Show previous record**. Professional File displays the previous record. As you can see, the purchase order number is 123. To return to the record you are currently working on, press F10.

Now you can continue typing entries. Type **456** in the PO# field. Then, continue typing the entries as shown in Figure 13-13.

Working with Records

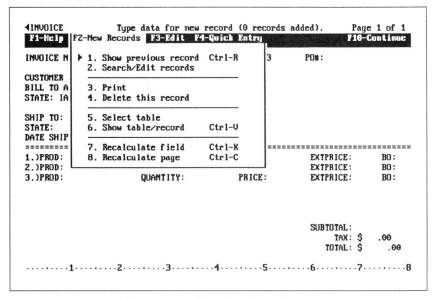

Figure 13-12 The New Records menu

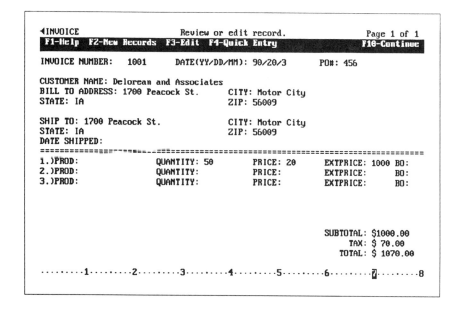

Figure 13-13 Completed record for INVOICE 1001

Chapter 13

Finding Records

Although you have only two records in the sample database, they are sufficient for learning how to use Professional File to find your records. First, you need to access the Search screen:

1. Choose option **3. Search/Update** from the Main menu.
2. Choose option **1. Search/Edit records** from the Search/Update menu. Professional File displays a screen that lets you specify the filename of the form you want.
3. If the default path is correct, type the filename and press Enter. If the default path is not correct, press Ctrl-E; then type the path and filename and press Enter. In either case, Professional File displays the Search/Update menu shown in Figure 13-14.
4. Choose option **1. Search/Edit records**, opening a Search screen that lets you enter search criteria in the various fields. The Search screen is identical to the form you created.

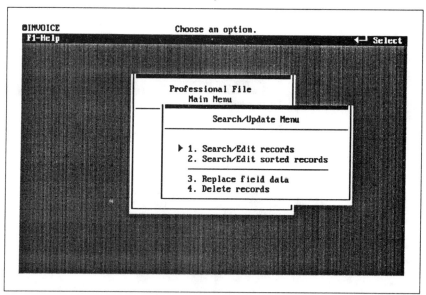

Figure 13-14   The Search/Update menu

At the top of the form is the message `Enter search instructions to find the records.` At this point you have two options. You can either browse (flip through the database record-by-record) or you can enter search criteria that specify which record or group of records you want to find.

Browsing

Use the browse method to make sure the data is being entered correctly; this method is not intended for use in searching through hundreds of records.

Browsing is the most basic way to find a record; you simply flip through the records page-by-page in the order they are stored. Let's browse through your invoice records. First, access the Search screen, but do not enter any search criteria. Then,

1. Press F10 to display the first INVOICE record.
2. Press F10 to see the next record.
3. Press F10 again.

What happened? Since you have only two records entered, Professional File displays the message No next match, as shown in Figure 13-15.

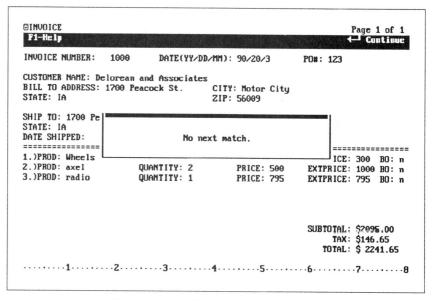

Figure 13-15 The No next match message

Using Search Criteria

The great thing about using a computerized database is that you *don't* have to flip through a stack of pages to find a single record. Professional File can search through the records quickly to find the record or group of records with a specific entry. All you need to do is tell File what to look for; Professional File then searches for one of the following matches:

- Numeric matches
- Character matches
- Date and time matches
- Combination matches
- Partial matches (the wild card)
- Not matches

Numeric Matches

You can use a numeric match to have Professional File match a specified set of numbers to the numbers in a given field. For example, use the numeric match to find the INVOICE record number 1000:

1. In the INVOICE NUMBER field, type =1000.
2. Press F10 to begin the search. Professional File displays the record for invoice number 1000.
3. Press F10 again, and Professional File responds with the **No next match** message.

Professional File switches from the Search mode to the Review or Edit Record mode. It assumes that you have searched for the record for the purpose of looking at it or making changes to it. To exit from this screen, press Esc, returning to the Search/Update menu.

Let's try a different type of numeric match. This time, use an operator symbol to search for records that have an entry greater than 2000 in the TOTAL field:

1. Choose option 1. **Search/Edit records** from the Search/Update menu, reopening the Search screen.
2. Move the cursor to the TOTAL field.
3. Type 2000.
4. Press F10. Professional File finds invoice number 1000. Note that the value entered in the TOTAL field is greater than 2000; $2241.65.
5. Press F10 again, and Professional File responds with the **No next match** message.
6. Press Esc. You are now in the Review or Edit Record mode.

Finding records by using operators is a fast way to find records with a range of entries. The following list sets out the kinds of search criteria you can use and what Professional File will look for.

Search Criteria	Will Find
<1000	999 or less
>50	51 or more
<=50	50 or less
>=50	50 or more
=20->40	20 to 40
=-50->50	-50 to +50

Character Matches

A character match lets you specify field entries that include letters, numbers, and symbols. During the search, Professional File:

- Ignores spaces before and after the entry.
- Considers up to 80 characters as a match.
- Treats upper- and lowercase as identical.

Suppose you want to see the records for all of your customers in Motor City:

1. Choose option `1. Search/Edit records` from the Search/Update menu, reopening the Search screen.
2. Move the cursor to the CITY field of the billing address.
3. Type `Motor City`.
4. Press F10 to start the search. Professional File displays invoice number 1001 first.
5. Press F10 again, and invoice number 1000 is displayed.

Partial Matches

So far, you've known exactly what you wanted Professional File to find. Many times, however, you won't know the exact spelling of an entry, or you'll only remember part of the entry. In such cases, you can use wild cards to have Professional File find a partial match. If you happen to play poker, you understand that a wild card can be used to take the place of any card you need. Here, a wild card can be used for any character except a blank.

Professional File offers two characters that can be used for wild card entries. The first wild card, the question mark (?), has a very specific role; it can substitute for a single letter only:

Search Criteria	Will Find	Will Not Find
?age	page, sage	mortgage
?ook	book, took	shook
?ook?	books, looks	bookend

A second wild card, two periods (..), serves a much more general purpose. This wild card comes in handy when you're not sure how many characters are missing. Simply type whatever portion of an entry you're sure of, and use the two periods to fill in the blank.

Search Criteria	Will Find	Will Not Find
..SMITH	SMITH, JOHN SMITH	SMITHSON
SMITH..	SMITHSON	JOHN SMITH
..SMITH..	JOHN SMITH, SMITHSON	JONES

Instead of browsing through your records when you're not sure what to look for, use the partial match to narrow your search.

As with numeric entries, you can use a math operator to search for a range of records. When searching for a range, keep in mind that Professional File sorts symbols before numbers and numbers before letters. The following list shows how the math operator can be used:

Search Criteria	Will Find
K-⟩W	Words beginning with K through W, but not A through J
Th-⟩To	Words beginning with Th through To
..-⟩1	Words starting with numbers or symbols, but not letters
..-⟩B	Words starting with A through B or numbers

Date or Time Matches

Format your DATE and TIME fields to help Professional File perform the search more quickly.

You can search your records for an exact date and time match, for a range of dates, or for a combination of dates and times. Suppose you entered several records in March of 1990, and you're receiving complaints about prices that were quoted in those records. You can have Professional File find the March records. Let's see how this search works on the INVOICE records:

1. Choose option 1. Search/Edit records from the Search/Update menu, reopening the Search screen.
2. Press the Tab key to move the cursor to the DATE field.
3. Type =90/../3.
4. Press F10. Professional File finds and displays invoice number 1001.
5. Press F10 again. Invoice number 1001 is displayed, because it too was entered in March of 1990.

Ranges work for times and dates, too:

Search Criteria	Will Find
⟨3/16/90	Any date prior to March 16, 1990; no dates after March 16, 1990
⟨12:00 AM	Any time earlier than midnight
⟨=12:00 AM	Midnight or any time earlier than midnight
=3/16/1990-⟩3/31/1990	Any record from March 16 to 31
=1:00-⟩5:00	Any record within the time period 1:00 to 5:00

Combination Matches

You can combine search criteria to broaden the scope of your search. Simply separate the criteria with a semicolon; Professional File reads the semicolon as "or." For example, to find all records with Motor City or Detroit, move the cursor to the CITY field and type Motor City;Detroit. You can use wild cards or math operators to further manipulate the search criteria.

Not-a-Match

Use not-a-match to find every record except the records you specify. The following list contains examples that illustrate how not-a-match works:

Search Criteria	Will Find
/=50	Any number *except* 50
/a..	Words that begin with any number, and any symbol or letter *except* "a"
/=90/20/3-⟩90/31/3	Any dates *not* between March 20, 1990 and March 31, 1990
/12:00AM	Any time that is *not* midnight

Sorting Records

You may encounter a situation in which you need to review a range of records in a particular sequence. For example, you may notice that a piece of information was incorrectly entered, and you need to determine when the error was introduced. You can use Professional File's Sort feature to sort the records in whatever order you specify. To review your records in a specified sequence,

1. Choose option **2. Search/Edit sorted records** from the Search/Update menu. Professional File displays a Sort screen very similar to the Search screen.
2. Press the Tab key to move the cursor to the field you want to sort first.
3. Type 1.
4. Move the cursor to the field you want to sort second.
5. Type 2. You can continue this process to sort up to 64 fields.

If you enter only a number in the field, Professional File sorts the records according to the following default order: blank records first, symbols next, numbers, then letters—all in ascending order.

According to the Sort entries in Figure 13-16, Professional File will sort the records according to the invoice number first. The "A" next to "1" indicates ascending order. The second sort is by date; this too will be sorted in ascending order.

You may not use the sort feature much during editing, but it will come in handy during the printing stage.

You can change the default sort order easily. Simply type the required code after the sort order number:

- To sort in numerical order, type n after the number, for example, type 1n.
- To sort in descending order, type d.
- To sort in numerical descending order, type nd.

Editing a Record

Once Professional File finds a record, it switches from Search mode to Edit mode. This allows you to edit individual records. Simply press the Tab key to move the cursor to the field you want to edit, and press F3 to open the Edit menu. Choose an item from the menu or use the shortcut keys to complete the edit.

Working with Records

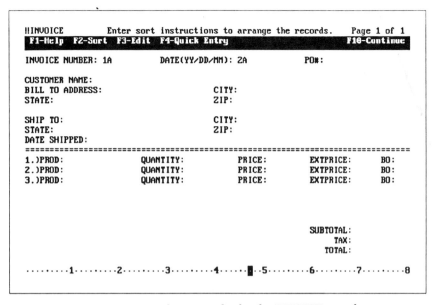

Figure 13-16 The sort order for the INVOICE records

Editing Several Records at Once

You may encounter a situation in which you need to make the same change in several records. For example, you may need to change the area code for all phone numbers in a particular city. Finding each record and entering the change could take a lot of time, even if you used search criteria. To simplify the process, Professional File lets you edit several records at once.

1. Choose option 3. Replace field data from the Search/Update menu. Professional File displays the form with the message Enter instructions to replace field data.

2. Move the cursor to the field you want to replace.

3. Type the new entry. (To erase the data in a field, type /.)

4. Press F10. Professional File displays the Search screen.

5. Enter the search criteria as explained in the previous sections. (To change all records, make no entry in the Search screen.)

6. Press F10. A warning screen appears, telling you that you are about to overwrite data.

7. Press Enter, starting the replacement.

Chapter 13

Deleting a Group of Records

In addition to letting you edit groups of records, Professional File lets you delete several records at once. The process is simple, but it includes a built-in safeguard to prevent accidental erasure of important information.

1. Choose option 4. Delete records from the Search/Update menu. Professional File displays the Search screen.
2. Enter search criteria as described in the previous sections. (If you want to delete all records in your database—be careful—do not enter criteria.)
3. Press F10. Professional File gives you one last chance before proceeding.
4. If you're sure you want to delete the specified records, press Enter. If not, press Esc.

Before deleting a group of records, make a backup copy of the database, just in case.

Summary

In this chapter, you learned how to create and edit records, find a specific record or group of records, and sort your records according to any of several criteria. In short, you have all the information you need to create and work with your database.

In the next chapter, you will learn how to lay out your data in a table format.

F O U R T E E N

Using Data Tables

In Chapters 12 and 13, you learned to enter and change information in your database through the use of forms. That's fine if you're working with a single record, but if you need to review and edit the same information in several records, the forms become difficult to manage.

To help deal with this problem, Professional File offers a feature that lets you display data from several records in a table. The table is set up like a spreadsheet; each column head represents a field name from the form, and each row represents the information from a single record. The column and row intersect to form an imaginary box that contains a single field entry.

In the table format, field entries for several records are on screen at the same time, letting you cross-check and edit information quickly.

When to Use a Table

The table is an excellent tool for narrowing the scope of your work. You can include only the fields you want to review in the order you want to review them, saving you the time it takes to search for a field on your form.

For example, you may receive a list of shipping dates from your warehouse, and you need to enter these dates in your invoice records. To simplify the process, you could create a two-column table with the invoice numbers in one column and the shipping dates in the other. If several of the dates are the same, you can use Quick Entry to save even more time.

You can also use a table if you need to type entries in two or more fields that are far apart on the form. If you tried to type the entries on the form, you would need to press the Tab key several times to move to the next field. With the table, however, you can put the fields in adjacent columns.

Creating a Table

Creating a table consists of copying field names from a form to the table format. Before you begin, however, you need to open a Table Design screen:

1. Choose option **1. Design** from the Main menu, opening the Design menu shown in Figure 14-1.
2. Choose option **4. Create/Edit table instructions**. Professional File displays a screen that lets you specify the file you want to open.
3. If the default path is correct, type the filename and press Enter. For example, type **invoice** and press Enter. If not, press Ctrl-E; then type the path and filename, and press Enter—for example,

   c:\fdata\invoice

   If you can't remember the filename, simply type the path and press Enter to see the directory listing. Then, highlight the file you want and press Enter.

   In any case, the blank INVOICE form appears, just as if you were going to enter a new record or search criteria. The only difference is that the top of the screen shows the message **Enter instructions for creating a table**.

Designing the Table

Now that the INVOICE form is on screen, you can begin entering instructions concerning the layout of the table. Two basic instructions must be entered:

- Order of the columns
- Width of the columns

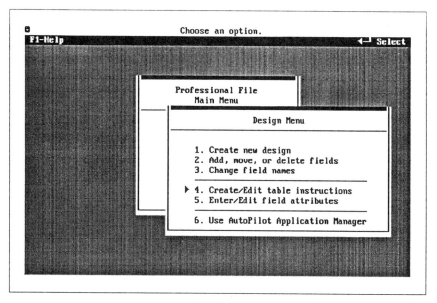

Figure 14-1 The Design menu

All field names in a table must come from the same page of the form; you cannot include a field name from page 1 and another from page 3.

Type numbers in the fields in the order you want them to appear in the table. For example, type 1 in the INVOICE NUMBER field to have the leftmost column head be INVOICE NUMBER. The column head appears exactly as it does on the form; you can modify the column heads later.

Unless you specify otherwise, Professional File creates columns that are just as wide as the fields on the form. If you want to specify a different width, type w and the number of characters wide you wish the column to be. For example, to create a column that's 24 characters wide, type w24.

A column can be no wider than 79 characters and no wider than the field on the form screen.

In the following example, you will create a table for the INVOICE database. The table will consist of three headings: DATE, CUSTOMER NAME, and TOTAL. You can use such a table to determine when sales peaks occur, so you can stock your inventory in advance. With the INVOICE form on screen, make DATE the first column head:

Professional File lets you use up to 64 fields in a table.

1. Press the Tab key to move the cursor to the DATE field.
2. Type **1w15**. (You must specify the width, because the formatted field is only eight characters wide, whereas the field name—DATE(YY/DD/MM):—is fifteen characters wide.)
3. Press the Tab key until the cursor is in the CUSTOMER NAME field.

Chapter 14

4. Type 2.
5. Press the Tab key several times, moving the cursor to the TOTAL field.
6. Type 3.

Saving Your Design

When you're satisfied with the instructions you entered in the Design screen, you're ready to save the design. Press F2 to open the Table menu shown in Figure 14-2. Take a quick look at the options on this menu:

Get Instructions: If you designed a table in the past and saved the instructions you used to design the table, this option lets you retrieve those instructions so you can recreate the table.

Save Instructions: After designing your table, you can choose this option to save the instructions.

Print Instructions: Choose this option to create a printout of your design instructions.

Delete Instructions: This option lets you delete your instructions from all the fields on the design screen.

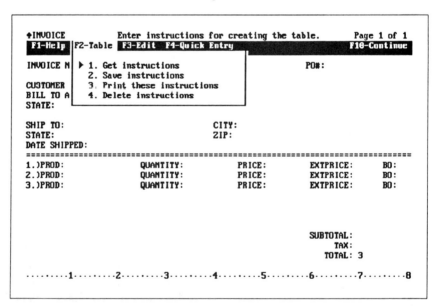

Figure 14-2 The Table menu

Using Data Tables

You can bypass the Table menu; when you're ready to save your design, press F10, then type a name for the file.

To save the instructions you just entered,

1. Choose option 2. Save instructions. Professional File displays an Instructions screen that lets you name the instructions.
2. Type a name (up to 10 characters). For example, type invtable as shown in Figure 14-3.
3. Press Enter to save the instructions and return to the Design menu.

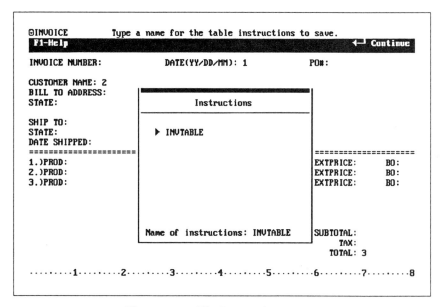

Figure 14-3 The Instructions screen

Viewing Data in the Table

With a large database, consider sorting the records before viewing the table.

Professional File does not allow you to proceed directly from creating the table instructions to displaying a table. You must go back to the Main menu:

1. Press Esc twice, returning to the Main menu.
2. Choose option 2. Add. Professional File displays the Add Record Form screen.
3. Press F2 to open the New Records menu.
4. Choose option 6. Show table/record. Professional File displays a list of previously saved table instructions.

5. Use the arrow keys to move the highlight to the instructions you want, and press Enter. Professional File displays the table.

 Use the shortcut keys Ctrl-V to bypass the New Records menu. Professional File displays the list of available instructions.

The table for the INVOICE form is shown in Figure 14-4. The field names are inserted across the top of the form, and the information from the two INVOICE records is displayed in the columns.

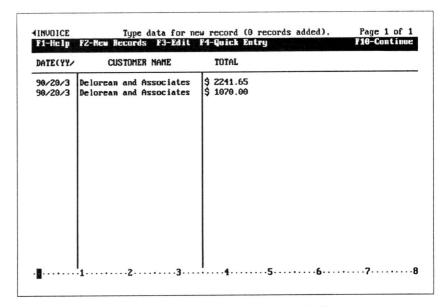

Figure 14-4 The table for the INVOICE form

Notice that the name of the table, INVTABLE, is not displayed in the upper left-hand corner of the screen; the name of the database, INVOICE, is shown. You can now begin moving the cursor from column to column to enter new data into the table.

Moving the Cursor in the Table

The Tab key operates the same as it does in the form; pressing Tab moves the cursor from one column to the next. Shift-Tab moves the cursor back one column. Other cursor movement keys are listed in Table 14-1.

Using Data Tables

Table 14-1   Cursor Movement Keys for the Table

Key	Cursor Movement
Home	First column in current row
Ctrl-Home	First entry in current column
End	Last column in current row
Ctrl-End	Last entry in current column
PgDn	Next screen of text
PgUp	Previous screen of text
Right Arrow	One space to right
Left Arrow	One space to left
Down Arrow	One line down
Up Arrow	One line up

Using the Table to Enter Data

On the Table screen you can see entries for the previous record, making Quick Entry a more viable option.

Now that you know how to move the cursor from one column to the next, try adding a record to see the effect on the database:

1. Move the cursor to the DATE column.
2. Type 90/20/1.
3. Move the cursor to the CUSTOMER NAME column.
4. Press Ctrl-F, copying "Delorean and Associates" from the previous record.
5. Move the cursor to the TOTAL column.
6. Type 4200.
7. To see the new entries in the INVOICE form, press Ctrl-V. Professional File displays the new record in the Form screen.
8. Press Ctrl-V again, returning to the Table screen.
9. Press F10 to save the new entries.

If your form has a validation formula that requires you to type an entry before you can save the record, be sure to include the field with the validation formula in your table. Otherwise, when you try to save a new record, Professional File opens the Form screen and waits until you type the entry.

Viewing the Table from Search/Update

You can use Professional File's Search feature together with the Table screen to view entries from a specified range of records. Here's how:

1. Choose option `3. Search/Update` from the Main menu, opening the Search/Update menu.
2. Choose option `1. Search/Edit records`. Professional File displays a screen that lets you specify the file you want to open.
3. If the default path is correct, type the filename and press Enter. For example, type `invoice` and press Enter. If not, press Ctrl-E; then type the path and filename, and press Enter—for example,

   `c:\fdata\invoice`

   In either case, the Search screen appears.
4. Enter search criteria as explained in Chapter 13.
5. Press F10 to conduct the search. Professional File displays the first record it finds.
6. Press F2 to open the New Records menu.
7. Choose option `5. Select table`. Professional File displays the list of available table instructions.
8. Move the highlight to INVTABLE and press Enter.
9. Professional File displays the table, including only those records specified in the search instructions.

Modifying Table Instructions

You can modify a set of table instructions at any time. Simply perform the following steps:

1. Choose option `1. Design` from the Main menu to open the Design menu.
2. Choose option `4. Create/Edit table instructions`. Professional File displays a screen that lets you specify the file you want to open.

3. If the default path is correct, type the filename and press Enter. For example, type `invoice` and press Enter. If not, press Ctrl-E; then type the path and filename, and press Enter—for example,

   `c:\fdata\invoice`

   Professional File displays the Table Design screen.
4. Press F2 to open the Table menu.
5. Choose option `1. Get instructions`. Professional File displays a list of available instructions.
6. Highlight the instructions you want to modify, and press Enter. Professional File displays the instructions.
7. Make whatever changes are necessary to the instructions.
8. Press F10 to save the changes. Professional File warns that you are changing the instruction set.
9. Press Enter to proceed with the modification. The new set of instructions is saved under the old name.

Printing a Table

If you need a printout of the table to send to your boss or to include in a report, you can print the entire table or a portion of it. If the records listed are the ones you want to print, you're ready to begin:

1. Move the cursor to the first record that you want to print. Professional File will print the records from this point on.
2. Press F2 to open the New Records menu.
3. Choose option `3. Print`. The Printing Options for Table screen appears, as shown in Figure 14-5.
4. Make sure the option choices are correct for your printing job. If they're not, use the Tab key to move the cursor to the option you want to change, and type the correction.
5. Press Enter, opening an abbreviated Printer Options screen.
6. Enter any required changes, and press Enter. Professional File prints the records as a table.

An interesting feature of the Printing Options for Table screen is that it lets you enter a header or footer for your table.

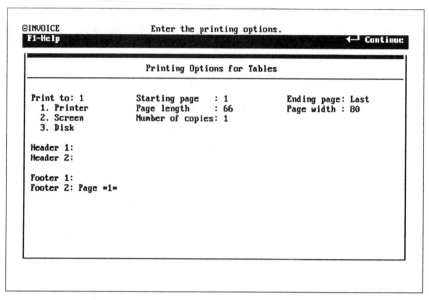

Figure 14-5 The Printing Options for Tables screen

After Professional File finishes printing your table, it returns you to the Table screen. The cursor is on the last record printed.

Summary

In this chapter, you learned to use the Table screen to view the information from several records at once. You can use the tables to track down errors and to see patterns or trends. You also learned to use tables with Quick Entry in order to copy information from one record to the next at the touch of a key. And you learned how to print your table or a section of it for use elsewhere.

The table can be a real time-saver when you're faced with the task of entering lists of data into your database. In the next chapter, you'll learn how to use macros with your database to save even more time.

FIFTEEN

Using Macros in Data Entry

Chapter 11 contains a thorough discussion of using macros as applied to word processing tasks. Macros operate no differently in the database; they are still short programs that can be executed through a two-key combination. The purpose of this chapter is to show how macros can be applied to the Professional File database.

Creating a Macro

You can create a macro at any point in Professional File. You simply tell Professional File to begin recording your keystrokes. When you're finished performing your task, save the record of your keystrokes and assign a two-key combination to the record. Whenever you want to perform the same task, just press the two keys. To begin:

1. Position the cursor where you want the macro to start. (You can even start from the Main menu.)
2. Choose option 7. Use macros from the Edit menu, or press Alt-0. This opens the Macro menu shown in Figure 15-1.
3. Choose option 2. Record a macro. Professional File displays a message screen, telling you that recording is in progress.
4. Press Enter, to return to the working copy. From this point on, Professional File records your keystrokes.

Chapter 15

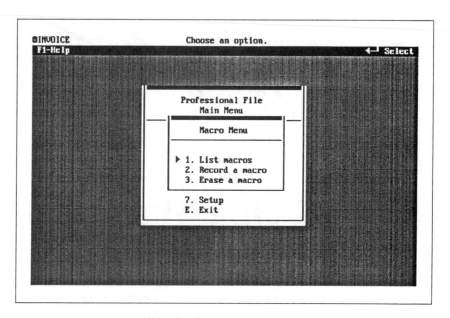

Figure 15-1 The Macro menu

Perform the task you want to record (up to forty keystrokes). For example, if you are creating a form, you can type an entire line of field names that you intend to repeat several times. You can also create a macro for typing field entries. If you need to repeat a long entry several times, record it as a macro. When you're finished, save and name your macro:

1. Press Alt-0, opening the Recording Options menu, as shown in Figure 15-2.

2. Choose option 2. End and save recorded keystrokes. Professional File responds with the Macro Definitions menu, as shown in Figure 15-3. This menu lists all of the keystrokes available for your macros. The keystrokes consist of Alt and a letter, or Alt and a number from 1 to 9. Use the PgDn key to see more of the menu.

3. Press the Up or Down Arrow key to highlight the keystroke you want to use. It's a good idea to choose a keystroke that reminds you of the task you want the macro to perform.

If you choose a keystroke that is already in use, Professional File overwrites the previous macro.

4. Type a brief description of the macro (up to twenty characters); for example, type Insert Line. The description serves a dual purpose: it helps you remember what the keystroke is used for, and it shows you that the keystroke is assigned to a macro.

5. Press Enter, assigning the keystroke combination to your macro.

Using Macros in Data Entry

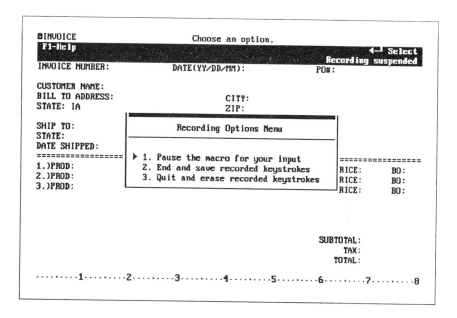

Figure 15-2 The Recording Options menu

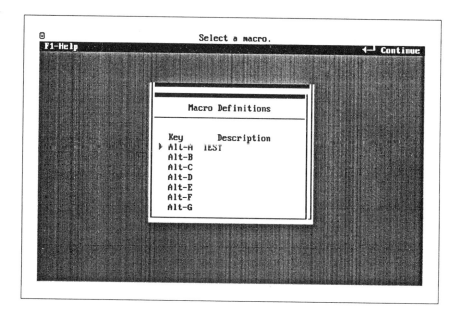

Figure 15-3 The Macro Defintions menu

The Get Database Macro

If you work on one database frequently, you may find that performing all the steps required to access that database is time consuming. You can use a macro to perform the required steps automatically. First, exit Professional File, then type pf restarting it. Then,

1. At the Main menu, press Alt-0 to open the Macro menu.
2. Choose option 2. Record a macro.
3. Press Enter. Professional File displays the Recording macro in the upper right corner of the screen.
4. Type 2, choosing Add from the Main menu. Professional File displays a screen that lets you specify the file you want to open.
5. If the default path is correct, type the filename and press Enter. For example, type invoice and press Enter. If not, press Ctrl-E; then type the path and filename, and press Enter—for example,

    c:\fdata\invoice

    This opens the Form screen for the specified form.
6. This is all you want the macro to do, so press Alt-0, opening the Recording Options menu.
7. Choose option 2. End and save recorded keystrokes. Professional File responds with the Save Recorded Keystrokes menu.
8. Use the PgDn key to see more of the menu.
9. Press the Up or Down Arrow key to highlight the key you want to use, and press Enter.
10. Type a brief description of the macro (up to twenty characters); for example, type Invoice.
11. Press Enter, assigning the keystroke combination to your macro.

Be sure to start playing back your macro at the same point you started creating it.

Now, whenever you want to access the INVOICE database, just start up Professional File and press Alt-I. For example, since you restarted Professional File before creating the macro, you could use the macro only after the initial startup.

The Merge Write and File Macro

If you have Professional Write and you want to insert information from your Professional File database into a letter you created using Professional Write, you can create a macro to eliminate some of the steps.

First, use Professional Write to create the form letter you want to use. You don't have to worry about making the field names in the form letter identical to those in the database. Save the letter as LETTER, and exit from Professional Write. Type pw, restarting Professional Write. Choose option 1. Create/Edit from the Main menu. Now you're ready to begin:

1. Press Alt-0, opening the Macros menu.
2. Choose option 2. Record a macro. Professional Write displays a message screen telling you that recording is in progress.
3. Press Enter, to return to the working copy.
4. Press F2 to open the File/Print menu.
5. Type 1, choosing option 1. Get file.
6. Press Ctrl-E and type the path and filename of the form letter.
7. Press Enter to get the form letter.
8. Press F2, opening the File/Print menu.
9. Type 5 choosing the Print Working Copy option. Professional Write displays the Print Options screen.
10. Press Tab, to move the cursor to Data file to merge:.
11. Type the path and directory of the Professional File database that contains the information you need.
12. Enter any other changes to the Print Options screen as required, and press Enter. Professional Write displays a Search screen.

Since you may want to search for a different letter or group of letters each time you want to use this merge macro, pause the macro here:

1. Press Alt-0, reopening the Recording Options menu.
2. Type 1, choosing option 1. Pause macro for your input, and press Enter.
3. Enter your search criteria, and press F10. Professional File displays a Sort and Identifier screen.
4. Enter your sort instructions. If you used a field name in your form letter that differs from the one in your database, type a semicolon after the sort instruction, and type the field name as it appears in your form letter.
5. Press F10. Professional File displays a Format screen.
6. Enter formatting instructions in any field you want formatted differently from the format in your database, and press F10.

Professional Write begins printing your form letters. When the printing is stopped, you're ready to save and name your macro:

1. Press F9 to resume recording your keystrokes.
2. Press Alt-0, opening the Recording Options screen.
3. Choose option 2. End and save recorded keystrokes, opening the Save Recorded Keystrokes menu. Use the PgDn key to see more of the menu.
4. Press the Up or Down Arrow key to highlight the keystroke you want to use; Alt-L may be a good one.
5. Type a brief description of the macro (up to twenty characters); for example, type Form letter.
6. Press Enter, assigning the keystroke combination to your macro.

To replay this macro, start with a clear Working Copy screen in Professional Write. Then, simply press Alt-L to start the macro. The macro will pause for you to enter search, sort, identifier, and format instructions, and then it will begin printing.

The Print Mailing Labels Macro

Suppose you print mailing labels for different records on a regular basis. The process could get a little tedious after a while. To save you some work, consider creating a macro within Professional File to perform some of those steps:

1. At the Main menu, press Alt-0 to open the Macro menu.
2. Choose option 2. Record a macro.
3. Press Enter. Professional File displays the Recording macro in the upper right corner of the screen.
4. Type 5, choosing option 5. Report/Print from the Main menu. This opens the Report/Print menu.
5. Type 5, choosing option 5. Print labels/selected fields. Professional File displays a screen that lets you specify the file you want to open.
6. If the default path is correct, type the filename and press Enter. For example, type invoice and press Enter. If not, press Ctrl-E; then type the path and filename—for example, c:\fdata\invoice—and press Enter.

Professional File diplays the INVOICE form. At the top of the screen is the message Enter instructions for printing mailing labels.

Using Macros in Data Entry

7. Type a field entry in each field you want to print on the mailing label. Refer to Table 16-1 in Chapter 16 for a list of field entries. For example, type an x in the CUSTOMER NAME and BILL TO ADDRESS fields, type + in the CITY and STATE fields, and type x 1 in the ZIP field.
8. Press F10, saving the label design and displaying the Search screen.
9. Press Alt-0, reopening the Recording Options menu.
10. Type 1, choosing option 1. Pause macro for your input and press Enter.
11. Enter your search criteria and press F10. Professional File opens the Printing Options for Mailing Labels screen.
12. Press F9, to resume recording of your keystrokes.
13. Change any of the settings on the Printing Options screen as required, and press Enter. Professional File displays an abbreviated Printer Options screen.
14. Change any settings as required, and press Enter.

Professional File begins printing your form letters. When the printing is stopped, you're ready to save and name your macro:

1. Press Alt-0, opening the Recording Options screen.
2. Choose option 2. End and save recorded keystrokes, opening the Save Recorded Keystrokes menu. Use the PgDn key to see more of the menu.
3. Press the Up or Down Arrow key to highlight the keystroke you want to use; Alt-M may be a good one. Press Enter.
4. Type a brief description of the macro (up to twenty characters); for example, type Mailing Label.
5. Press Enter, assigning the keystroke combination to your macro.

To replay this macro, start at the Main menu. Then, simply press Alt-M to start the macro. The macro will pause for you to enter search instructions, and then it will begin printing your labels automatically.

Summary

As you gain experience, you will begin to notice yourself performing several time-consuming tasks on a regular basis. You will notice lines of field names that you need to repeat and common entries that you're getting tired of retyping. With macros, you can do away with some of the drudgery of data entry, and save time in the process. The key to learning macros is to experiment; creating them may take some time at first, but you'll save time in the long run.

S I X T E E N

Printing Records and Reports

If you have Professional Write, refer to Chapter 10 for a detailed discussion of using Professional Write and File together to create form letters.

Up to this point, you've been concerned with creating the Professional File database. You've learned how to fill this vast storage tank with raw information. This chapter teaches you how to use that raw data in more practical, meaningful applications. You'll learn to use your field entries to print forms, lists, and mailing labels. You will even learn to use your database to analyze information.

Printing Records

It is important to differentiate between records and reports. A record consists of all the entries on a single form. A report, on the other hand, uses information from several records. Professional File offers three basic ways to print records:

- As they appear in record form
- On mailing labels
- On preprinted business forms, such as a bill of lading or a bank statement

Throughout this chapter, you'll see that even though Professional File offers only a few basic printing options, these options are flexible enough to handle just about any printing job you'll encounter.

Chapter 16

Printing a Record as a Form

The easiest way to print a record is to print it as it appears on the computer screen. You just specify which records you want to print, and the order in which you want to print them. Professional File takes care of the rest. Let's print a record from the INVOICE database. First, display the INVOICE form:

1. Choose option `5. Report/Print` from the Main menu. This opens the Report/Print menu shown in Figure 16-1.
2. Choose option `4. Print records`. Professional File displays a screen that lets you specify the file you want to open.
3. If the default path is correct, type the filename and press Enter. For example, type `invoice` and press Enter. If the default path is not correct, press Ctrl-E; then type the path and filename, and press Enter—for example,

   `c:\fdata\invoice`

   If you can't remember the filename, simply type the path and press Enter to see the directory listing. Then, highlight the file you want and press Enter. In any case, Professional File displays the INVOICE form.

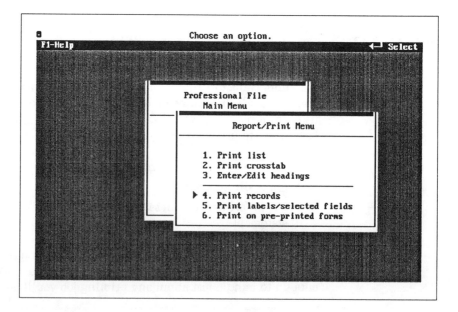

Figure 16-1 The Report/Print menu

You can enter sorting instructions in up to 64 fields, but three or four is usually sufficient.

NOTE

At the top of the INVOICE screen is the message `Enter sort instructions for printing specific records.` Enter sorting instructions in each field you want to sort. For example, type 1 in the INVOICE NUMBER field and 2 in the PO# field, so Professional File will sort the records first according to invoice number and second according to purchase order number.

Sorting is a little unnecessary here, since the database contains only two records. If you were working with a large database, however, the sorting would come in handy. Refer to Chapter 13 for more information on sorting records.

To save the sorting instructions for future use, press F2 to open the Sort menu and choose option `2. Save instructions` and type a name for the instructions. (This step is optional.) Later, when you want to reuse the instructions, choose the first option `Get instructions` from the Sort menu. Now, enter your sorting instructions and any search instructions you want to include:

1. Press F10, entering the sort instructions and displaying the Search screen. This Search screen is identical to the one used in Chapter 13.
2. Enter your search instructions on the Search screen. To print all the records in your database, make no entries.
3. Press F10, entering the search instructions and opening the Printing Options for Records as Displayed screen. See Figure 16-2.

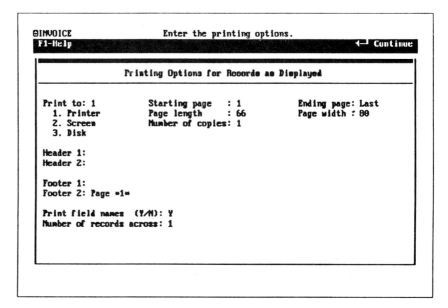

Figure 16-2 The Printing Options for Records as Displayed screen

Printing Options for Records

The first option asks you to specify where to print the records. If you're unsure of which records your search instructions will find or how your sort instructions will work, type 2 to print the records to the screen. This lets you preview the output before printing.

Alternatively, you can type 3 to print the records to disk. Use this setting if you want to send the records via modem, or import the records into a Lotus 1-2-3 spreadsheet.

The second option lets you specify on which page you want to begin and end printing. For example, if you have already printed a multipage report and you edit an entry on a single page of the report, this option lets you print only the edited page.

Adding an optional header or footer to a report is always a good idea. You can add a header to indicate the purpose and scope of the report. If you wish, you can specify a footer, but you're pretty safe accepting the default page number entry.

The next option lets you omit the field names in cases where the column headings are obvious. Be careful, however; omitting field names can make interpretting the data difficult. In general, you'll want to keep field names as column heads.

Finally, the Print Options screen lets you specify how many records you want printed across the page. Unless your record is very narrow, stick with the default choice of 1.

When you're satisfied with the settings on the Print Options screen, press Enter. This opens an abbreviated Printer Options screen. Change any of the settings as required, and press Enter to start printing.

Printing Mailing Labels

Mailing labels can be printed in much the same way as the records were in the previous example. The difference is that a mailing label uses the information from only a few fields in the record. If you used Professional Write's Address Book to print mailing labels, the following steps will look familiar:

1. Choose option `5. Report/Print` from the Main menu. This opens the Report/Print menu.

2. Choose option `5. Print labels/selected fields`. Professional File displays a screen that lets you specify the file you want to open.

3. If the default path is correct, type the filename and press Enter. If not, press Ctrl-E; then type the path and filename and press Enter.

Professional File diplays the INVOICE form. At the top of the screen is the message `Enter instructions for printing mailing labels`.

4. Type a field entry in each field you want to print on the mailing label. Table 16-1 provides a list of possible entries. For example, type an x in the CUSTOMER NAME and BILL TO ADDRESS fields, type + in the CITY and STATE fields, and type x 1 in the ZIP field, so Professional File will sort the records by zip code and print the labels in order. See Figure 16-3.
5. Press F10, saving the label design and displaying the Search screen.
6. Enter your search instructions on the Search screen. To print all the records in your database, make no entries.
7. Press F10, opening the Printing Options for Mailing Labels screen.

Table 16-1 Field Entries for Mailing Labels

Entry	Result
x	Print field and move to the next line on the label.
+	Print field, skip two spaces, and print the next designated field on the same line of the label.
1,2	Sort field: first order, second order, etc. This entry can be as great as 64.
n	Sort field numerically.
d	Sort field in descending order.
@1, @2, @3	This entry determines the order for printing fields.

Printing Options for Mailing Labels

After you save your label design, Professional File displays a screen that lets you set the print options. See Figure 16-4. You should be concerned with the following options:

- Label length
- Label width
- Print field names (Y/N)
- Number of records across

Use the Tab key to move the cursor from one field to the next. Press Shift-Tab to move to the previous field.

Chapter 16

```
@INVOICE        Enter instructions for printing mailing labels.   Page 1 of 1
F1-Help  F2-Label  F3-Edit  F4-Quick Entry                        F10-Continue
INVOICE NUMBER:          DATE(YY/DD/MM):            PO#:

CUSTOMER NAME: x
BILL TO ADDRESS: x
STATE: +                 CITY: +
                         ZIP: x 1

SHIP TO:                 CITY:
STATE:                   ZIP:
DATE SHIPPED:
==============================================================================
1.)PROD:      QUANTITY:         PRICE:         EXTPRICE:      BO:
2.)PROD:      QUANTITY:         PRICE:         EXTPRICE:      BO:
3.)PROD:      QUANTITY:         PRICE:         EXTPRICE:      BO:




                                               SUBTOTAL:
                                                    TAX:
                                                  TOTAL:

........1........2........3........4.....▌.5........6........7........8
```

Figure 16-3   The Mailing Label Design screen

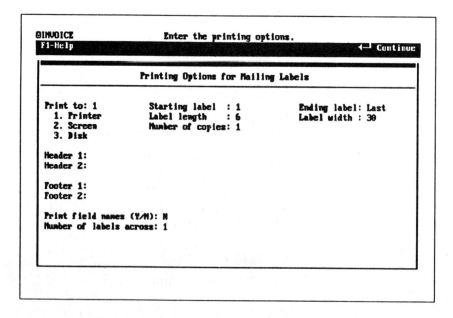

Figure 16-4   The Print Options for Mailing Labels

You can sort labels on a field without printing the field on your mailing label. Enter the sort number, but do not include any other instructions in the field.

Label Length: Default setting is 6 lines, for a label that's one inch long (vertically). If the label is longer, measure its length and multiply by 6 to determine the setting. Enter the correct setting.

Label Width: Default setting is 30, for a label that's 3 inches wide. If your label is wider or narrower, measure its width and multiply by 10. Enter the correct setting.

Print Field Names: If you want the field names printed on your label, change this setting to Y.

Number of Records Across: If your roll or sheet of labels has more than one label across, enter the correct setting for the number of labels across.

Printing the Current Record

You can print a single record in the Add, Search, or Update mode. Professional File can print the record as it appears on screen, as a mailing label, or on a pre-printed form.

To print the record that's on screen, press F2, opening the Records menu. Choose option 3. Print, opening the Print Records menu shown in Figure 16-5. This menu offers three options:

- Print record
- Print label/selected fields
- Print on pre-printed form

Print Record

Choose option 1. Print record to open the Print Options screen. Change the settings as required, and press Enter. Professional File prints only the record displayed.

Print Label/Selected Fields

Selecting this option lets you print a mailing label from the record displayed. If you choose this option, Professional File displays the Design Mailing Label screen. Enter the instructions as explained in the section above and press Enter.

Chapter 16

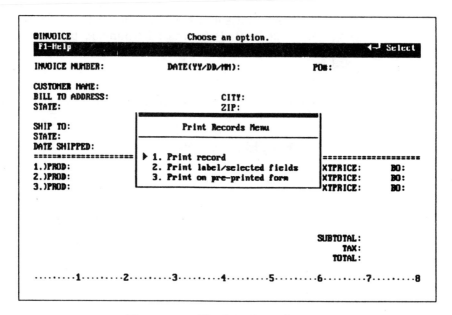

Figure 16-5 The Print Records menu

Print on Pre-Printed Form

This option lets you print a record on a pre-printed form, such as a check or an invoice. Before you choose this option, however, you must print a grid on a blank form to give yourself some idea of where the information will be printed.

Printing the Grid: The grid consists of rows and columns that intersect to indicate where specific information will be printed. To print the grid on a form:

1. Load the pre-printed form into your printer.
2. Choose option 5. Report/Print from the Main menu.
3. Choose option 6. Print on pre-printed forms. Professional File displays a screen that lets you specify the file you want to open.
4. If the default path is correct, type the filename and press Enter. If not, press Ctrl-E; then type the path and filename, and press Enter. Professional File displays the data entry form, with the message Enter instructions for printing on pre-printed forms.
5. Press F2 to open the Coordinates menu.
6. Choose option 6. Print grid, opening the Printing Options for Pre-printed Forms screen.

Printing Records and Reports

7. Enter the settings for page length and width, and press Enter. This opens a second Printer Options screen that lets you select a printer, select compressed print, and insert printer control codes.

8. Press Enter. Professional File prints the grid on the pre-printed form. Figure 16-6 shows an example of such a grid.

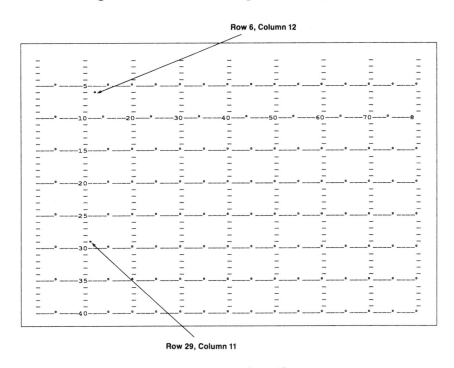

Figure 16-6 The grid

Entering Instructions: To tell Professional File where to print information on the form, you need to enter coordinates from the grid into the INVOICE form on screen. For example, say the blank space for the invoice number begins at row 5, column 10:

1. Press Esc to display the INVOICE form.
2. Type any sorting instructions you want to use. (This step is optional.)
3. Type @5,10 as shown in Figure 16-7. To print the same information in more than one location, separate the entries with @; for example

@5,10 @20,32

Chapter 16

When entering coordinates for printing, the syntax is important. All instructions must be entered as:

`row coordinate,column coordinate`

4. Enter any additional instructions (use Table 16-2 for reference).
5. Press F10, saving the instructions and displaying the Search screen.

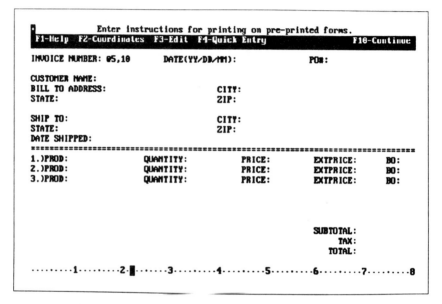

Figure 16-7 The coordinates for the invoice number

Table 16-2 Field Entries for Pre-Printed Forms

Entry	Result
@5,10,5	Prints five characters
@5*,10	Prints in specified row unless it is filled; if filled, prints in next blank row, same column.
@5,10a	Aligns decimal point in specified column (make sure you leave enough room for the digits that are to the left and right of the decimal point).
@5,10n	Prints numbers only, including plus and minus signs, decimal points, parentheses, and brackets.
@5,10e	Spells out number.

6. Enter search instructions, and press F10, opening the Printer Options screen.
7. Enter the required settings, and press F10 to start printing.

Printing Messages

With Professional File, you can print up to six special messages not included in your database. For example, you could print "Happy Holidays" on your Christmas bonus checks. To include a message:

1. Choose option **5. Report/Print** from the Main menu. This opens the Report/Print menu.
2. Choose option **6. Print on pre-printed forms**. Professional File displays a screen that lets you specify the file you want to open.
3. If the default path is correct, type the filename and press Enter. If not, press Ctrl-E; then type the path and filename, and press Enter.
4. Press F2 to open the Coordinates menu.
5. Choose option **5. Show/Hide messages**, opening the Messages screen shown in Figure 16-8.
6. Enter the coordinates for each message you want to include, as explained in the previous section. Type the message as you want it to appear.
7. Press F2, and choose option **5. Show/Hide messages**.
8. Press F10, saving the coordinates and messages, and opening the Search screen.
9. Enter search instructions, and press F10, to open the Printer Options screen.
10. Enter the required settings, and press F10.
11. Change any settings as required in the Printer Options screen, and press Enter.

Printing Reports

Reports differ from records in that reports contain information from several records. Professional File offers two ways to organize this information:

List	A report that lists information in columns
Crosstabs	A report that summarizes data

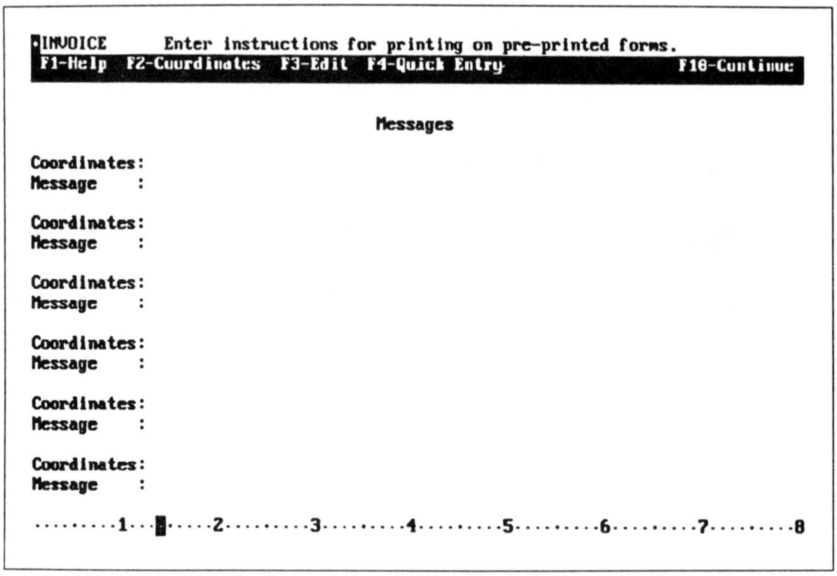

```
▌INVOICE      Enter instructions for printing on pre-printed forms.
 F1-Help  F2-Coordinates  F3-Edit  F4-Quick Entry           F10-Continue

                              Messages

Coordinates:
Message     :

Coordinates:
Message     :

Coordinates:
Message     :

Coordinates:
Message     :

Coordinates:
Message     :

Coordinates:
Message     :
........1..▌....2........3.........4.........5.........6.........7.........8
```

Figure 16-8   The Messages screen

Printing a List

The list report is closely related to the table format explained in Chapter 14; the key difference is that the list lets you calculate formulas using data from the fields.

The procedure required for printing a list is similar to the procedures described above for printing records. You simply access a special form and enter printing instructions in each field that you want to include in the list. To access the form:

1. Choose option 5. Report/Print from the Main menu.
2. Choose option 1. Print list. Professional File displays a screen that lets you specify the file you want to open.
3. If the default path is correct, type the filename and press Enter. If not, press Ctrl-E; then type the path and filename, and press Enter.

   Professional File displays a screen that lets you enter the instructions for creating a list. At the top of the screen is the message Enter instructions to create the list report.

4. Type the list instructions in each field that you want to include in the list (refer to Table 16-3). Figure 16-9 shows the INVOICE form with sample entries.

Printing Records and Reports

5. Press F2 and choose option 2. Save instructions.
6. Type a name for the instructions.
7. Press F10, opening the Search screen.
8. Enter search instructions. To print all records, leave the Search screen blank.
9. Press F10, opening the Printing Options screen.
10. Move the cursor to the Select Printer option, and type 2 to print the list to screen. (This lets you review the list before printing it.)
11. Enter the other required settings on the Printing Options screen.
12. Press F10 to print the list to screen. Figure 16-10 shows the INVOICE list printed to screen.

Note the printing option Print summaries only (Y/N). This gives you the option of printing only the total for each record. Therefore, if you have 50 customers or accounts, each with multiple records, Professional File prints only the total for each customer.

Table 16-3 List Instructions

Entry	Result
1,2,3	Prints the field in the order specified, from left to right.
a	Calculates the average of all entries in a field and prints the result.
c	Counts the number of entries in a field and prints the total.
d	Sorts data in descending order.
h	Turns word wrap on or off.
i	Uses the column only for sorting—does not print or display the column.
k	Sorts data by keyword (use only with column one).
l	Leaves a blank line when the data in column one changes (column one).
max	Finds the maximum entry in a field and prints it.
min	Finds the minimum entry in a field and prints it.
n	Sorts text or unformatted data numerically.
p	Begins printing on a new page when the data in column one changes.
r	Repeats duplicate entries (column one or two).
sa	Calculates and prints the subaverage of values in a field when the data in column one changes; prints a total at the end of the list.

(continued)

Table 16-3 (continued)

Entry	Result
sc	Calculates and prints a subcount for the number of entries in a field when the data in column one changes; prints a total at the end of the list.
smax	Finds the largest entry in a field and prints it when the data in column one changes; prints the largest value at the end of the list.
smin	Finds the smallest value in a field and prints it when the data in column one changes; prints the smallest value at the end of the list.
st	Calculates and prints the subtotal of values in a field when the data in column one changes; prints the total at the end of the list.
t	Calculates and prints the total of entries in a field.
w1 to w255	Sets column width (must be entered after the column number—for example, 1 w23.

Note: Notice that several of the instructions are keyed to the data in column one. Whenever you create a list report, carefully select the field for column one. Otherwise, you may limit your choice of instructions.

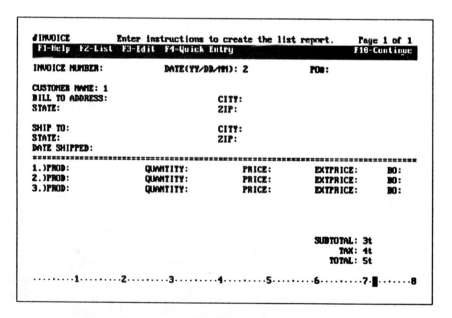

Figure 16-9 The INVOICE form with list instructions

Printing Records and Reports

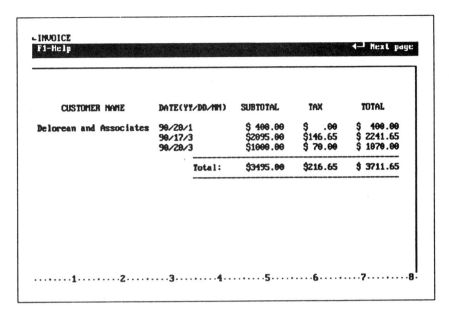

Figure 16-10 The List Report on screen

Notice that there is only one customer name in column one. The reason for this is that all the records in our database are for the same customer. Professional File leaves this column blank until it encounters a new CUSTOMER NAME entry; this lets you see the breaks in the list more easily. If you want to print every occurrence of the customer name, you must type r in the field as part of your instructions.

Since all the customer name entries are the same, Professional File has sorted the records according to the secondary sort field: DATE. If there were several different customers in the database, their respective invoices would be sorted into groups; the records in each group would then be sorted by date.

If your report is too wide for the screen, use the Right Arrow key to see the rest of the form.

The final three columns contain values from the invoices. At the bottom of each column is a total. Professional File lines up the decimal points and inserts dollar signs as specified by the format attributes.

If two asterisks appear in a column, they indicate that the entry is wider than the column. To see the entire entry, you must go back to the Instruction screen and specify a wider column.

Invisible Columns

Invisible columns come in handy when you're calculating a markup, and you don't want the customer to know how you determined the markup. For example, if you charge 50% over cost for parts, you can use an invisible column to determine the calculation. To make a column invisible, type i in the field on the Design screen.

You can also make a column invisible if you want to sort your records according to the entries in that field, but you don't want the field printed.

Derived Columns

A derived column is one that does not exist in the database form, but is created for the list by utilizing information from other fields. To create a derived column:

1. Choose option 5. Report/Print from the Main menu.
2. Choose option 1. Print List.
3. Press F2 and choose option 1. Get instructions.
4. Type the name of the instructions you want to get, and press Enter.
5. Press F2 and choose option 5. Show/Hide Derived columns, opening the Derived Columns screen shown in Figure 16-11.
6. Type a name for the column heading in the Heading field. (If you leave this field blank, Professional File uses whatever formula you enter as the heading.)
7. Press Tab, moving the cursor to the Formula field.
8. Enter the formula. Keep the following guidelines in mind when entering the formula:
   - You do not need to type an equal sign before the formula.
   - Use column numbers as field identifiers—for example, #4 and #5.
   - The derived column must come after all other columns.
9. Press the Tab key, moving the cursor to the Instruction field.
10. Type a number indicating the next column on the list. For example, if this additional column is the sixth column, type 6t, indicating that the total of columns 4 and 5 will be displayed.
11. Press F10, opening the Search screen.
12. Enter search instructions and press F10, opening the Printing Options screen.
13. Move the cursor to the Select Printer option, and type 2 to print the list to screen. (This lets you review the list before printing it.)

Printing Records and Reports

14. Enter the other required settings on the Printing Options screen.
15. Press Enter, printing the list to screen.

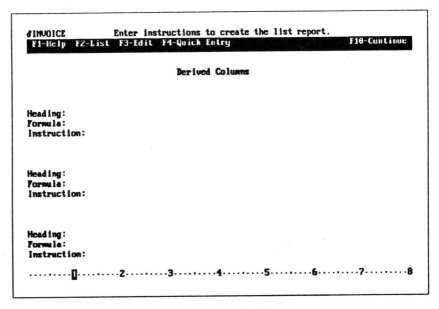

Figure 16-11 The Derived Columns screen

Figure 16-12 illustrates an example of the settings required in the Derived Columns screen. These settings will create a column called COST OF GOODS. The formula multiplies the entry in column three, the subtotal, by 75% to determine the actual cost of materials used to produce the item. Figure 16-13 shows the result of the new settings.

Creating Crosstab Reports

The term "crosstab" refers to *cross-tabulation*. A crosstab report is a tool for summarizing information in the database and displaying the information in a well-focused form. It consists of a minimum of three elements:

- rows
- columns
- summary values

Chapter 16

```
∂INVOICE          Enter instructions to create the list report.
     F1-Help  F2-List  F3-Edit  F4-Quick Entry                F10-Continue

                              Derived Columns


     Heading: COST OF GOODS
     Formula: #3 *.75
     Instruction: 6



     Heading:
     Formula:
     Instruction:



     Heading:
     Formula:
     Instruction:

     .........0.........2.........3.........4.........5.........6.........7.........8
```

Figure 16-12 Settings entered

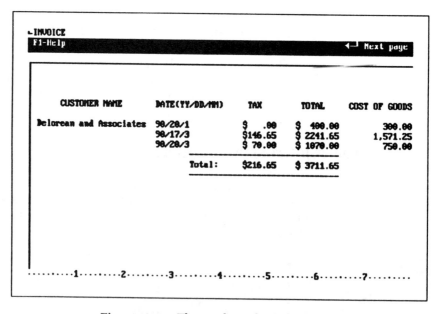

Figure 16-13 The resulting derived column

Suppose you had the following form that charts voter preference:

Age	Sex	Voter Preference
45–60	Male	Jones
18–25	Female	Smith
62–67	Female	Jones
29–43	Male	Smith

You could create a crosstab to indicate voter preference for a particular group, using Age for columns, Sex for rows, and Voter Preference for the summary value. Instead of displaying the information in columns, each crosstab would focus on a distinct group. For example, the following crosstab might be used:

Age: 45-60
Sex: Male
Preference: Jones

Crosstab reports enable you to focus on particular market segments and patterns that you can't look at using a table or list. To create a crosstab report:

1. Choose option `5. Report/Print` from the Main menu.
2. Choose option `2. Print crosstab`. Professional File displays a blank form that lets you type instructions for the crosstab.
3. Type `r` in the field you want to use for a row.
4. Type `c` in the field you want to use as a column.
5. Type `s` in the field you want to use for the summary.
6. Press F10. Professional File displays the Sort screen.
7. Enter the sort instructions and press F10. The Search screen appears.
8. Enter search instructions and press F10, opening the Printing Options screen shown in Figure 16-14.
9. Enter the required settings on the Printing Options screen. The summary functions at the bottom of the screen let you format the numbers in a variety of ways depending on your needs. The term *cell* refers to the box formed by the intersection of a row and column.
10. Press Enter to print the crosstab.

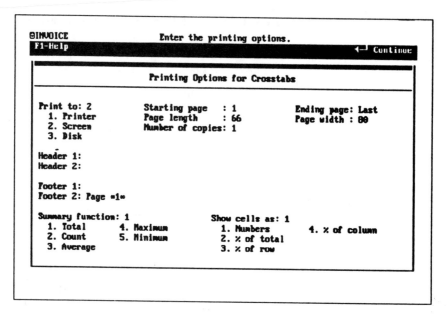

Figure 16-14 The Crosstab Printing Options menu

Modifying Column Headings

With Professional File, you can change a heading in a list or crosstab report without affecting your database:

1. Choose option 5. Report/Print from the Main menu.
2. Choose option 3. Enter/Edit headings. Professional File displays the Instructions screen, where you can edit the headings.
3. Press the Tab or Shift-Tab to move to the field you wish to change.
4. Type the new heading in the field.
5. Press F10 to save the new headings.

Professional File will now use the new headings in reports. These headings have no effect on the database except in report functions.

Summary

In this chapter, Professional File revealed its flexibility in dealing with a database. You learned to use only the information you need to create effective reports. You can print records or portions of records to create mailing labels or to fill out pre-printed forms. And you can use Professional File's Sort and Search features to organize and find records quickly.

The only thing left for you to do is to practice and experiment. If you have Professional Write, go back to Chapter 10 and try to insert information from your newly created database into a form letter. Then, you will experience the full power and flexibility of Professional Write and File.

Chapter 16

APPENDIX

Installing Professional Write and Professional File

If computers are new to you, don't let the word "installing" scare you off. When I first saw that word, I thought it meant something like putting central air conditioning in my house or putting a new engine in my car.

It's not that at all. Installation, in this case, simply means copying and loading the program files you bought, and answering any questions that Professional Write and File might have concerning your particular computer.

Installing Professional Write and Professional File

The installation process for Professional Write varies depending on whether you have a hard disk or a floppy disk system. Professional File, on the other hand, can only be run on a hard disk system.

Installing on a Hard Disk

The following instructions refer specifically to installing Professional Write, but you can use the same instructions to install Professional File. To install Professional Write, you must perform three basic steps:

- Make a directory to keep your Professional Write files separate from the other files on the disk.
- Activate the new directory.
- Copy the Professional Write files to the new directory.

Appendix

Making a Directory Using DOS

1. Start up your computer with DOS.
2. Make sure the drive where you want to store your Professional Write program files is active. For example, if your hard disk drive is drive C, C should be displayed.
2. Type md pro to tell DOS, "Make a directory called PRO."
3. Press Enter.

Activating a Directory

1. Type cd\pro to tell DOS, "Change the directory to PRO."
2. Press Enter.

DOS will probably respond with a prompt indicating that you are now in the PRO subdirectory. If your system is not set up to display the active subdirectory, you won't see the prompt, but you will be in the new subdirectory.

Copying Files to a Directory

1. Insert the Professional Write Start Up Disk (Disk 1) into drive A.
2. Type copy a:*.* to tell DOS, "Copy all files from the disk in drive A."
3. Press Enter. DOS displays a list of the files as they are copied, and then tells you when it's done.

Replace the disk in drive A with the next disk you want to copy, and repeat the process until all of your program files are copied to the hard disk.

Creating a Directory for Your Data Files

While you're at it, create a directory to store the files you'll create using Professional Write. That way, you won't get your personal files mixed in with Professional Write's program files.

Name the new directory WDATA, as suggested by the designers of Professional Write. The idea behind this directory is that it will keep the files you create using Professional Write separate from the files you create using Professional File and Professional Plan. If you have these programs, it's a good idea to create three data directories: WDATA for Write files, FDATA for File files, and PDATA for Plan files.

Under the WDATA directory heading, you will create a subdirectory called EXAMPLES to store the sample files you'll create using this book. If you need more information about directories and subdirectories, refer to Chapter 4.

Creating a Data Directory

1. Make sure the drive in which you want to create the data directory is active. For example, if you want to create the directory in drive C, the DOS prompt C should be displayed.
2. Type md wdata and press Enter. This tells DOS to make a directory called WDATA.
3. Type cd\wdata, telling DOS to activate the new subdirectory.
4. Type md examples and press Enter, making a subdirectory under the WDATA directory called EXAMPLES.

Make a new subdirectory before you begin a project. That way, the directory will be ready when you decide to save a file.

Installing on a Floppy Disk System

Installing Professional Write on a floppy disk system is fairly simple, but you must perform some precautionary steps before you begin.

Before You Begin

Never use the original disks you purchased for your daily work. Make a copy of the original and use the copy. Software Publishing Corporation authorizes you to make copies for your own use. However, it is illegal to make copies for someone else.

To copy your original disks for use as backups, you'll need several blank disks. (The number and type of disks you need depends on the number and type of disk that your originals are on.)

Copying Disks Using DOS

1. Make sure the disks do not contain any information you care to lose. The copying process will overwrite any information on the disk.
2. If the DOS prompt shows that drive A is active (DOS A), go on to step 5. If not, type a: at the DOS prompt and press Enter, activating drive A.
3. Type diskcopy a: a: telling DOS that you want to copy a disk using drive A.

4. Press Enter. DOS responds by telling you to insert the source diskette in drive A.
5. Insert the original disk you want to copy in drive A and press Enter. DOS copies the disk into your computer's memory, then tells you to insert the target diskette in drive A.
6. Replace the original disk in drive A with a blank disk, and press Enter. DOS copies the information from the original disk to the disk in drive A and tells you when it's done.

Remove the disk, label your copy, and repeat the copying process until you have a copy of each program disk.

Installing Professional Write

Now that you have a backup copy of Professional Write, you can safely use the copies to install Professional Write. Just perform the following steps:

1. Insert your DOS startup disk in drive A, and turn on your computer. DOS loads itself into your computer, and displays the prompt A to tell you it's ready.
2. Remove the DOS disk, and insert the Professional Write Start Up Disk (Disk 1) in drive A.
3. Type pw and press Enter. After a few seconds, Professional Write tells you to insert the Program Disk (Disk 2) into a specified drive and press Enter.
4. Insert the Program Disk into the specified drive and press Enter. In a few seconds, the Professional Write main menu appears.

You can now begin working with Professional Write or you can go on to customize it.

Customizing Professional Write

In this section, you'll see how to customize Professional Write for your particular equipment and for your personal way of doing things. To get started, perform the following steps:

1. At the PRO prompt, type pw and press Enter, launching the program. In a moment, the Professional Write main menu will appear as shown in Figure A-1.
2. Press the Down Arrow key once, highlighting option 2. Setup, and press Enter, opening the Setup menu shown in Figure A-2.

Installing Professional Write and Professional File

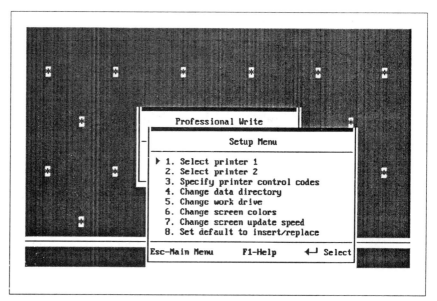

Figure A-1 The main menu

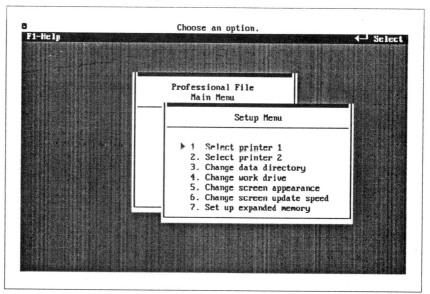

Figure A-2 The Setup menu

As you can see, the Setup menu consists of a list of options. To choose an option, you can either use the Up and Down Arrow keys to highlight the option and press Enter or simply type the option's number. We will go through the setup process step-by-step, handling each option as it appears on the menu.

Select Printer 1

The first thing to do is to designate the type of printer you will be using. Professional Write is preset to print on a parallel printer through the PRN printer port. If that's how your system is set up, the following steps are not necessary, but you may want to perform them to take advantage of Professional Write's type styles and fonts. If you're using a serial printer or if your printer is connected to a different port, however, you must perform the following steps.

Professional Write lets you connect two printers so you don't have to spend time typing in new settings every time you want to use another printer. For example, you may have a brand new laser printer that you want to use only for high-quality output. You can set this printer up as Printer 1, since only the Printer 1 setup supports fonts. You can then set up the printer you use for rough drafts as Printer 2.

Professional Write includes a booklet that contains information about how Professional Write interacts with a wide variety of printers. It's a good idea to read the booklet before you begin, to find out if your printer has any quirks. To connect your printer, perform the following steps:

1. Choose option 1. Select printer 1, opening the Printer 1 Selection screen shown in Figure A-3. This screen lists the model names of several printers. You can scroll through the list by pressing the PgUp or PgDn key.

2. If your printer is listed, use the Up and Down Arrow keys to highlight it. If it's not listed, you can move the highlight to Unlisted Printer, to an earlier model from the same manufacturer, or to a similar printer. Your selection is shown next to Printer: near the bottom of the screen.

3. The printer port is displayed just below your selection. If that's the correct port, press Enter. If it's not, press the Tab key to move to the Printer Ports column and use the Up or Down Arrow keys to highlight the correct port. Then press Enter.

If you're not sure which printer port to use, choose PRN. If that's the wrong port, Professional Write will tell you it's the wrong port when you try to print. You can then go back to the Printer 1 Selection screen and try another port.

If you chose a serial port, Professional Write displays the Serial Port Settings screen, which lets you type information concerning your printer. Refer to the manual that came with your printer to determine if any of these settings needs to be changed. To change a setting, press the

Installing Professional Write and Professional File

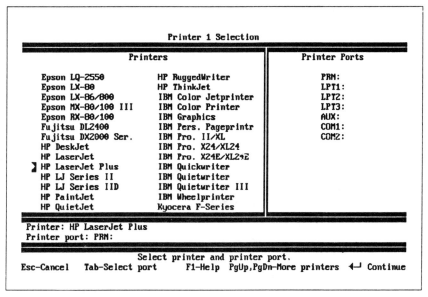

Figure A-3 The Printer 1 Selection screen

Tab key to move the cursor to the setting you want to change. Then, type the new setting.

This gets you started, but Professional Write provides additional options to support your printer's capabilities. We'll explore these setup options in more depth in Chapter 7 and Chapter 9.

Select Printer 2

If you have a second printer, choose option 2. Select Printer 2 from the Setup menu, and repeat the steps above.

Specify Printer Control Codes

If you have a sheet feeder or other fancy equipment hooked up to your printer, you may want to send codes before and after printing to turn the equipment on and off or to initiate and shut down an operation. Normally, you would have to type these codes in your working copy, but with Professional Write, you can type them just once. Here's how:

1. Choose option 3. Specify printer control codes from the Setup menu, opening the Printer Control Codes screen shown in Figure A-4.

299

Appendix

2. Type the ASCII decimal values for the codes you want sent. If the code consists of several numbers, separate them with commas. (These codes are listed in the printer manual that came with your printer.)
3. Press the Tab key to move to the next code, and continue typing codes.
4. Press Enter, saving the codes and returning to the Setup menu.

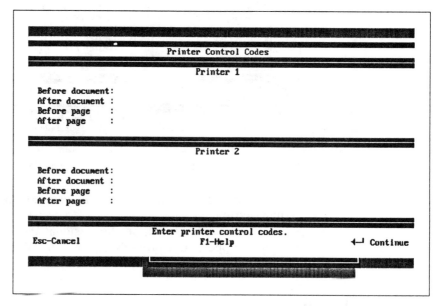

Figure A-4 The Printer Control Codes screen

 If your special equipment is built in, Professional Write automatically sends codes to the printer. In this case, there's no need to enter new codes.

Change Data Directory

This setup option is one you'll use often. It lets you specify the subdirectory in which you'll be working, so you don't have to type the name of the drive and subdirectory every time you try to get or save a file. To change the default, perform the following steps:

1. Choose option 4. Change data directory from the Setup menu, opening the Current Data Directory screen.

2. Press Ctrl-E, deleting the directory shown.
3. If you want to make a floppy disk drive the default, type the letter of the drive followed by a colon—for example, `B:`. If you want to make a subdirectory the default, type the complete path and subdirectory that you want to be the default. For example, type `c:\wdata\examples`. This gives Professional Write directions to your subdirectory.
4. Press Enter.

Now, whenever you try to get or save a file, Professional Write will automatically access the new default drive or subdirectory.

Change Work Drive

Occasionally, Professional Write needs a little elbow room to do its work. When you're creating form letters or converting Professional Write documents to Microsoft Word, for example, Professional Write creates a file in the work drive to perform its task.

Professional Write is set up to use drive C as its work drive. If you're using a floppy disk system and you don't have a drive C or if you want to use another drive as the work drive, you can specify a different work drive. To specify a different work drive, perform the following steps:

1. Choose option `5. Change Work Drive` from the Setup menu, opening the Current Work Drive screen.
2. Type in the letter of the drive you want to use as the work drive.
3. Press Enter, saving your entry and returning to the Setup menu.

Change Screen Colors

If you have a color monitor, you can change the color of the display to suit your personal preference.

1. Choose option `6. Change Screen Colors` from the Setup menu, opening the Change Screen Colors screen.
2. Highlight the color you want and press Enter. This returns you to the Setup menu, which is now displayed in the new color.

Change Screen Update Speed

If you have a color monitor, sometimes a fast screen change will distort the appearance of what is on the screen. For color monitors, the initial setting is slow; for monochrome monitors, it's fast. If you have a color monitor and you find that the screen changes are too slow for you, you can choose speed over appearance. Just perform the following steps:

1. Choose option `7. Change screen update speed` from the Setup menu.
2. At the `Fast screen update?` prompt, type y and press Enter. This returns you to the Setup menu.

Perform the same steps to change back.

Set Default to Insert/Replace

If you usually type in the Overstrike mode, you can make that mode the default.

1. Choose option `8. Set Default to Insert\Replace` from the Setup menu.
2. At the `Insert/Replace` prompt, type r for Replace, and press Enter.

Making a Laptop Display Readable

When you start Professional Write the first time on a laptop computer, you may not be able to read the screen. To make the screen readable, you need to experiment with the color options to see what works best. Perform the following steps:

1. Start up Professional Write. On a hard disk system, you need to access the directory that contains the Write files and type pw. On a floppy disk, you need to load the Start Up disk in drive A, type pw, and press Enter. When the disk drive stops, replace the Start Up Disk with the Program Disk and press Enter. Wait for the drive to stop before going to step 2.
2. Type 2, but do not press Enter. This opens the Setup menu, although you can't see it.

3. Type 6, but do not press Enter. This chooses option `6. Change screen colors`, but again you can't see the display.
4. Type 4 selecting monochrome.

You should now be able to see the Setup menu. If not, try choosing some of the other colors from options 1 to 3.

Index

A

accessing forms, 231-232
Address Book
    adding records, 179
    creating, 175-177
        multiple books, 186
    deleting records, 185
    editing records, 184-185
    entering records, 178-179
    exporting to Professional File, 193
    finding records, 180
    merging with form letters, 175, 183-184, 187-190
    printing envelopes/mailing labels, 194-195
addresses (F4 key), 9
Alt-0 (macro menu) key, 197
Alt-A (display fonts) key, 155
Alt-D (list fonts) key, 155
Alt-S (print styles) key, 151
Alt-V (view) key, 153
Alt-X (leave preview) key, 155
application programs, xviii
arrow keys, 10
ASCII
    control codes, printer support, 138-139
    file, print to, 169
    format, 25, 100
    saving files, 87-89
asterisk character (*), 140
attributes
    field, 218-221
    format, 220-224
averages
    calculating, 130-131
    F8 key, 131

B

Backspace key, 10
beginning of block (Ctrl-Q key), 56
blocks, 51
    printing, 65
    rectangular, 52, 67-70
        calculating, 70
        copying, 70
        erasing, 67-69
        shifting, 70
    text, 52-66
        fonts, 61, 70, 139-140
        indentation, 64
        line spacing, 65
        margins, 61-64
        printing, 66
        saving, 66
        typestyle, 59-61, 70
boldface (Ctrl-B key), 17, 20
book formatting conventions, xx-xxi
    icons, xxi
    keys, xx
    options, xx
bottom margins, setting, 42
bulleted lists, 21

C

calculate, 117
    averages, 130-131
    blocks, rectangular, 70
    F9 key, 125
    function, 125-131
calculator, 125-131
capitalization, 106
cartridge fonts, setting up, 136
centering text, 39-41

305

characters
    asterisk (*), 140
    deleting, 14-15
    formatting, 19-20
    wildcard (..), 84-85, 114-115
clearing the screen, 90-91
clipboard functions, 55-58
close-up view, cursor movement, 156-157
columns
    derived, 286-287
    headings, modifying, 290
    invisible, 285-286
combining documents, 95-96
commands
    FORMAT NO, 162
    FORMAT YES, 162
    GRAPH, 172
    JOIN, 171-172
    NEW PAGE, 34-35, 159
    PRINTER, 170
    embedded, 34-35
    Print page number, 45-46
comments
    adding to forms, 238
    validation, 229
composing form letters, 186-187
compressed print style, 151, 169
conditional formulas, 227, 237
context-sensitive help, 6
control codes, printer, 170, 299-300
conventions, book format, xx-xxi
copying
    between files, 58
    blocks
        rectangular, 70
        text, 57-58
    documents, 93-94
    files, 93-94
    records, quick entry, 241-242
criteria, search
    Address Book, 180-182
    database files, 190, 245-249
crosstab reports, printing, 287-290
Ctrl-B (boldface) key, 17, 20
Ctrl-D (double space) key, 18
Ctrl-E (erase path) key, 29

Ctrl-E (erase) key, 24
Ctrl-F (find) key, 113
Ctrl-F1 (help) key, 7
Ctrl-G (get file) key, 28
Ctrl-J (jump to page) key, 13-14
Ctrl-L (delete line) key, 17
Ctrl-M (math) key, 17
Ctrl-O (print options) key, 25, 165
Ctrl-P (paste) key, 57
Ctrl-Q (beginning of block) key, 56
Ctrl-R (mark rectangular block) key, 67
Ctrl-S (save) key, 43
Ctrl-spacebar (hard space) key, 19
Ctrl-T (mark text) key, 53-54, 59-60
Ctrl-U (underline) key, 17, 20
Ctrl-W (delete word) key, 17
Ctrl-Y (drawing function) key, 122-124
Ctrl-Z (end of block) key, 56
cursor movement, 5, 12-14
    close-up view, 156-157
    drawing function, 121-124
    previewing document, 147-148
    tables, 258-259
customizing Professional Write, 296-303
cutting and pasting, 51, 58

D

data
    files, merging, 168
    tables, 253-261
        creating, 254-255
        cursor movement, 258-259
        designing, 254-257
        entering data, 259
        modifying, 260-261
        printing, 261
        saving, 256-257
        viewing, 257-258, 260
database, 205-223, 228-229, 231-252
    files
        merging with form letters, 188-192
        search criteria, 190

forms, 206-217
formulas, 224-227
date
   entering, 233-235
   format, 221
dBASE database files, merging
   letters, 189-190
decimal tabs, 35, 37-39
defaults, 218-219
   data directories, 76-77
   margins, 33
   settings, changing, 43
   tab stop, 35
Del (Delete) key, 10
deleting
   characters, 14-15
   documents, 92
   fields, database forms, 217
   files, 92
   lines, 15-17
      Ctrl-L key, 17
   macros, 203
   records,
      database, 252
      Address Book, 185
   words, 15-17
      Ctrl-W key, 17
derived columns, 286-287
dictionary, 99-106
   F5 key, 8, 100, 109-110
   adding words, 102
   personal, 107-108
directories, 71-78
   changing, 300-301
      defaults, 76-77
   creating, 294-295
   removing, 93
   sorting, 79-85
Disk Operating System (DOS), xviii
disks
   copying, 93-94
   directories, 72-75
   getting files, 28-29
   installing application programs, 293-300
   saving documents, 22-24
   starting Professional Write, 2-3

display fonts
   Alt-A key, 155
   on screen, 140
document formats
   ASCII, 100
   list, 21
   outline, 21
documents, xviii
   combining, 95-96
   copying, 93-94
   editing, preview mode, 157-163
   deleting, 92
   inserting, 95-96
   previewing, 143-163
   printing, 25
   saving, 86-89
   spell checker, 103-106
double space (Ctrl-D key), 18
downloading fonts, 134, 170
drawings, 117-124
   creating, 119-124
   Ctrl-Y key, 122-124
   cursor movement, 121-124
   editing, 122-124

E

editing
   document, preview mode, 157-163
   drawings, 122-124
   F3 key, 215-216, 232
   forms, 214-217
   macros, 203
   menu, 19-20, 215-216, 232
   records
      Address Book, 184-185
      database, 250-251
embedded commands, 34-35
encrypted files, 25
end key, 10
end of block (Ctrl-Z key), 56
Enter key, 6, 11
envelopes, 167, 194-195
erase (Ctrl-E key), 24, 29
erasing
   blocks, rectangular, 67-69
   fields, 232-233

words, 115
working copy, 90-91
Esc (Escape) key, 5, 9
exporting, Address Book to
  Professional File, 193

F

F1 (help) key, 6, 149-150, 232
F2 (file/print) key, 7, 22-25, 73-75
F2 (new records menu) key, 232
F2 (options) key, 149-152
F3 (edit) key, 8, 215-216, 232
F3 (fonts) key, 149, 153-155
F4 (format) key, 8, 18
F4 (quick entry menu) key, 232
F4 (return) key, 149, 155
F5 (dictionary) key, 8, 100, 109-110
F6 (addresses) key, 9
F8 (average) key, 131
F8 (fonts) key, 47
F8 (margin setting) key, 62-63
F8 (sort order) key, 79-80
F9 (calculate) key, 125
F9 (search multiple documents) key, 82
F10 (text block operations) key, 53-55, 59-60
fields
  adding, database forms, 216
  attributes
    default, 218-221
    index, 218
    unique data entry, 218
  deleting, database forms, 217
  formatting, 191-192
  moving, database forms, 217
  names, 178, 210-213
    changing names, database forms, 217
  validating, 228-229
File/Print
  F2 key, 7, 22-23, 25, 73-75
  macro, 199-201
files
  copying, 93-94
    between, 58

deleting, 92
directories, 71-88
  sorting, 79-85
getting, 27-29, 89-90
joining for printing, 171-172
managing, xviii-xix
naming, 78-79
PERSONAL.SPC, 107-108
PFS.DIR, 24
PW.DEF, 43
saving, 24-25, 86-89
  ASCII format, 87-89
searching, 82-85
final formulas, database, 227
find and replace, 111-115
finding
  records
    Address Book, 180
    database, 244-249
  text, 111-115
    Ctrl-F key, 113
fixed-pitch spacing, 134
floppy disks
  copying from hard disk, 93-94
  directories, 74-75
  getting files, 28
  installing application programs, 295 300
  saving documents, 22-23
  starting Professional Write, 3
fonts, 47, 133-141
  adjusting, 141, 161-162
  blocks, changing, 61, 70
  cartridge, 136
  changing, 138-139
    document preview, 153
  displaying, 140
  downloading, 134
  F3 key, 149, 153-155
  F8 key, 47
  internal, 134
  large, 141
  listing, 153-155
  menu, 149, 153-155
  setting up, 134-139
  soft, 134, 137
    downloading, 170

footers
    creating, 44
    formatting, 45, 47-49
form letters
    composing, 186-187
    merging with database files, 188-192
FORMAT NO command, 162
FORMAT YES command, 162
formats
    ASCII, 87-89, 100
    attributes, 220-224
        date, 221
        numeric, 222-223
        text, 224
        time, 221-222
    book conventions, xx-xxi
    documents
        list, 21
        outline, 21
    F4 key, 8, 18
    menu, 18
formatting
    characters, 19-20
    fields, 191-192
    footers, 45, 47-49
    headers, 45, 47-49
forms
    accessing, 231-232
    adding comments, 238
    creating, 207-209
        naming fields, 210-213
    designing, 206-209
    editing, 214-217
    entering data, 232-238
    erasing fields, 232-233
    modifying, 239-240
    saving, 214
formulas, 224
    conditional, 227-237
    database, 225-227
    final, 227
    subtotal, 226
    testing, 235
    what-if entries, 236
function keys, 5-9

G

Get Database macro, 266
getting files, 27-29, 89-90
    Ctrl-G key, 28
GRAPH command, 172
graphs, inserting during printing, 172

H

hard disks
    copying to floppy, 93
    directories, 72-75
    getting files, 28-29
    installing application programs, 293-294
    saving documents, 23-24
    starting Professional Write, 2
hard spaces, 19, 158
    Ctrl-spacebar key, 19
hardware, xviii, 144
headers
    creating, 44
    formatting, 45, 47-49
headings, column, 290
help
    Ctrl-F1 key, 7
    F1 key, 6, 149-150, 232
    menu, 4, 149-150
Hewlett-Packard LaserJet printer, 135-137
Home key, 10

I

icons, xxi
importing
    files from Address Book, 193
    worksheet files, 96
indentation, changing blocks, 64
indexed fields, 218
insert mode, 14
inserting
    documents, 95-96
    hard spaces, 19
    numbers into calculator, 128-130
    page breaks, 34-35
    printer control codes, 170

worksheet files in documents, 95-96
installing, Professional Write and File, 293-303
internal fonts, 134
invisible columns, 285-286

J

JOIN commands, 171-172
joining files for printing, 171-172
Jump to Page key, 13-14
justified print style, 151, 169

K

keys, xx
    Alt-0 (macro menu), 197
    Alt-A (display fonts), 155
    Alt-D (list fonts), 155
    Alt-S (print styles), 151
    Alt-V (view), 153
    Alt-X (leave preview), 155
    arrow, 10
    Backspace, 10
    Ctrl-B (boldface), 17, 20
    Ctrl-D (double space), 18
    Ctrl-E (erase), 24, 29
    Ctrl-F (find), 113
    Ctrl-F1 (help), 7
    Ctrl-G (get file), 28
    Ctrl-J (jump to page), 13-14
    Ctrl-L (delete line), 17
    Ctrl-M (math), 17
    Ctrl-O (print options), 25, 165
    Ctrl-P (paste block), 57
    Ctrl-Q (beginning of block), 56
    Ctrl-R (mark rectangular block), 67
    Ctrl-S (save), 43
    Ctrl-spacebar (hard space), 19
    Ctrl-T (mark text), 53-54, 59-60
    Ctrl-U (underline), 17, 20
    Ctrl-W (delete word), 17
    Ctrl-Y (drawing function), 122-124
    Ctrl-Z (end of block), 56
    Del (delete), 10
    End, 10
    Enter, 6, 11
    Esc (escape), 5, 9
    F1 (help), 6, 149-150, 232
    F2 (file/print), 7, 22-23, 25, 73-75
    F2 (new records menu), 232
    F2 (options), 149-152
    F2 (print/file), 27
    F3 (edit), 8, 215-216, 232
    F3 (fonts), 149, 153-155
    F4 (Addresses), 9
    F4 (Format), 8, 18
    F4 (quick entry menu), 232
    F4 (return), 149, 155
    F5 (dictionary), 8, 100, 109-110
    F8 (average), 131
    F8 (font), 47
    F8 (margin setting), 62-63
    F8 (sort order), 79-80
    F9 (calculate), 125
    F9 (search multiple documents), 82
    F10 (text block operations), 53-55, 59-60
    function, 5-9
    Home, 10
    PgDn (page down), 11
    PgUp (page up), 11
    special, 9-11
    Tab, 11

L

landscape orientation, 134
laptop readability, 302-303
LaserJet printer, 135-137
leave preview (Alt-X key), 155
left margin
    setting, 29-33
    temporary, 33-34
letter quality print style, 151, 169
letters
    form, 186-187
    inserting addresses from Address Book, 183-184
line spacing, blocks, 65
lines
    deleting, 15-17
    reformatting, 159-163
    ruler, 5

Index

status, 5
listing
    fonts, 153-155
        Alt-D key, 155
    format, 21
    macros, 203
lists, printing, 282-286

M

macros, 197-203
    creating, 197-202, 263-269
    deleting, 203
    editing, 203
    File/Print, 199-201
    Get Database, 266
    listing, 203
    menu (Alt-0 key), 197
    Merge Write and File, 266-268
    Pause, 201-202
    Print Mailing Labels, 268-269
mailing labels
    macro, 268
    printing, 194-195, 274-277
Main menu, 5-6
managing files, xviii-xix
margins
    bottom, 42
    changing, blocks, 61-64
    setting, 29-33
        F8 key, 62-63
        resetting, 32-34
        temporary, 33-34
        top and bottom, 42
    top, 42
marking blocks
    rectangular, 67-70
        Ctrl-R key, 67
    text, 52-66
        Ctrl-T key, 53-54, 59-60
mathematical operations, 127
    Ctrl-M key, 17
menus
    Edit, 19-20, 215-216
    Fonts, 149
    Format, 18
    Help, 4, 149-150
    Main, 5-6

    making selections, 3-4
    Options, 149-152
    preview, 149-155
    Repeated words, 105
    Return, 149-155
Merge Write and File macro, 266-268
merging
    data files, 168
    documents, 175, 183-184, 187-192
    database files, 188-192
messages
    printing, 281
    validation, 228
modes
    insert, 14
    overstrike, 14
moving
    blocks of text, 56-57
    cursor, 5, 12-14
        close-up view, 156-157
        drawing function, 121-124
        previewing document, 147-148
        tables, 258-259
    fields, database forms, 217

N

naming
    fields, database forms, 210-213
    files, 78-79
NEW PAGE command, 34-35, 159
new records menu (F2 key), 232
normal print style, 151, 168
numbers
    page 45-46
    rounding, 131
numeric format, 222-223

O

operations, order of mathematical, 127
options, xx
    F2 key, 149-152
    menu, 149-152
    print, 25
    setup, 300-301
order of mathematical operation, 127

orientation
    landscape, 134
    portrait, 134
orphans, 159
outline format, 21
overstrike mode, 14

P

pages
    breaks, inserting, 34-35
    numbering, 45-46
    size, setting, 43
paper size, 152
pasting text blocks, 56-58
    Ctrl-P key, 57
Pause macro, 201-202
personal dictionaries, 107-108
PERSONAL.SPC file, 107-108
PFS.DIR file, 24
PgDn (page down) key, 11
PgUp (page up) key, 11
pitch, 133
portrait orientation, 134
preprinted forms
    messages, 281
    printing, 278-281
previewing document, 143-146
    close-up, 155-157
    cursor movement, 147-148
    editing, 157-163
    full page, 147-148
    menus, 149-155
    split screen, 148
Print Mailing Labels macro, 268-269
print/file (F2 key), 27
PRINTER command, 170
printers
    control codes, 170, 299-300
        ASCII, 138, 139
    Hewlett-Packard LaserJet, 135-137
    selecting, 298-299
printing, 165-170
    blocks of text, 65-66
    data tables, 261
    documents, 25
    envelopes, 167, 194-195
    inserting, graphs, 172

joining files, 171-172
mailing labels, 194-195, 274-277
    macro, 268
merging data files, 168
options
    setting, 165-170
    Ctrl-O key, 25, 165
page numbers, 45-46
preprinted forms, 278-281
records, 271-273
    current record, 277
    options, 274-281
reports, 271, 281
    crosstab, 287-290
    lists, 282-286
styles
    Alt-S key, 151
    changing, 150-152
    compressed, 151, 169
    font format, 151
    justified, 151, 169
    letter quality, 151, 169
    normal, 151, 168
    to ASCII files, 169
Professional File, database files
    importing Address Book data, 193
    merging with letters, 189-190
Professional Write
    customizing, 296-303
    database function, 231-252
    starting from disk, 2-3
    installing, 293-303
proportional spacing, 134
PW.DEF file, 43

Q

quick entry
    copying records, 241, 242
    current date and time, 234, 235
    F4 key, 232

R

RAM (random access memory), 56
records
    adding Address Book, 179

deleting
    Address Book, 185
    database, 252
editing
    Address Book, 184-185
    database, 250-251
entering
    Address Book, 178-179
    data, 240-243
finding
    Address Book, 180
    database, 244-249
    paging through Address Book, 180-182
    printing, 271-273
        current record, 277
        options, 274-281
    show previous record, 242
    sorting, 217
        database, 250
        forms, 218
rectangular blocks, 52
    calculating, 70
    copying, 70
    erasing, 67-69
    marking, 67-70
    shifting, 70
reformatting lines, 159-163
repeated words, spell checker, 104-106
reports, printing, 271, 281
    crosstabs, 287-290
    lists, 282-286
resetting margins, 32-34
retrieving files, 27-29
Return menu, 149, 155
    F4 key, 149, 155
right margin, setting, 29-33
rounding results, 131
ruler line, 5

S

saving
    Ctrl-S key, 43
    data tables, 256-257
    documents, 86-89
        floppy disk, 22-23

        hard disk, 23-24
    files, 24-25, 86-89
        ASCII format, 25
        encrypted format, 25
    forms, 214
    text blocks, 66
search criteria
    Address Book, 180-182
    database files, 190, 244-249
searching for files, 82-85
    F9 key, 82
selecting
    items from menus, 3-4
    printers, 298-299
setting
    format defaults, 43
    margins
        left and right, 29-33
        temporary, 33-34
        top and bottom, 42
    page size, 43
    print options, 165-170
    tabs, 35-39
setup options, 300-301
size
    page, setting, 43
    paper, changing, 152
soft fonts, 134
    downloading, 170
    setting up, 137
software, xviii
sorting
    directories, 79-85
    F8 key, 79-80
    forms, 217-218
    records, 250
spacing
    fixed-pitch, 134
    hard, 19, 158
    proportional, 134
special keys, 9-11
spell check, 99-108
    entire document, 103-106
    repeated words, 104-106
    single word, 100-102
split screen, document preview, 148
starting Professional Write, 2-3

status line, 5
subdirectories, 28-29, 72-75
    creating, 86-88
subtotal formulas, 226
synonym screen, 110

T

Tab key, 11
tables
    adjusting font changes, 141
    cursor movement within, 258-259
    data, 253-261
        viewing, 257-258, 260
    entering data, 259
    modifying, 260-261
    printing data, 261
tabs
    adjusting font changes, 141
    decimal, 35, 37-39
    setting, 35-39
    traditional typewriter, 35-37
testing formulas, 235
text
    blocks, 52
        changing fonts, 139-140
        copying, 57-58
        marking, 52-66
        moving, 56-57
        operations (F10 key), 53-55, 59-60
    centering, 39-41
    double-spacing, 18
    entering, 11-12
    finding, 111-115
    format, 224
    replacing, 113-115
thesaurus, 99, 108-116
time format, 221-222
title pages, 48-49
toggle command, 18
top margins, setting, 42

traditional tabs, 35-37
typefaces, 133
typestyle, 47
    changing, 59-61

U

underline (Ctrl-U key), 17, 20
unique data entry fields, 218

V

validating fields, 228-229
validation, 228-229
    messages, 228
viewing
    Alt-V key, 153
    document before printing, 143-163
    table data, 257-260

W

What-if, using formulas, 236
widows, 158-159
wild card (..), 114-115, 84-85, 181-182, 190
words
    counting, 115-116
    deleting, 15-17
    erasing, 115
    repeated, 104-106
    spell checker, 100-102
word-wrapping, 12
work drive, 301
worksheet files
    importing, 96
    inserting in documents, 95-96
write screen, 4, 5

Z

zoom, 155-157